High Notes

High Notes

Selected Writings of Gay Talese

Introduction by Lee Gutkind

BLOOMSBURY

NEW YORK · LONDON · OXFORD · NEW DELHI · SYDNEY

Bloomsbury USA
An imprint of Bloomsbury Publishing Plc

1385 Broadway	50 Bedford Square
New York	London
NY 10018	WC1B 3DP
USA	UK

www.bloomsbury.com

BLOOMSBURY and the Diana logo are trademarks of Bloomsbury Publishing Plc

First published 2017

ISBN: PB: 978-1-63286-746-9
        ePub: 978-1-63286-747-6

LIBRARY OF CONGRESS CATALOGING-IN-PUBLICATION DATA
Names: Talese, Gay, author.
Title: High notes : selected writings of Gay Talese / Gay Talese.
Description: New York : Bloomsbury USA, 2017
Identifiers: LCCN 2016031081 (print) | LCCN 2016047904 (ebook) |
ISBN 978-1-63286-746-9 (paperback) | ISBN 978-1-63286-747-6 (e-book)
Subjects: | BISAC: LITERARY COLLECTIONS / General.
Classification: LCC AC8.5 .T35 2017 (print) | LCC AC8.5 (ebook) | DDC 814/.6—dc23
LC record available at https://lccn.loc.gov/2016031081

10 9 8 7 6 5 4 3 2 1

Typeset by RefineCatch Limited, Bungay, Suffolk
Printed and bound in the U.S.A. by Berryville Graphics Inc., Berryville, Virginia

For George Gibson, my editor and publisher,
with my gratitude and admiration always

Contents

Introduction

Lee Gutkind

We are in a New York City recording studio, early one Sunday afternoon. Tony Bennett, the legendary and ageless pop singer, is rehearsing a duet of the Rodgers and Hart classic "The Lady Is a Tramp" with the flamboyant singer-songwriter Lady Gaga. The two performers are having fun—and flirting shamelessly. It's a great scene:

Bennett is characteristically bronze, smiling and majestic in a Brioni tux with a red pocket square, a white shirt, and a black tie, and Gaga is in a long black lace see-through gown under a sleeveless black leather motorcycle jacket with studded lapels. She's sipping whiskey and affecting a slight Southern redneck drawl, and she's teasing Bennett about the way his mere presence captivates women. "Do they always get really nervous and stand there, sweating and blushing?" She herself is clearly not immune.

I will never forget this scene, which appeared in the *New Yorker* half a dozen years ago. I found it so authentic and affecting, these two legends from different generations coming together, the moment captured by a legend and superstar in his own right, Gay Talese. Since then, whenever I hear either Gaga or Bennett on the radio, I flash back to that studio in New York, and their charming connection.

This is what Gay Talese can do for a reader. Of course, his stories are all diligently reported and elegantly developed throughout, but in every piece there is also this "you are here" element, a brilliant flash that thoroughly illuminates the characters he profiles.

It happens when I hear a Frank Sinatra song—suddenly I am in a billiard room in a swank private club, as Ol' Blue Eyes confronts a stranger wearing a green shaggy-dog Shetland sweater, a tan suede jacket, and Game Warden boots, and says: "I don't like the way you're dressed." Or when I see an image of Charles Manson, and I am instantly visualizing the owner of the ranch where the Manson clan took refuge, George Spahn, old and blind, who is transfixed by the killer's power over his disciples. These high notes sometimes make you uncomfortable, but they are Talese's own elegant way of capturing the lifeblood of the people he is profiling.

That scene that so perfectly nails Sinatra's arrogance is, of course, from "Frank Sinatra Has a Cold"—Talese's seminal work and the one for which he is most acclaimed. And we connect with George Spahn, perplexed by the mysterious Manson, in "Charlie Manson's Home on the Range," first published in *Esquire* in 1971.

These articles, with their high notes, exemplify the enduring legacy of Gay Talese's writing, how he informs his reader, brings to life a distinctive cast of characters, weaves a story through a montage of ideas and anecdotes, and establishes a cinematic impression that is unforgettable.

The longer pieces in this collection represent the best of Talese's journalism for *Esquire*, a multilayered blend of history, anecdote, and scenes gathered during long stints of boots-on-the-ground contact with his subjects, an intensive approach for which Talese is rightfully celebrated. Talese called it "the art of hanging out," and it's the foundation of his work. He doesn't parachute into a situation; rather, he lives in it and also, instinctively, on the edges of it, making himself available when he senses opportunity, and scarce when his presence becomes a distraction. In another of his more recent *New Yorker* profiles, "Travels with a Diva," you can see Talese negotiating his involvement with the opera singer Marina Poplavskaya so that he is with her when she wants him and nearly invisible when she doesn't. There's a defining moment in that story when the diva complains that Talese's attention is making her nervous—and he backs off while revealing the contradictions of her personality, and her complicated relationship to fame.

Similarly, Talese sometimes finds himself, without fanfare, at the center of a defining moment. In "The Kingdom and the Tower" we see Arthur Gelb, veteran managing editor of the *New York Times*, in a restaurant, commemorating his last day in the old *Times* headquarters before the move to their current location. Surprisingly, Gelb, leading his guests, reveals a key to a secret entrance to the building. Gelb observes that he has used this secret key a thousand times and the last time he will use it is now. This is how we enter the mayhem of the final celebratory night at 229 West Forty-third Street.

Whether he is part of the story—or not—his presence as the architect of the multidimensional world he recreates, and his mastery of intimate detail, is always apparent. You live inside every character and find a place for yourself in each venue because Talese puts you there. In "A Matter of Fantasy," Harold Rubin, who was to become the king of Chicago pornography, leafing through a magazine, first sees the image that would change his life, and we see it as though through his eyes: "She wore no jewelry, no flowers in her hair; there were no footprints in the sand, nothing dated the day or spoiled the perfection of this photograph." In "The Kingdoms, the Powers, and the Glories of the *New York Times*" the notorious *New York Times* editor Clifton Daniel remembers the day he met Margaret Truman, the woman who was to become his wife: "the way she wore her hair, her shoes, the dark blue Fontana dress with the plunging neckline." And then Talese adds a memorable detail that Daniel had confided to a friend years later, "I looked down the neck of that dress, and I haven't looked back since."

As in the instance of Daniel's friend, Talese's journalistic tendrils extend beyond his subjects to characters at the edges of his stories. This, too, is a mark of his persistence as a reporter. His access to Sinatra's milieu, we learn in "On Writing 'Frank Sinatra Has a Cold,'" was, at first, stonewalled. Sinatra would not see him—because he had a cold. Faced with a seemingly insurmountable challenge, Talese worked around his subject, connecting with people who knew the best and the worst of the singer. Incredibly, he fashioned his enduring and revealing profile by following but never actually speaking to Sinatra.

On a more personal note, in "Wartime Sunday," Talese leads the reader on an engaging journey from his own clumsy attempts to fulfill obligations as an altar boy at Sunday mass in Ocean City, New Jersey, through youthful baseball experiences, and continuing with a riff on the proper technique (according to Talese's father, at least) for eating spaghetti. The personal story concludes with a wonderful high note: A young soldier in a restaurant, at a table not far from Talese and his family, eating spaghetti—the wrong way! Oh, and the soldier was Joe DiMaggio.

Extraordinary moments like these emerge throughout this collection, adding color and context to the stories Talese tells. Like the doorman in "The Kidnapping of Joe Bonnano," who saw everything—and nothing—on the night the gangster was snatched.

Near the end of the studio session and the end of the article, an onlooker asks Gaga why the song was such a fitting tune for her to sing with Bennett, and Gaga replies, "Well, 'cause I am a tramp." She then gestures to Bennett, and adds, "He knows it."

But Bennett, cool and collected, shakes his head. "I know you're a lady," he replies emphatically. "Playing a tramp."

The spontaneous and intimate interactions between Gaga and Bennett, which occur throughout the piece, are indicative of the way Gay Talese designs and times everything he writes. He brings to life the famous, the infamous, and the unknowns in a subtle series of evocative cinematic interactions. Long after you read Talese, the high notes ring on.

High Notes

Wartime Sunday

As the dutiful only son of an exacting tailor who presumed to possess the precise measure of my body and soul, it was my unavoidable birthright to wear the customized clothes that reflected my father's taste, advertised his trade, and reaffirmed his art with a needle and thread.

I became my father's miniature mannequin soon after I learned to walk, and during winter I was draped in sturdy worsted coats and jackets with squarish shoulders and hand stitching on the edges of the lapels; on my head was a feathered felt fedora—slanted at an angle favored by my father—that was occasionally knocked off by the rowdy students with whom I rode the bus to parochial school.

Nearly all of my classmates were the children of the Irish-Catholic families that lived along the south Jersey marshlands on the other side of the bay. Catholicism was still a minority religion on this island, settled during the previous century by Protestant prohibitionists, yet the Irish-Catholics brandished absolute authority over my early education and my often-flattened fedora.

Each night I went to bed dreading the next morning's ride on the bus, a rusting vehicle of a purplish-black shade that precisely matched the color of the robes worn by the nuns who dominated the classrooms. The school's bus driver, Mr. Fitzgerald, was a crusty Dublin-born janitor who wore a tweed cap and whose breath exuded a sour blend of oatmeal and whiskey. In addition to his weekday job as driver and school janitor, he appeared each Sunday in the vestry of the church to help the elderly pastor dress for Mass and to help himself surreptitiously to the sacramental wine.

One Sunday morning in the vestry before the 10:15 Mass, as I was buttoning up my cassock in preparation for my duties as an altar boy, I watched as Mr. Fitzgerald (while lifting a lace-trimmed gown over the pastor's head and shoulders) took quick, squint-eyed swallows from a tiny silver flask that he slipped in and out of his jacket. He assumed that his furtive drinking was observed by no one—until he turned to catch me staring at him from the far corner of the room.

Though I was momentarily stunned, I knew that I should convey some gesture of apology. But as I took a step toward him, Mr. Fitzgerald signaled with an upraised palm that I should keep my distance. Then he jabbed his index finger in the air toward me and pointed to a wall hook from which was hung a thin, six-foot-long wooden pole topped by a taper, used to light the tall candles that stood above the altar. I realized that I had forgotten to light the candles.

Quickly I moved through the doorway and, after lighting the taper at the end of the pole, entered the main body of the church. Among the waiting parishioners were my mother and father, sitting close to each other in the third row, two well-tailored Italians in a humble Irish-Catholic parish on a Protestant island, a minority within a minority.

Holding the front hem of my cassock, I climbed five steps to the base of the altar. I could barely see the highest points of the six towering candles; I had no view whatsoever of the wicks, because they were concealed within heavy gold rings that encircled the candle tips to prevent dripping.

Standing on my toes, I extended the long pole above my head toward the first candle. I waited resolutely, expectantly, while gazing up at the burning end of the pole and watching as it emitted wispy black veils of smoke. But the obstinate wick failed to ignite. I stood there patiently, stretching high, as my arms began to ache and my eyes watered. I heard the rustle of the congregation. Everyone was no doubt watching me. I took perverse satisfaction in the fact that I now commanded the attention of the entire church.

I now envisioned the wick as a poisonous spider lodged in the head of the candle whose long white neck I wanted to choke and singe in the manner that I had seen uncooperative enemy conspirators tortured in war films.

Hearing someone snicker, I glanced back toward the Mother Superior. But she had now taken her seat, and her eyes were rigidly focused straight ahead into vacant space.

Before I could further indulge my diabolical fantasy, I was startled by a snapping sound coming from behind me. Lowering the pole and turning toward my audience, I saw eight dark-robed nuns in the front row tilted forward in their seats, frowning; standing above them was the Mother Superior, snapping her fingers and leaning over the altar rail, trying to direct my attention to the candle that held the spider of my imagination.

Moving back a few paces on the platform, I looked up to see that the wick was burning brightly above the candle's ring—and it had been burning for three or four minutes while I had stood daydreaming.

Hearing someone snicker, I glanced back toward the Mother Superior. But she had now taken her seat, and her eyes were rigidly focused straight ahead into vacant space. Behind the nuns were dozens of parishioners who sat with their faces pinched in expressions of pique, or with their mouths opened as they yawned—except for my parents, who sat with their heads slightly bowed, their eyes lowered as if in prayer.

Aware that I had lost my audience as well as whatever was left of my aplomb, I turned to face the five other candles—but not before noticing Mr. Fitzgerald at the vestry door, pointing anxiously at his wristwatch. Mass was now ten minutes late, thanks to my incompetence, and seeing Mr. Fitzgerald in such a fit of agitation caused me to panic; in haste, I began to swipe my fiery pole back and forth through the air within a fraction of an inch of the five unlit candle wicks.

Without looking up to see whether or not I had ignited the wicks, I headed toward the side door into the vestry. But as I disappeared through the doorway, my curiosity made me turn at the final moment to glance over my shoulder to sneak a peek at the upper ledge of the altar. The wicks of the candles were all miraculously aglow.

As Father Blake feebly picked up his chalice and readjusted his tricornered black cap, I took my place and walked out to the altar to begin the Mass that was now almost twenty minutes late.

For most of the next hour I fulfilled my prescribed functions by rote. I held the hem of Father Blake's long vestments as he climbed the altar steps. I genuflected at the proper times. And I adroitly handled and poured from the cut-glass cruets the consecration water and the red wine that Mr. Fitzgerald had mercifully not consumed. I did not fail to ring the bell three times when the priest raised the host—nor did I forget my liturgical responses to the priest, even though, like most altar boys in the parish, I could translate hardly a word of the Latin I had been forced to memorize.

But at the point when I was to lift a heavy, cumbersome prayer book with its wooden stand and carry it from the right side of the altar to the left, I tripped on the hem of my cassock. My body fell heavily across the book and its stand, and I heard the sharp sound of splintered wood—and the groans of the congregation as my chin hit the floor behind the black heels of Father Blake.

Gallantly, he did not turn around, possibly because of his partial deafness, and as I slowly rose to my feet I hoisted the book on its fractured stand and carefully placed it atop the altar—where it rested at a lopsided angle. I shamefully slinked down the steps, fully prepared to occupy my rightful place in the purgatory of errant altar boys.

How I continued to serve out the rest of the Mass on that most miserable Sunday of my young life I will never know. For years thereafter the recollection of that morning could bring a blush to my face. When Mass finally ended, I felt relief but no escape from my humiliation. I pulled off and hung up my short white surplice and my cassock, then put on my topcoat and fedora and departed through the side door without saying goodbye.

I went directly to our car, which was parked a block away. It was a 1941 blue Buick coupe that my father had bought one month before the government's metal-rationing policy. Opening the door and climbing into the back seat, I slumped low and pulled my hat forward, hoping to avoid notice by the passing pedestrians who might have witnessed my pathetic performance in church.

Through the windshield, I saw my parents approaching with my sister, and I moved up in the seat and awaited them with feelings of mild resentment. I did not want them to invade the quiet enclosure of the car.

My mother was wearing a beaver coat that my father had recently made slimmer and remodeled with a mink collar and cuffs—a coat that had hung unclaimed for years in the fur-storage vault of my parents' store. This was one of several fur coats my mother had, some having been purchased new from a designer friend of my father's, others having been inherited from storage customers who died without claimants or had bartered their furs in exchange for new dresses and suits during the Depression, or who had long abandoned them in the vault because the coat or cape or boa had now become outmoded and was no longer considered worth the cost of several years of unpaid storage bills.

Thus did my family's legacy become festooned with fur pieces of every size and shape, and during sweltering summer afternoons I liked nothing better than to unlock the frosty vault that extended along one side of the store and to sidle swiftly down the rows of coats while nuzzling my face into the variegated pelts: the luxurious mink, the curly broadtail, the bristly raccoon, the deep, incredibly cool softness of chinchilla.

The car door opened, and my mother, in her beaver coat, entered the front seat.

"We were outside the church all this time looking for you," my mother said, seeming more concerned than irritated. "Why didn't you wait for us in front of the church?"

"I was too tired and cold," I replied.

She said nothing as we all waited for my father to finish wiping the windshield. The sunlight that had shown through the glass was now subdued by clouds, and a sudden breeze blew dust and sand across the hood of the car, causing my father to close his eyes and hold on to his hat. He then opened the door and glanced at me in the back seat as if assessing my mood.

"We could drive to Philadelphia and have a good dinner, if we had the gas," he said, alluding to the wartime fuel shortage. "But instead we'll go tonight to Atlantic City."

"They have homework," my mother said.

"They have all afternoon to do their homework," my father said. "We'll go early enough and be back before ten." Smiling at me through the rearview mirror, he seemed to understand my desire to escape, however briefly, the narrow boundaries of this island.

My mother unbuttoned my sister's snowsuit as my father started up the Buick. We began the ten-minute ride to our apartment above the store. I gazed at my family in the front seat—my father in a tweed overcoat and brown fedora, my mother with her fur coat and black leather curved-brim hat, and my sister in a pink snowsuit trimmed with pieces of white rabbit fur that had been left over from one of my father's alteration jobs.

He wasted nothing. The fur scraps left on his cutting table after he had shortened one customer's coat would later reappear to decorate the pocket flaps or the collar or the hem of another customer's cloth coat he had been paid to remodel. The creative skill he had once exhibited as a designer and cutter of men's custom-made suits, a skill that in the current economy was reduced to a pauper's art, was now put to profit in the repair and restyling of ladies' furs.

Earlier that year, when fabric of every kind was rationed due to the war, I had watched my father one afternoon tear about one hundred small swatches of woolen material out of several sample books; then, after he had laid out the swatches on a table and arranged them into an interesting mosaic, he sewed the varicolored swatches together to form a large section of material from which he created a most uncommon hacking jacket. After lining it with satin, he proceeded to wear it around town with a vivid silk handkerchief sprouting immodestly from his breast pocket.

The Buick continued slowly uptown past the small hotels and rooming houses now closed for the winter. Most of the houses had turrets, dormered roofs, finials that seagulls stood upon, and spacious porches cluttered with upturned wicker sofas and deck chairs tied down against the whip of the wind.

Hardly anyone walked along the sidewalks. Except for the pharmacy and cigar store, there was a Sabbath ban on all businesses, including the town's single cinema, where the marquee's lettering read: THE HUNCH-BACK OF NOTRE DAME . . . CHARLES LAUGHTON, MAUREEN O'HARA

I listened absently while my parents exchanged shoptalk over my sister's head as she snuggled between them reading the comics. The radio was tuned to a Philadelphia station that specialized in classical music, but there was so much static that the music was barely audible. Still, I knew that my father's uncompromising commitment to that kind of music would prevent him from switching to one of the clearer stations featuring such popular bands as Benny Goodman's or Tommy Dorsey's, or the vocalists I liked to hear, such as Bing Crosby, Nat King Cole, or Frank Sinatra.

The fact that Sinatra was an Italo-American gained no concession from my father, who seemed irrationally resistant to any and all performers who appealed primarily to a youthful spirit or exemplified the latest fad. The objects of his displeasure included not only crooners but also the most celebrated new stars of Hollywood and the heralded figures of the sports world.

When my father was growing up, there were no games to be played. He passed through his adolescent years without knowing what it was like to be young. Among athletes, he regarded baseball players as the most excessively praised and the sport itself as the most tediously time-consuming, and his weary response to the game was escalated to an active dislike of it after I became, at the age of nine, a baseball addict.

I became hooked on baseball during the summer of 1941, as the New York Yankees' center fielder, Joe DiMaggio, was breaking a major-league record by hitting in fifty-six successive games. Even on my provincial island, where the fans were exceedingly partial to the teams from Philadelphia, the New York slugger was admired by the crowds of people that gathered on the boardwalk or under the green-striped awning of a midtown grocery market where a radio loudly played a new song recorded by Les Brown's band:

From Coast to Coast, that's all you hear
Of Joe the One-Man Show
He's glorified the horsehide sphere,
Jolting Joe DiMaggio . . .
Joe . . . Joe . . . DiMaggio . . . we
Want you on our side

One day as I strolled into my parents' store whistling that tune, my father, who recognized it immediately, turned away and walked back to the cutting room, slowly shaking his head. I continued with my whistling, albeit less forcefully, throughout the day. I recognize this as perhaps my first sign of rebellion against my father, one that would intensify during the next two years, until I began to plan my escape from parochial school for when the Yankees would begin spring training in March 1944.

I would not have to go far. It had recently been announced that, due to wartime restrictions on travel, the Yankees would forgo Florida to train in Atlantic City. After reading this, I secretly marked the passage of each grim, cold day, anticipating a glorious spring in which I would travel by trolley across the marshlands to the rickety little stadium that would be ennobled by the presence of baseball's World Champions. I revealed none of these plans to my father, of course, and I vowed that my rendezvous would be realized no matter what he said or did to justify his abnormal aversion to the national pastime.

If truth be told, however, I would one day understand my father's lack of appreciation of sports. When he was a boy growing up during the First World War, there were no games to be played. Child labor was not only accepted but demanded by the destitute conditions of the day, and my father passed through his adolescent years without knowing what it was like to be young.

As he was quick to remind me whenever I complained about having to help out in the store, he had been forced to hold down two demanding jobs while attending grammar school. He rose at dawn to serve as a tailor's apprentice in his uncle's shop; later, after school, he toiled in the valley on his grandfather's farm, which was short of workers because men had been conscripted by the Italian army since 1914.

Among those summoned was my father's older brother, Sebastian, who would return from the front in 1916 feeble-minded and crippled from inhaling poisonous gas and being bombarded by artillery shells during trench warfare against the Germans. Since Sebastian never fully recovered, and since my father's father, Gaetano, had died two years earlier of asbestosis shortly after returning to Italy from his factory job in America, my father became prematurely responsible for the welfare of his widowed mother and her three younger children.

Two of these children (my father's brothers Nicola and Domenico) were now Italian infantrymen, united with the Germans against the Allied armies attacking Italy. Almost every night after I went to bed, I could overhear my father's whispered prayers as he knelt on the prie-dieu in our living room, under the wall portrait of Saint Francis di Paola, begging the medieval monk to save his brothers from death, and pleading also for the protection of his family members who were now trapped in the war zones of southern Italy. Sicily had surrendered by this time, but the Allies had not yet conquered southern Italy, and throughout 1943, in our apartment and in the store, I was aware of my father's volatile behavior, his moods abruptly shifting between resignation and peevishness, tenderness and aloofness, openness and secrecy. On this flag-waving island where my father wished to be perceived publicly as a patriotic citizen, I instinctively sympathized with his plight as a kind of emotional double agent.

After returning from school, I would see his uneasiness when the postman walked into the store to drop a pack of mail on the counter. When the postman had left, my father would approach the mail tentatively and sift through it to see whether it contained any of those odd, flimsy envelopes sent from overseas. If he found any, he would place them unopened next to the cash register in my mother's dress department.

After the doors of the store were closed and locked, my mother would open and silently read each overseas letter, while my father watched her face for any sign of shock or sadness. If she showed neither, he would be reassured that there had been no disaster and would quietly take the letter from her and read it himself.

I was disturbed by these scenes and wished to remain as detached as possible from the complex reality that embraced my life. There were many times when I wished that I had been born into a different family, a plain and simple family of impeccable American credentials—a no-secrets, non-whispering, no-enemy-soldiers family that never received mail from POW camps, or prayed to a painting of an ugly monk, or ate Italian bread with pungent cheese.

I would have preferred having a mother who spent less time in the store with the island's leading Protestant ladies, to whom she sold dresses, and more time playing parish politics with the nuns and the offshore Irish women who invaded our school on PTA evenings and Bingo Nights. And I would have welcomed a father who could have become more relaxed and casual, and on weekends would have removed his vest and tie and played ball with me on the beach.

But I knew this last wish was pure fantasy on my part—a discovery I had made the summer before, after I had spent a half hour bouncing a red rubber ball against a brick wall in the parking lot behind our shop. I was supposed to be working in the store at the time, affixing long, thin cardboard guards to the bottom of wire hangers, then lining these hangers up on a pipe rack within reach of two black men who were pressing trousers and jackets. But after I had hung up about fifty hangers with the guards attached, I disappeared through the clouds of steam rising from the pressing machines and, with the ball in my pocket, slipped out the back door into the cool breeze of the parking lot. There I began to fling the ball against the wall and practice fielding it on the short hop in imitation of the Yankees' star second baseman, the acrobatic, dark-eyed Joe Gordon, to whom I fancied I bore some resemblance.

I assumed that my father was away from the store having lunch, which he always did in the middle of Saturday afternoon; I was therefore suddenly shaken by the sight of him opening the back door, then walking toward me with a frown on his face. Not knowing what to do, but nonetheless compelled by nervous energy to do something, I quickly took the ball in my right hand, cocked my arm, and threw it at him.

The ball soared forty feet in a high arc toward his head. He was so startled to see it coming that he halted his step and stared skittishly up at the sky through his steel-rimmed glasses. Then—as if not knowing whether to block the ball or try and catch it—he extended his arms upward, cupped his soft tailor's hands, and braced himself for the impact.

I stood watching anxiously from the far corner of the lot, no less shocked than he that I had chosen this moment to confront him—perhaps for the first time in his life—with the challenge of catching a ball. I cringed as I saw the ball hit him solidly on the side of the neck, carom off a shoulder, rebound against the wall behind him, and come rolling slowly back to his feet, where it finally stopped.

As I waited, holding my breath, he lowered his head and began to rub his neck. Then, seeing the ball at his feet, he stooped to pick it up. For a moment he held the rubber ball in his right hand and examined it as if it were a strange object. He squeezed it. He turned it around in his fingers. Finally, with a bashful smile, he turned toward me, cocked his arm awkwardly, and tried to throw the ball in my direction.

But it slipped from his grip, skidded weakly at an oblique angle, and rolled under one of his dry-cleaning trucks parked idly along the edge of the lot.

As I hastened to retrieve it, I saw him shrug his shoulders. He seemed to be very embarrassed. He who cared so much about appearances had tried his best, and yet the results were pitiful—it was a sorrowful moment for both of us.

But I heard my father make no excuses as I crawled under the truck to get the ball. And when I got up again, I saw that he was gone.

. . .

The Buick turned the corner past the bank into the business district and stopped in front of our store. It was almost 12:15, and I should have been hungry when my father announced cheerfully, "I'm making pancakes—who wants some?" My sister Marian jumped and cheered, but I remained silent.

I followed as Marian skipped up the steep, carpeted, indoor staircase with its beige stone walls, which ascended past two landings to an arched entrance. A black cast-iron chandelier hung above the entrance, and the outer wall at each landing contained a four-foot niche encasing a holy statue and an ever-burning red votive candle.

In one niche was a serenely composed figure of the Virgin Mary, who stood exquisitely unruffled while under her bare feet a snake squirmed. In the other niche was the brown-robed statuette of Saint Francis di Paola, who, though his sandaled feet were free from snakes, possessed a characteristically grim and sulky facial expression—just as depressing as that in his wall portrait in our apartment and in the living rooms of most of my father's Philadelphia friends. This wretched-looking monk was the leading spoilsport in all of sainthood, a horror since my earliest childhood; today he reminded me somewhat of myself, and I loathed him more than usual.

In the apartment, I hung up my hat and my coat, and after politely refusing my mother's offer to bring me lunch while I did my homework, I closed my bedroom door—to resume working on one of my model airplanes. It was a Lockheed P-38 fighter with a twin fuselage. Carefully pasting crisp, thin sections of paper onto the balsa-wood frame, I could hear the sounds of Puccini rising softly from my father's Victrola. I pictured him seated in the living room in his favorite chair, reading the newspaper—and also my mother, at the other end of the apartment, in her usual seat at the dining-room table, helping my sister with spelling, reading, and arithmetic.

A typical Sunday—so different from the rest of the week because there were no bonging sounds in the apartment every time someone opened the door of the shop; the upstairs telephone extension was not ringing every minute with customers' calls; and if I turned on my small radio there would not be the usual static that existed whenever the electric sewing machines were zipping along in the cutting room.

Often on summery Saturday afternoons, when the Yankees' games were being broadcast from New York, I would sneak down to the front of the store and turn off the two principal lights that caused most of the static, then quickly return upstairs to press my right ear against the warm radio and hope that the voice of the Yankees, Mel Allen, would fill me in on whatever action I had missed.

When my father became aware of my gamesmanship with the lights, he would quietly enter the apartment and sometimes catch me hunched against the radio—and after snapping off the dial, he would furiously shove me by the shoulders down the rear steps into the back of the store, near the pressing machines and the sweating black men partly obscured in the clouds of steam. There on the floor were huge boxes of cardboard guards waiting to be hooked onto the bottom of new wire hangers. Or, worse, there were piles of rusty, used hangers that my father had bought cheaply from customers (to offset the limited supply of metal hangers produced in wartime). These entangled hangers that clung together like a basket of crabs had to be separated, bent into proper shape, scraped clear of rust, then affixed one by one with a cardboard guard. The game proceeded without me, its eventual conclusion unknown to me until, on the following day, I anxiously reached for the sports section of the paper.

But on this static-free Sunday, since the broadcasts of professional football held little appeal, I concentrated on my model airplanes—I razor-cut the wood, fit it to the pattern, and slowly succumbed to the etherlike effect of the powerful glue that soon put me to sleep.

Hours passed before my mother, with a soft nudge, whispered so that my father could not hear: "Hurry, dress—we're leaving for Atlantic City."

The Buick moved through the darkened streets toward the bay bridge, avoiding the coastline. All lighting was prohibited along the ocean. Houses within view of the ocean had their window shades pulled down, and the beach was now occupied only by mounted Coast Guardsmen, whose horses could move in water reaching up to their necks and were trained not to become alarmed by the sight of the phosphorous flashes that sometimes jumped above the waves.

Over the marshlands, past the pine trees, beyond the frosted farmlands and country roads that barely reflected the blue-tinted headlights of our car, we finally reached the circular boulevard with its central granite monument that marked the entrance, away from the coast, into Atlantic City.

After a few blocks on the main avenue, over which a silvery span of Christmas decorations devoid of lights framed the night, my father turned into a side street where there were bars and nightclubs with black men and women standing in front. Two blocks beyond, without a black person in sight, we were in the Italian neighborhood, with its locally renowned Venice Restaurant.

Nearly every table was occupied by Italo-American families with babies in high chairs (I recognized a red chair that I had once occupied); and the waiters, wearing tuxedos and clip-on bow ties, moved swiftly up and down the aisles with their trays, conversing with their customers and with one another in a dialectical blend of English and Italian. Though called the Venice, there was little Venetian about it, the aroma of cooking was clearly Neapolitan, and prominently displayed behind the bar was a mural of the Bay of Naples—the last view of Italy that many of these people had had before embarking for America.

My father took our orders, as he always did, then conveyed them in Italian to one of the waiters, who never wrote anything down. As usual, my first plate was spaghetti with clam sauce—and my usual way of consuming this was with a fork and a round tablespoon, which I held like a catcher's mitt to scoop up the fallen bits of clam and to stabilize my fork as I attempted to twirl the spaghetti strands into a tight and tidy mouthful.

My father, I'd noticed, never ate spaghetti in this fashion. He used only the fork, with which he masterfully twirled the strands without any of them dangling as he lifted them to his mouth. But on this occasion, after my plate had arrived and I had begun in my customary style with the spoon, he sat watching with an almost pained look on his face. Then he said, patiently: "You know, I think you're old enough now to learn how to do it right."

"To do what right?"

"To eat spaghetti right," he said. "Without the spoon. Only people without manners eat spaghetti that way—or people who are ignorant, like most Americans, or those Italian-Americans who are *cafoni* [country bumpkins]—but in Italy the refined Italians would never be seen in public using the spoon."

Putting aside the spoon, I tried two or three times to spin the spaghetti around the fork, but each time, the strands fell off the plate and slipped onto the tablecloth or onto the floor.

"Forget it," my father said, finally. "Forget it for today—but from now on, practice. One day you'll learn to get it right."

Soon the second course arrived, then dessert and the black coffee in the small cup that my father drank. My parents talked business, and my sister and I shifted restlessly.

My wandering attention was drawn to a large table near the bar, around which a festive crowd of middle-aged men and women were laughing and applauding, raising their wineglasses toward a young soldier who was with them.

The soldier sat very tall in his khaki uniform. His hair was shiny black and precisely parted. His shoulders were huge, his long face lean and hard, and his brown eyes were alert. He seemed to be fully aware of how special he was. The people around him could hardly stop watching him, or touching him, or patting him gently on the back as he bent forward to eat. Only he was eating. The others ignored their plates to concentrate on watching him, applauding and toasting his every move.

As the waiter arrived with our check, I held his sleeve and asked: "Who's that soldier over there?"

The waiter's eyebrows rose with a slight flutter, and leaning into my ear he replied: "That's Joe DiMaggio!"

Bolting to my feet, I stared at the tall soldier who continued to eat, and I imagined in the distance the solid sound of the bat, the roar of the crowd, the spirited rhythm of Les Brown's band.

Tapping my father's shoulder, I said: "That's Joe DiMaggio!"

Looking up from the check he had been scrutinizing for any sign of error, my father glanced casually at the big table. Then he turned back and replied: "So?"

Ignoring my father, I remained standing, in prolonged appreciation. And before we left the restaurant I took one final look, closer this time, and I noticed that on the table in front of my hero was a steaming plate of spaghetti. Then his head leaned forward, his mouth opened, and everybody around him smiled—including me—as he twirled his fork in midair and scraped it unabashedly in a large silver spoon.

The Kidnapping of Joe Bonanno

Knowing that it is possible to see too much, most doormen in New York have developed an extraordinary sense of selective vision: they know what to see and what to ignore, when to be curious and when to be indolent—they are most often standing indoors, unaware, when there are accidents or arguments in front of their buildings, and they are usually in the street seeking taxicabs when burglars are escaping through the lobby. Although a doorman may disapprove of bribery and adultery, his back is invariably turned when the superintendent is handing money to the fire inspector or when a tenant whose wife is away escorts a young woman into the elevator—which is not to accuse the doorman of hypocrisy or cowardice but merely to suggest that his instinct for uninvolvement is very strong, and to speculate that doormen have perhaps learned through experience that nothing is to be gained by serving as a material witness to life's unseemly sights or to the madness of the city. This being so, it was not surprising that on the night when the reputed Mafia chief, Joseph Bonanno, was grabbed by two gunmen in front of a luxury apartment house on Park Avenue near Thirty-sixth Street, shortly after midnight on a rainy Tuesday in October, the doorman was standing in the lobby talking to the elevator man and saw nothing.

It all happened with dramatic suddenness: Bonanno, returning from a restaurant, stepped out of a taxicab behind his lawyer, William P. Maloney, who ran ahead through the rain toward the canopy. Then the gunmen appeared from the darkness and began pulling Bonanno by the arms toward an awaiting automobile. Bonanno struggled to break free but he could not. He glared at the men, seeming enraged and stunned—not since Prohibition had he been so abruptly handled, and then it had been by the police when he had refused to answer questions; now he was being prodded by men from his own world, two burly men wearing black coats and hats, both about six feet tall, one of whom said: "Com'on, Joe, my boss wants to see you."

Bonanno, a handsome gray-haired man of fifty-nine, said nothing. He had gone out this evening without bodyguards or a gun, and even if the avenue had been crowded with people he would not have called to them for help because he regarded this as a private affair. He tried to regain his composure, to think clearly as the men forced him along the sidewalk, his arms numb from their grip. He shivered from the cold rain and wind, feeling it seep through his gray silk suit, and he could see nothing through the mist of Park Avenue except the taillights of his taxicab disappearing uptown, and could hear nothing but the heavy breathing of the men as they dragged him forward. Then, suddenly from the rear, Bonanno heard the running footsteps and voice of Maloney shouting: "Hey, what the hell's going on?"

One gunman whirled around, warning, "Quit it, get back!"

"Get out of here," Maloney replied, continuing to rush forward, a white-haired man of sixty waving his arms in the air, "that's my client!"

A bullet from an automatic was fired at Maloney's feet. The lawyer stopped, retreated, ducking finally into the entrance of his apartment building. The men shoved Bonanno into the back seat of a beige sedan that had been parked on the corner of Thirty-sixth Street, its motor idling. Bonanno lay on the floor, as he had been told, and the car bolted toward Lexington Avenue. Then the doorman joined Maloney on the sidewalk, arriving too late to see anything, and later the doorman claimed that he had not heard a shot.

• • •

Bill Bonanno, a tall, heavy, dark-haired man of thirty-one whose crew cut and button-down shirt suggested the college student that he had been in the 1950s, but whose moustache had been grown recently to help conceal his identity, sat in a sparsely furnished apartment in Queens listening intently as the telephone rang. But he did not answer it.

It rang three times, stopped, rang again and stopped, rang a few more times and stopped. It was Labruzzo's code. Frank Labruzzo was in a telephone booth a few blocks away signaling that he was on his way back to the apartment. On arriving at the apartment house, Labruzzo would repeat the signal on the downstairs doorbell and the younger Bonanno would then press the buzzer releasing the lock. Bonanno would then wait, gun in hand, looking through the peephole of the apartment to be sure that it was Labruzzo getting out of the elevator. The furnished apartment the two men shared was on the top floor of a brick building in a middle-class neighborhood, and since their apartment door was at the end of the hall they could observe everyone who came and went from the single self-service elevator.

Such precautions were being taken not only by Bill Bonanno and Frank Labruzzo but by dozens of other members of the Joseph Bonanno organization who for the last few weeks had been hiding out in similar buildings in Queens, Brooklyn, and the Bronx. It was a very tense time for all of them. They knew that at any moment they could expect a confrontation with rival gangs trying to kill them or with government agents trying to arrest them and interrogate them about the rumors of violent plots and vendettas now circulating through the underworld. The government had recently concluded, largely from information obtained through wiretapping and electronic bugging devices, that even the top bosses in the Mafia were personally involved in this internal feud and that Joseph Bonanno, a powerful don for thirty-three years, was in the middle of the controversy. He was suspected by other dons of excessive ambition, of seeking to expand at their expense, and perhaps over their dead bodies, the influence that he already had in various parts of New York, Canada, and the Southwest. The recent elevation of his son, Bill, to the No. 3 position in the Bonanno organization was also regarded with alarm and skepticism by a few leaders of other gangs as well as by some members of Bonanno's own gang of about three hundred men in Brooklyn.

The younger Bonanno was considered something of an eccentric in the underworld, a privileged product of prep schools and universities, whose manner and methods, while not lacking in courage, conveyed some of the reckless spirit of a campus activist. He seemed impatient with the system, unimpressed with the roundabout ways and Old World finesse that are part of Mafia tradition. He said exactly what was on his mind, not altering his tone when addressing a mafioso of superior rank, and not losing his sense of youthful conviction even when speaking the dated Sicilian dialect he had learned as a boy from his grandfather in Brooklyn. The fact that he was six-feet-two and more than two hundred pounds, and that his posture was erect and his mind very quick, added to the formidability of his presence and lent substance to his own high opinion of himself, which was that he was the equal or superior of every man with whom he was associating except for possibly one, his father. When in the latter's company, Bill Bonanno seemed to lose some of his easy confidence and poise, becoming more quiet, hesitant, as if his father were severely testing his every word and thought. He seemed to exhibit toward his father a distance and formality, taking no more liberties than he would with a stranger. But he was also very attentive to his father's needs and seemed to take great pleasure in pleasing him. It was obvious that he was awed by his father, and, while he no doubt had feared him and perhaps still did, he also worshiped him.

During the last few weeks he had never been very far from Joseph Bonanno's side, but last night, knowing that his father wished to dine alone with his lawyers and that he planned to spend the evening at Maloney's place, Bill Bonanno passed a quiet evening at the apartment with Labruzzo watching television, reading the newspapers, and waiting for word. Without knowing exactly why, he was mildly on edge. Perhaps one reason was a story he had read in the *Daily News* reporting that life in the underworld was becoming increasingly perilous and claiming that the older Bonanno had recently planned the murder of two rival dons, Carlo Gambino and Thomas (Three Finger Brown) Luchese, a scheme that supposedly failed because one of the triggermen had betrayed Bonanno and had tipped off one of the intended victims. Even if such a report were pure fabrication, being based possibly on the FBI's wiretapping of low-level Mafia gossip, the publicity given to it was of concern to the younger Bonanno because he knew that it could intensify the suspicion that indeed did exist among the various gangs that ran the rackets (which included numbers games, bookmaking, loan-sharking, prostitution, smuggling and enforced protection), and the publicity could also inspire the outcry of the politicians, provoke the more vigilant pursuit of the police, and result in the issuing of more subpoenas by the courts.

The subpoena was now dreaded more in the underworld than before because of a new federal law requiring that a suspected criminal, if picked up for questioning, must either testify if given immunity by the court or possibly face a sentence for contempt. This made it imperative for the men of the Mafia to remain inconspicuous if wishing to avoid subpoenas every time there were newspaper headlines, and the law also impeded the Mafia leaders' direction of their men in the street because the latter, having to be very cautious and often detained by their caution and evasiveness, were not always where they were supposed to be at the appointed hour to do a job, and they were also frequently unavailable to receive, at designated telephone booths at specific moments, prearranged calls from headquarters seeking a report on what had happened. In a secret society where precision was important, the new problem in communications was grating the already jangled nerves of many top mafiosi.

The Bonanno organization, more progressive than most partly because of the modern business methods introduced by the younger Bonanno, had solved its communications problem to a degree by its bell-code system and also by the use of a telephone-answering service. It was perhaps the only gang in the Mafia with an answering service. The service was registered in the name of a fictitious Mr. Baxter, which was the younger Bonanno's code name, and it was attached to the home telephone of one member's maiden aunt who barely spoke English and was hard of hearing. Throughout the day various key men would call the service and identify themselves through agreed-upon aliases and would leave cryptic messages confirming their safety and the fact that business was progressing as usual. If a message contained the initials "IBM"—"suggest you buy more IBM"—it meant that Frank Labruzzo, who had once worked for IBM, was reporting. If the word "monk" was in a message it identified another member of the organization, a man with a tonsured head who often concealed his identity in public under a friar's robe. Any reference to a "salesman" indicated the identity of one of the Bonanno captains who was a jewelry salesman on the side; and "flower" alluded to a gunman whose father in Sicily was a florist. A "Mr. Boyd" was a member whose mother was known to live on Boyd Street in Long Island, and reference to a "cigar" identified a certain lieutenant who was never without one. Joseph Bonanno was known on the answering service as "Mr. Shepherd."

• • •

One of the reasons that Frank Labruzzo had left the apartment that he shared with Bill Bonanno was to telephone the service from a neighborhood coin box and also to buy the early edition of the afternoon newspaper to see if there were any announcements or developments of special interest. As usual, Labruzzo was accompanied by the pet dog that shared their apartment. It had been Bill Bonanno who had suggested that all gang members in hiding keep dogs in their apartments, and while this had initially made it more difficult for the men to find rooms, since some landlords objected to pets, the men later agreed with Bonanno that the presence of a dog not only made them more alert to sounds outside their doors but a dog was also a useful companion to have when going outside for a walk—a man with a dog aroused very little suspicion in the street.

Bonanno and Labruzzo also happened to like dogs, which was one of the many things that they had in common and it contributed to their compatibility in the small apartment. Frank Labruzzo was a calm, easy-going, somewhat stocky man of fifty-three with glasses and graying dark hair; he was a senior officer in the Bonanno organization and also a member of the immediate family—Labruzzo's sister, Fay, was Joseph Bonanno's wife and Bill Bonanno's mother, and Labruzzo was close to the son in ways that the father was not. There was no strain or stress between these two, no competitiveness or problems of vanity and ego. Labruzzo, not terribly ambitious for himself, not driven like Joseph Bonanno nor restless like the son, was content with his secondary position in the world, recognizing the world as a very much larger place than either of the Bonannos seemed to think that it was.

Labruzzo had attended college and had engaged in a number of occupations, but he had pursued none for very long. He had, in addition to working for IBM, operated a dry-goods store, sold insurance, and had been a mortician. Once he had owned, in partnership with Joseph Bonanno, a funeral parlor in Brooklyn near the block of his birth in the center of a neighborhood where thousands of immigrant Sicilians had settled at the turn of the century. It was in this neighborhood that the elder Bonanno had courted Fay Labruzzo, daughter of a prosperous butcher who had manufactured wine during Prohibition. The butcher had been proud to have Bonanno as a son-in-law even though the wedding date, in 1930, had had to be postponed for thirteen months due to a gangland war involving hundreds of newly arrived Sicilians and Italians, including Bonanno, who were continuing the provincial discord transplanted to America but originating in the ancient mountain villages that they had abandoned in all but spirit. These men had brought with them to the New World their old feuds and customs, their traditional friendships and fears and suspicions, and they not only consumed themselves with these things but they also influenced many of their children, sometimes their children's children—and among the inheritors were such men as Frank Labruzzo and Bill Bonanno, who now, in the middle 1960s, in the age of space and rockets, were fighting a feudal war.

It seemed both absurd and remarkable to the two men that they had never escaped the insular ways of their parents' world, a subject that they had often discussed during their many hours of confinement, discussing it usually in tones of amusement and unconcern, although with regret at times, even bitterness. Yes, we're in the wagon-wheel business, Bonanno had once sighed, and Labruzzo had agreed—they were modern men, lost in time, grinding old axes; and this fact was particularly surprising in the case of Bill Bonanno: he had left Brooklyn at an early age to attend boarding schools in Arizona, where he had been reared outside the family, and had learned to ride horses and brand cattle, had dated blonde girls whose fathers owned ranches; and he had later, as a student at the University of Arizona, led a platoon of ROTC cadets across the football field before each game to help raise the American flag prior to the playing of the national anthem. That he could have suddenly shifted from this campus scene in the Southwest to the precarious world of his father in New York was due to a series of bizarre circumstances that were perhaps beyond his control, perhaps not. Certainly his marriage had been a step in his father's direction, a marriage in 1956 to Rosalie Profaci, the pretty dark-eyed niece of Joseph Profaci, the millionaire importer who was also a member of the Mafia's national commission.

Bill Bonanno had first met Rosalie Profaci when she was a young student attending a convent school in upstate New York with his sister. At that time he had had a girlfriend in Arizona, a casual American girl with a flair for freedom; while Rosalie was appealing, she also was demure and sheltered. That the young couple would meet again and again, during summer months and holidays, was largely due to their parents, who were very close, and whose approval was bestowed in subtle but infectious ways whenever Rosalie and Bill would converse or merely sit near to one another in crowded rooms. At one large family gathering months before the engagement, Joseph Bonanno, taking his twenty-one-year-old daughter Catherine aside, asked her privately what she thought of the likelihood that Bill would marry Rosalie. Catherine Bonanno, an independent-minded girl, thought for a moment, then said that while she was extremely fond of Rosalie personally she did not feel that Rosalie was right for Bill. Rosalie lacked the strength of character to accept him for what he was and might become, Catherine said, and she was about to say something else when, suddenly, she felt a hard slap across her face, and she fell back, stunned, confused, then had burst into tears as she ran, having never before seen her father so enraged, his eyes so fiery and fierce. Later he had tried to comfort her, to apologize in his way, but she remained aloof for days although she understood as she had not before her father's desire for the marriage. It was a wish shared by Rosalie's father and uncle. And it would be fulfilled the following year, an event that Catherine Bonanno would regard as a marriage of fathers.

The wedding, on August 18, 1956, had been extraordinary. More than three thousand guests had attended the reception at the Astor Hotel ballroom in New York following the church wedding in Brooklyn, and no expense had been spared in embellishing the occasion. Leading orchestras had been hired for the dancing, and the entertainment included the singing of the Four Lads and Tony Bennett. Pan American Airways was engaged to fly in thousands of daisies from California because that flower, Rosalie's favorite, was then unavailable in New York. A truckload of champagne and wine had been sent as a gift by a distributor in Brooklyn. The guest list, in addition to the legitimate businessmen and politicians and priests, included all the top men of the underworld. Vito Genovese and Frank Costello were there, having requested and received inconspicuous tables against the wall. Albert Anastasia was there, it being a year before his murder in the Park Sheraton Hotel barbershop, and so was Joseph Barbara, whose barbecue party for nearly seventy mafiosi at his home in Apalachin, New York, three weeks after the murder, would be discovered by the police and would result in national publicity and endless investigations. Joseph Zerilli had come with his men from Detroit, and so had the Chicago delegation led by Sam Giancana and Tony Accardo. Stefano Magaddino, the portly old don from Buffalo, cousin of Joseph Bonanno, had been given an honored table in front of the dais, and seated near to him were other relatives or close friends of the Bonannos and Profacis. All of the twenty-four semi-independent organizations that formed the national syndicate had been represented at the wedding, meaning that there were men from New England to New Mexico, and the group from Los Angeles alone had totaled almost eighty.

. . .

Bill Bonanno, smiling next to his bride on the dais, toasting the guests and being toasted in turn, had often wondered during the evening what the FBI would have done had it gotten its hands on the guest list. But there had beeh little chance of that since the list, in code, had been in the careful custody of Frank Labruzzo and his men who had been posted at the door to receive the guests and to escort them to their tables. There had been no intruders on that night, nor had there been a great deal of public concern over the Mafia in 1956, the Kefauver hearings of 1951 having been forgotten, and the Apalachin fiasco being one year away. And so the wedding and reception had proceeded smoothly and without incident, with Catherine Bonanno as the maid of honor and Joseph Bonanno, elegant in his cutaway, had presided over the gathering like a medieval duke, bowing toward his fellow dons, dancing with the women, courtly and proud.

After the reception, during which the bridal couple had received in gift envelopes about $100,000 in cash, they had flown to Europe for a honeymoon. They had stayed for a few days at the Ritz Hotel in Paris, then at the Excelsior in Rome, receiving special attention in each place and having been ushered quickly through customs at the airport. Later they had flown to Sicily, and as the plane slowly taxied toward the terminal building in Palermo, Bill Bonanno noticed that a large crowd had gathered behind the gate and that a number of carabinieri were among them, standing very close to Bonanno's aging bald-headed uncle, John Bonventre, who seemed rather grim and tense. Bill Bonanno's first thought was that Bonventre, who had once served in the United States as an under-boss in the Bonanno organization, was about to be deported from his native Sicily, to which he had gone the year before to retire, having taken with him from America a lifetime's supply of toilet paper, preferring it to the coarse brands produced in Sicily. As the plane had stopped, but before the door had opened, a stewardess stood to ask that Mr. and Mrs. Bonanno please identify themselves. Slowly, Bill Bonanno had raised his hand. The stewardess had then asked that the couple be the first to leave the plane.

Walking down the ramp into the hot Sicilian sun, mountains rising in the distance behind sloping villages of tan stone houses, Bonanno had sensed the crowd staring at him, moving and murmuring as he got closer. The old women were dressed in black, the younger men had fixed dark expressions, children were milling everywhere, and the statuesque carabinieri, flamboyantly dressed and brandishing gleaming silver swords, stood taller than the rest. Then the uncle, Bonventre, bursting with a smile of recognition, had run with arms outstretched toward the bridal couple, and the crowd had followed, and suddenly the Bonannos had been surrounded by clutching kissing strangers, and Rosalie, blushing, had tried without success to conceal the awkwardness she had felt in the center of swarming unrestrained affection. Her husband, however, had seemed to enjoy it thoroughly, reaching out with his long arms to touch everyone that he could, leaning low to be embraced by the women and children, basking in the adoration and salutations of the crowd. The carabinieri had watched impassively for a few moments, then had stepped aside, clearing a path that led toward a line of illegally parked automobiles waiting to take the couple to the first of a series of celebrations that would culminate with a visit on the following day to Castellammare del Golfo, the town in western Sicily where Joseph Bonanno had been born and where earlier Bonannos had long ruled as *uomini rispettati*—men of respect.

Rosalie had hoped that they would also visit her father's birthplace, a town just east of Palermo called Villabate, but her husband, without ever explaining why, indicated that this was impossible. Moments after he had landed at Palmero his uncle had whispered a message just received from the United States from the elder Bonanno insisting that the couple avoid Villabate. A number of friends and distant relatives of the Profacis still living in Villabate were then struggling with a rival gang for control over certain operations, and there had already been seven murders in the last ten days. It was feared that the enemies of Profaci's friends in Villabate might seek revenge for their dead upon Bill Bonanno or his wife, and although Rosalie had persisted in her request to see Villabate, her husband had managed to avoid the trip after making endless excuses and offering a busy itinerary of pleasant distractions. He had also been relieved that Rosalie had not questioned, nor had even seemed to notice, the quiet group of men that followed them everywhere during their first day of sight-seeing in Palermo. These men, undoubtedly armed, were serving as bodyguards for the Bonanno couple, even sitting outside the couple's hotel door at night to guarantee that no harm would come to them in Sicily.

The journey to Castellammare del Golfo, sixty miles west of Palermo, had been the high point of the Sicilian visit for Bill Bonanno. As a boy he had seen framed photographs of his father's town hanging on the walls at home, and he had later noted references to it in history books and travel guides, although the references had been very brief and superficial—it was as if the writers, with few exceptions, had quickly driven through the town without stopping, being perhaps intimidated by one published report, claiming that eighty percent of Castellammare's adult male population had served time in prison.

There was no social stigma attached to this, however, because most of the local citizens regarded the law as corrupt, representing the will of invaders who had long sought to control the islanders, and exploit the land through conqueror's law. The history of Castellammare, as with most of Sicily, had been turbulent for centuries, and Bonanno had remembered reading that the island had been conquered and reconquered no less than sixteen times—by Greeks, Saracens, and Normans, by Spaniards, Germans, and English, by various combinations and persuasions ranging from Holy Crusaders to Fascists: they had all come to Sicily and did what men do when away from home, and the history of Sicily was a litany of sailors' sins.

As the caravan of cars had arrived at Castellammare, having driven for two hours along narrow mountain roads above the sea, Bonanno felt a sudden sense of familiarity with the landscape that was beyond mere recognition from pictures; he felt united with all that he had imagined for years, all that he had heard as a boy from the reminiscing men gathered around his father's dinner table on Sunday afternoons. The town was actually quite beautiful, a tranquil fishing village built along the bottom of a mountain, and at the very tip of the land, on a jagged rocky edge splashed by waves, stood the old stone castle that had given the town its name.

The castle, built many centuries ago by the Saracens or Aragons, no one was absolutely certain, had served as the town's lookout post for spotting invading ships; but now it was a decaying structure of no purpose, and the elder Bonanno and the other men had recalled playing in it as boys.

Near the castle, along the small beach, were the fishermen, weather-worn and ruddy, wearing black berets; they had been pulling in their nets as the Bonanno party had passed but had been too busy to notice the line of cars. In the town square, near a church built four hundred years ago, were many men walking slowly, arm in arm, making many gestures with their hands. The stone houses, most of them two or three stories high with balconies in front, were arranged in tight rows along narrow cobbled roads over which was heard the clacking sounds of donkeys pulling colorfully painted wagons between the motor traffic. Here and there, sunning themselves in front of their doors, had been groups of women, the unmarried ones seated with their backs to the street, possibly following a fashion inherited a thousand years ago when the Arabs had occupied Sicily.

. . .

In front of one particularly well-constructed house, on Corso Garibaldi, a crowd had gathered. When the procession of cars had been spotted, the people had stepped up to the curb, waiting. They were about thirty in number, dressed in dark clothes except for the children, one of whom held a bouquet of flowers. They had been standing in front of the home where Joseph Bonanno had been born, and the arrival of his son had been regarded as a historical event. An indication of the Bonanno family status in Castellammare had been the fact that the ceremony surrounding Joseph Bonanno's baptism in 1905 had marked the end of a shooting war between the local mafiosi and those in the neighboring village of Alcamo; and when Joseph Bonanno's father, Salvatore Bonanno, had died in 1915, he had been buried in the most prominent plot at the base of the mountain.

After the bridal couple had been greeted by, and had disentangled themselves from, the embracing crowds, and had had coffee and pastry with their cousins and compari, they had gone to the cemetery; and Bill Bonanno, standing before a large gravestone that exhibited a proud picture of a man with a handlebar moustache, had sensed something more about his own father's relationship to the past. The eyes looking out from the gravestone were penetrating and dark, and Bill Bonanno could readily accept what he had heard of his grandfather's persuasive power, although he found it difficult to believe that this authoritative-looking photograph was of a man who had died at thirty-seven. His grandfather seemed to be a tall man, lean and tall unlike Sicilians; although the Bonannos were not Sicilians by origin. They had lived hundreds of years ago in Pisa, according to Joseph Bonanno, but had left rather hastily following a dispute with the ruling family. Joseph Bonanno, who kept a family coat-of-arms hanging in his home in the United States, a shield decorated with a panther, had compiled a history of his ancestry that claimed kinship with Charles Bonanno, engineer of the leaning tower of Pisa.

After Bill Bonanno had returned from his honeymoon, in September of 1956, he had urged his father to visit Castellammare. And a year later, the elder Bonanno had done so. But the pleasant experiences of that trip had been curtailed by negative events that had followed in 1957, and had continued to follow into the 1960s. There had been the publicity attached to the Anastasia murder and the Apalachin meeting, and then there had been the Senate testimony of Joseph Valachi, the Mafia defector, who had identified Joseph Bonanno as his sponsoring godfather and as the leader of one of New York's five "families," as well as a member of the nine-man national commission. Finally, in 1963, there had been the dissension within Bonanno's organization, internal differences between a few old friends who had left Castellammare forty years before. And now, in October of 1964, hiding in the apartment, Bill Bonanno, the son, was a partner in the tension and intrigue.

He was tired of it, but there was little he could do. He had not seen Rosalie or his four young children in several days, and he wondered about their welfare and wished that his relationship with his in-laws, the Profacis, had not declined as it had in recent years. He and Rosalie had now been married for eight years, and much had happened since their honeymoon, too much, and he hoped that he could successfully repair the damage done. What was required, he felt, was a new start, a second attempt in another direction, and he had thought that they were moving toward this earlier this year, in February, when they had moved into their new home, a ranch-type house on a quiet tree-lined street in East Meadow, Long Island. They had finally left Arizona, a state that Rosalie had come to hate for a number of reasons, not the least of which was a certain woman in Phoenix, and they had come East to live for a few months in the mansion of Rosalie's uncle, Joe Magliocco, in East Islip, Long Island, prior to getting their own home. The time spent at Magliocco's place had been hectic, not only for them but for their children.

The mansion was on a sprawling estate protected by high walls and trees, by watchdogs and gunmen. Joe Magliocco, a muscular fat man of three hundred pounds, had taken over the Profaci operation, including its control over the Italian lottery in Brooklyn, after the death in 1962 of Joseph Profaci. (Rosalie's father, Salvatore Profaci, was also dead at this point, having been killed before her wedding due to an explosion he had caused while working on an engine in his motorboat.) Magliocco, an impulsive man who lacked great organizational ability, had also inherited many problems when he took over, the worst of which had been an internal revolt by younger members led by the Gallo brothers. The dissension caused by the Gallo faction, among other issues, was still unresolved when Rosalie and Bill Bonanno had moved in with Magliocco in 1963, and they had sensed that things were becoming almost desperate for Magliocco in the late summer and fall of that year—men were coming and going at odd hours, the dogs were on constant alert, and Magliocco was rarely without his bodyguard even when walking short distances through his estate.

One morning in December, as the Bonanno's two-year-old son, Joseph, was crawling through the dining room, he reached between the china closet and the wall, and pulled the trigger of a rifle that had been left standing there. The rifle blast blew a hole in the ceiling, hitting through the upper floor not far from where Magliocco lay sleeping. The fat man bolted out of bed, yelling; and Rosalie, who had been feeding her newly born infant in another part of the house, began to scream. The big house suddenly vibrated with a flurry of bodies running in panic, chasing and shouting—until the little boy was discovered downstairs, sitting on the rug wearing his red pajamas, stunned but safe, with a smoking rifle at his feet. Two weeks later, Joe Magliocco had died of a heart attack.

• • •

On hearing Frank Labruzzo ringing the downstairs bell, Bill Bonanno pressed the buzzer and then watched through the peephole of the apartment door. He saw Labruzzo step out of the elevator with newspapers under his arm, and he could tell by the pale expression on Labruzzo's face that something had gone wrong.

Labruzzo said nothing as he entered the apartment. He handed the papers to Bonanno. On the front page of every one, in large headlines at the very top, was the news:

JOE BANANAS—CALL HIM DEAD

JOE BONANNO IS KIDNAPED BY 2 HOODS IN NEW YORK

MOB KIDNAPS JOE BANANAS

FBI JOINS KIDNAPER SEARCH

Bill Bonanno felt feverish and dizzy. He sank finally into a chair, his mind racing with confusion and disbelief. The headlines, large letters spreading across the entire page, more prominent than the war in Vietnam and the social revolution in America, seemed to be screaming at him and demanding a reply, and he wanted to react quickly, to run somewhere to do something violent, hating the feeling of being helpless and trapped. But he forced himself to sit and methodically read every paragraph. Most of the newspaper articles suggested that Joseph Bonanno was already dead, possibly encased in concrete and resting in a river. There was some speculation that he was perhaps being held hostage until he made certain concessions, and there was finally a theory that the kidnapping was a hoax arranged by Joseph Bonanno himself as a way of avoiding an appearance before a Federal grand jury meeting in Manhattan later in the week.

The younger Bonanno discounted this last point as absurd. He was convinced that his father had intended to appear before this grand jury as he had before others in the past—revealing nothing, of course, but at least appearing and pleading his innocence or seeking refuge in his constitutional rights. Bill Bonanno also did not believe that his father would have attempted anything so tricky as a staged kidnapping without first consulting with Labruzzo and himself.

He watched Labruzzo pacing back and forth through the room like a caged animal. Labruzzo still had said nothing. Normally very calm, he seemed at this moment very nervous and fearful. Finally aware that he was being observed, Labruzzo turned and, as if trying to reestablish his position as a cool man under pressure, said, almost casually, "Look, if it's true that he's dead, there is nothing we can do about it."

"If it's true," Bonanno replied, "they're going to be looking for us next."

Labruzzo was again silent. Bonanno got up to turn on the television set and radio for late news. He wondered if the location of their apartment was known to outsiders, and he also tried to figure out which men from his own organization might have collaborated in his father's capture, feeling certain that it had been handled partly from the inside. How else would they have known that Joseph Bonanno had planned to spend the night at Maloney's place? Everything had been so neatly done, the two gunmen appearing on Park Avenue just as the elder Bonanno had stepped out of a cab, and Maloney, having gotten out first, running ahead through the rain and not seeing anything until after it had happened. Although these suspicions were later to be proved unfounded and Bill was to come to feel guilty about them, he even thought Maloney might have been part of the deal.

Because Bill Bonanno, like his father, was suspicious of most lawyers. Lawyers were servants of the court, part of the system, which meant they could never be trusted entirely——or they were crime buffs, men who enjoyed being on the fringe of the gangsters' world, were fascinated no doubt by the occasional glimpses they got into the secret society. Sometimes they even became involved in Mafia intrigue, giving advice to one don or another, and shifting sides as the odds changed—it was a kind of game with them.

And no matter which faction won or lost, the lawyers survived. They lived to accompany their clients to the courthouse as photographers took pictures, and they later made statements to the press—they were a privileged clique, highly publicized, highly paid, often crooked but rarely caught, they were the untouchables. Bonanno remembered having heard years ago of how the Mafia dons had complained among themselves about the exorbitant fees charged by certain lawyers after the police had raided the Apalachin conference. A few dons claimed to have paid about $50,000 each for their legal defense, and since much of this had been paid in cash, as the lawyers had requested, the mafiosi could only guess at the amount on which no taxes had been paid. While Bonanno knew that Maloney was not this sort of lawyer, he nevertheless suspected the worst until future evidence proved otherwise; he was a lawyer, after all— and they lived off other people's misery.

As for the men who had provided the muscle in the kidnapping, Bonanno assumed that they had had the prior approval of the Mafia's national commission, which had recently suspended Joseph Bonanno from its membership. He also assumed that they had acted under the personal direction of the Mafia boss in Buffalo, the senior member of the commission, seventy-three-year-old Stefano Magaddino, his father's cousin and former friend from Castellammare. The apparent bitterness on Magaddino's part toward his father was a subject often discussed within the Bonanno organization in 1963 and 1964. It was believed to be based partly on the fact that Magaddino, whose territory extended from western New York into the Ohio Valley and included links with Canadian racketeers in Toronto, had felt threatened by Joseph Bonanno's ambitions in Canada. For decades the Bonanno organization had worked in partnership with a group of mafiosi in Montreal, sharing most profitably in the importation of untaxed alcohol as well as in gambling and other illegal activities, including the control of the pizza trade and various protection rackets in Montreal's large Italian community. In 1963, when Joseph Bonanno went to Montreal and later applied for Canadian citizenship, Magaddino interpreted this as further evidence that Bonanno's Canadian interests were going to extend into Magaddino's territory, and the latter was overheard one day complaining of Bonanno: "He's planting flags all over the world!"

Even though Bonanno's petition for Canadian citizenship was denied and was followed by his expulsion, Magaddino's suspicions had persisted. It was a feeling not based on any one issue, Bonanno's men believed, but was inspired by a combination of fear and jealousy. They remembered Magaddino's dark mood on the night of Bill Bonanno's wedding reception in 1956, how he had stood near the dais surveying the great gathering of mafiosi who had come from all parts of the nation out of respect for Joseph Bonanno, and Magaddino had said in a loud voice to a man at his table: "Look at this crowd. Who the hell's going to be able to talk to my cousin now? This will go to his head."

Bill Bonanno also had sensed how little Magaddino had thought of him, and how upset the Buffalo boss had become when the elder Bonanno had sanctioned his elevation to No. 3 man in the Bonanno organization and had overlooked a member that Magaddino considered more worthy of promotion—namely, Magaddino's own brother-in-law, Gasper Di Gregorio. Di Gregorio had been a member of the Bonanno organization for thirty years, and until recent months Bill Bonanno had believed that Di Gregorio was one of his father's most loyal followers. He was a quiet, unassuming gray-haired man of fifty-nine who ran a coat factory in Brooklyn and was virtually unknown to the FBI; born in Castellammare, he had fought alongside the elder Bonanno in the famous Brooklyn gang war of 1930, and a year later he had been the best man when Joseph

Bonanno had married Fay Labruzzo. He was also Bill Bonanno's godfather, a friend and adviser during the younger Bonanno's years as an adolescent and student, and it was difficult for Bonanno to figure out when and why Di Gregorio had decided to pull away from the Bonanno organization and lure others with him. Di Gregorio had always been a follower, not a leader, and Bill Bonanno could only conclude that Magaddino had finally succeeded after years of effort to use Di Gregorio as the dividing wedge in the Bonanno organization. Di Gregorio had taken with him perhaps twenty or thirty men, perhaps more—Bill Bonanno could only guess, for there was no easy way to know who stood where at this point. Maybe fifty of the three-hundred-man Bonanno family had defected in the last month, influenced by the commission's decision to suspend the elder Bonanno and encouraged by Magaddino's assurance that the commission would protect them from reprisals by Bonanno loyalists.

No matter what the situation was, Bill Bonanno knew that he could only wait. With his father gone, perhaps dead, it was important that he remain alive to deal with whatever had to be done. To venture outdoors at this point would be foolish and maybe suicidal. If the police did not spot him, Magaddino's men might. So Bonanno tried to suppress the fury and the despair that he felt and to resign himself to the long wait with Labruzzo. The phone was ringing now, the third code call in the last five minutes—the captains were reporting in from other apartments, available for any message he might wish to leave with the answering service. He would call it in a few moments to let them know that he was all right.

It was noon. Through the Venetian blinds he could see that it was a dark, dreary day. Labruzzo was sitting at the kitchen table drinking coffee, the dog at his feet. The pantry was well stocked with canned goods and boxes of pasta, and there was plenty of meat and sauce in the refrigerator. Bonanno, a fair cook, would now have lots of practice. They could exist here easily for several days. Only the dog would miss the outdoors.

Bonanno and Labruzzo lived in confinement for nearly a week, sleeping in shifts with their guns strapped to their chests, and being visited at night by the few men they trusted. One of these was a captain named Joe Notaro. He had been close to the Bonannos for years, and was respected for his sound judgment and caution. But on his first visit to the apartment, Notaro admitted with regret and embarrassment that he had probably been indirectly responsible for the elder Bonanno's capture.

He recalled that on the day of the kidnapping he had been sitting in his car discussing Joseph Bonanno's plans for the evening with another officer, speaking in a tone loud enough to be heard by the driver. Notaro's driver was a meek little man who had been with the organization for a number of years, and had never been taken very seriously by the members. As Notaro was later astonished to discover, the driver was then working as an informer for the Di Gregorio faction. The driver had apparently held a grudge against the organization ever since one of the captains had taken away his girlfriend, and Joseph Bonanno had been too preoccupied at the time with other matters to intercede in the driver's behalf. The fact that the offending captain had later been sentenced to a long jail term on a conspiracy charge in a narcotics case had not soothed the driver's wounded ego. After Bonanno's capture, the driver had disappeared, and Notaro had just learned that he was now driving for Di Gregorio's group.

Among other bits of information picked up by Notaro and his fellow officers from their sources around town—from bookmakers and loan sharks, from the men who work in nightclubs and in related businesses linked socially to the underworld—was that Joseph Bonanno was not yet dead and was being held by Magaddino's men at a farm somewhere in the Catskill Mountains in upstate New York. The FBI and the police were reported to be concentrating their efforts in that area, and had also visited Bonanno's home in Tucson and were keeping watch on the late Joe Magliocco's mansion, considering it an ideal hideaway because of its protective walls and the private dock. As for the status of the organization, Bonanno's officers believed that more than two hundred men were still loyal and that their morale was very high. Most of the men were remaining indoors, the officers said, and were sleeping in shifts and doing their own cooking in their apartments and rented rooms. Bonanno and Labruzzo were told that at one apartment the men had complained at dinner the previous evening that the spaghetti had a metallic taste— they later learned that the cook, while vigorously stirring the meat sauce, had knocked his pistol out of his chest holster into the pot.

. . .

With each visit the officers brought the latest papers, and Bonanno and Labruzzo could see that the kidnapping episode was continuing to receive enormous coverage. Pictures of the younger Bonanno had appeared in several papers, and there was speculation that he, too, had been taken by his father's enemies, or that he was hiding in New York or Arizona, or that he was in the protective custody of federal agents. When a reporter had telephoned FBI headquarters to verify this last item, an agency spokesman had refused to comment.

The headline writers were having fun with the story, Bonanno could see—YES, WE HAVE NO BANANAS—and reporters were also keeping a close watch on his wife and children at home in East Meadow, Long Island. One paper described Rosalie as leaning out of a window to reply to a reporter, in a "trembling voice," that she knew nothing of her husband's whereabouts, and her eyes were said to be "red-rimmed" as if she had been crying. Another newspaper, describing her as very pretty and shy, said she had spent part of the afternoon in a beauty parlor. A third paper reported that Bonanno's seven-year-old son, Charles, while playing on the sidewalk in front of the house, had been approached by a detective asking questions about his father; but the boy had replied that he knew nothing. Bill Bonanno was very pleased.

He had trained his children well, he thought. He had cautioned them, as his own father had once cautioned him, to be careful when speaking with strangers. He did not want his children to be curt or disrespectful to anyone, including the police, but he warned them to be on guard when asked about matters pertaining to their home or parents, their relatives or the friends of relatives. He had also conveyed to his children his disapproval of tattletales. If they saw their brothers, sisters, or cousins doing something wrong, he had said, it was improper for them to go talebearing to adults, adding that nobody had respect for a stool pigeon, not even those who gained by such information.

Sitting quietly in the apartment, after Notaro had left and Labruzzo was sleeping, Bonanno remembered an incident earlier in the year when his advice to his children had seemed to boomerang. The family had been spending the day at a relative's home in Brooklyn, and during the afternoon one of the aunts had complained that the little wagon she kept in the backyard for hauling laundry had been taken, and that the children, who had been playing with it earlier, had claimed not to know who had taken it out of the yard. Bonanno had then approached the children,

lining them up for questioning; and when none had given any information about the wagon, he had said in a forceful tone that he was going to
take a walk around the block, and that when he returned he wanted to
see the wagon in the yard where it had been. He did not care who had
taken it, there would be no punishment; he just wanted it back. After his
walk, Bonanno returned to the yard. The children were out of sight, but
the wagon had reappeared.

While Bonanno was not overly concerned about his children's welfare
during his absence, knowing Rosalie's capabilities as a mother, he was
worried about the loneliness and anxiety that she would undoubtedly
feel each night after the four children had gone to sleep. Her mother,
who lived forty-five minutes away in Brooklyn, would certainly visit; but
Mrs. Profaci did not drive a car, and it would not be easy for her to
arrange transportation. Her relatives, as well as most relatives on the
Bonanno side of the family, were hesitant about appearing at Bill
Bonanno's home, fearing the publicity and the police investigation that
might follow. Bonanno's sister, Catherine, who feared neither publicity
nor the police, would have been a great comfort to Rosalie but she lived
in California with her husband and young children.

. . .

Bonanno's mother was probably in Arizona, or else living in seclusion with
friends; and his nineteen-year-old brother, Joseph Jr., was a student at
Phoenix College. Knowing Joseph, he doubted that he was attending classes
very often. Joseph was the wild one of the family, a drag racer, a bronco
rider, a nonconformist who was so thoroughly undisciplined that he could
never become a member of the organization, Bill Bonanno felt sure. The
elder Bonanno had been on the run during much of his younger son's
adolescence, dodging the Kefauver committee or the McClellan committee
or some other investigation or threat; and Joseph Jr. had been left under the
supervision of his mother, who could not control him. In any case, Joseph
Jr. was now in Phoenix, and Rosalie was in Long Island, and Bill Bonanno
only hoped that she could manage things alone and not crack under the
continued pressure that she had been forced to face in recent years.

He knew that Rosalie would probably be surprised if she knew his
thoughts at this moment, having heard her accuse him so often of caring
only about "those men" and never about her. But he sincerely was
concerned about her, and was also aware of a certain guilt within himself

which would be hard for him to admit, at least to a wife. That he loved her, he had no doubt, but the responsibilities that he felt toward his father's world, and all that had happened to him because of it, had destroyed a part of him, perhaps the better part. He knew that he could not justify much of what he had done with regard to Rosalie since their marriage, nor would he try. To himself he saw it all as a temporary escape from the tight terrifying world that he had inherited, an indulgence to his restlessness between the brief moments of action and interminable hours of boredom, the months of waiting and hiding and the machinations attached to the most routine act, like making a telephone call or answering a doorbell—in such a strange and excruciating world, he had done some damnable things, but now he could only hope that his wife would concentrate on the present, forgetting the past temporarily. He hoped that she would efficiently run the home, borrowing money from her relatives if necessary, and not become overly embarrassed by what she read in the newspapers, saw on television, or heard in the street. This was asking a lot, he knew, particularly since she had not really been prepared as a girl for the life she was now leading. He remembered her description of how her family had sought to protect her from reality, and how accustomed she had become as a girl to finding holes in the newspapers around the house, sections cut out where there had been photographs or articles dealing with the activities of the Profaci organization.

His homelife as a boy had been different. His father had never seemed defensive about any aspect of his life, seeming only proud and self-assured. The elder Bonanno had somehow suggested the nature of his life so gradually and casually, at least to Bill, that the ultimate realization of it was neither shocking nor disillusioning; although as a boy Bonanno had noticed his father's rather odd working hours. His father seemed either to be home all day and out at night, or to be at home constantly for weeks and then gone for weeks. It was very irregular, unlike the routines of the fathers of the boys with whom Bill had first gone to school in Long Island. But he was also aware that his father was a busy man, involved in many things, and at first this awareness satisfied his curiosity about his father, and seemed to explain why his father kept a private office in the house.

During this period of Bill Bonanno's life, in the 1940s, his father had a cheese factory in Wisconsin, coat factories and a laundry in Brooklyn, and a dairy farm in Middletown, New York, on which were forty head of cattle and two horses, one named after Bill and the other after Catherine. The family's home was in Hempstead, Long Island, a spacious two-story red brick Tudor-style house with lovely trees and a garden, not far from East Meadow, where Rosalie and Bill now lived. The family had moved to Hempstead from Brooklyn in 1938, and Bill had attended school in Long Island for four years, until a serious ear infection, a mastoid condition that had required operations, had led to his being transferred to schools in the dry climate of Arizona. His father had selected a boarding school in Tucson and would come to Arizona with his wife to visit Bill for the entire winter, renting an apartment there at first, later buying a house; and within four or five years Bill gradually became aware of the many men who frequently visited his father there, men who seemed very respectful and deferential. These were many of the same men that he had remembered seeing around the house as a boy in Long Island; and he also recalled a particular cross-country automobile trip that the Bonanno family had taken years before, when Bill was about eight years old, traveling from New York to California, visiting the Grand Canyon and other sites, and in every large city in which they stopped his father had seemed to know numbers of people, very friendly men who had made a great fuss over Bill and his sister.

After Bill Bonanno had gotten his driver's license, which was obtainable at sixteen in Arizona, his father had sometimes asked him to meet certain men arriving at the Tucson train station or the airport, men whom Bill knew very well now and had become fond of—they were like uncles to him. When he eventually began to recognize these same men's photographs in newspapers and magazines, and to read articles describing them as thugs and killers, he concluded, after a brief period of confusion and doubt, that the newspapers were uninformed and very prejudicial. The characterization of the men in the stories bore little resemblance to the men that he knew.

Perhaps his first personal involvement with his father's world occurred at Tucson High School, in 1951, on a day when he was called out of class and told to report to the principal's office. The principal seemed upset as he asked, "Bill, are you in any kind of trouble with the law?"

"No," Bonanno had said.

"Well, there are two men from the FBI in my outer office," the principal said, adding, "Look, Bill, you don't have to talk to them if you don't want to."

"I have nothing to hide," he said.

"Would you prefer that I be present?"

"Sure, if you want to."

The principal led Bill Bonanno into the outer office and introduced him to the agents, who asked if he knew anything about the disappearance and possible murder of the Mafia boss, Vincent Mangano. Bill Bonanno said that he knew nothing about it. He had heard that name before, but it had been in connection with James Mangano, who had an asthmatic daughter and had rented the Bonanno's Tucson home one summer when they were away. The agents took notes, asked a few more questions, then left. Bill Bonanno returned to his classroom, somewhat shaken. He felt the eyes of the other students on him, but he did not face anyone as he took his seat, although he felt separated from his classmates in a way he had not felt before.

It was a feeling, he was sure, that Rosalie had never had as a girl, and he even wondered if she had it now. She seemed totally unaware and naïve about his world. While he occasionally interpreted this as self-protectiveness on her part, a determination to ignore what she disapproved of, he also believed sometimes that his wife was genuinely remote from reality, as if her parents had really fulfilled their ambition to separate Rosalie from the embarrassing aspects of their own past. But this could not be entirely true, for if they had really wished to separate her from themselves they would never have condoned her marriage to him.

Still, for whatever reason, his wife's quality of detachment irritated him at times, and he hoped that now, following his father's disappearance, she would respond to the emergency and do nothing foolish or careless. He hoped, for example, that when she left their house with the children she would remember to lock the front and back doors, and would be certain that all the windows were securely bolted. He was worried that FBI men, posing as burglars, would break into the house and infest the interior with electronic bugs. They often did this, he had heard; they would enter a house and overturn a few pieces of furniture, and plow through the bureau drawers and closets, giving the impression that they were thieves looking for valuables, but what they really were doing was installing bugs. Once the agents got into a house, he knew, it was nearly impossible to detect their little handiwork, conceding that in this area the FBI was very creative and clever. He knew of a case in which the agents had even bugged a house before the carpenters had finished building it. It had happened to Sonny Franzese, an officer in the Profaci organization; the agents had apparently gone to the construction site of Franzese's new home in Long Island after the workmen had left for the day, inserting bugs into the framework and foundation. Franzese later wondered why the agents knew so much about him.

Bill Bonanno kept an electronic debugging device in his closet at home, a kind of plastic divining rod with an antenna that was supposed to vibrate when sensing bugs, but he was not sure how trustworthy it was. If the agents did get into his house, he was sure that they could find some things that would serve as evidence against him. They would find a few rifles in the garage, and pistols in his bedroom bureau. They might find a false identification card or two, and various drivers' licenses and passports. They would discover his vast collection of quarters, several dollars' worth neatly packed in long thin plastic tubes that fit into the glove compartment of his car, and were used for long-distance calls at telephone booths. The agents would probably help themselves to the excellent Havana cigars that he remembered having left on the top of his bedroom bureau, in a jar that also contained Q-tips cotton swabs on sticks that he used for draining his left ear in the morning, the infected ear that had gotten him to Arizona, where he wished he was at this moment. The agents might be interested in some of the books in his library, which included three books on the FBI and all the books about the Mafia, including ones by Senators Kefauver and McClellan; and several other books that he suspected would be over the agents' heads— the Churchill volumes, books by Bertrand Russell, Arthur Koestler, Sartre, and the poetry of Dante; but there was one book that they would surely like to thumb through: the large photo album of his wedding. The album, which consisted of several photographs of the reception, including the crowded ballroom scene at the Astor, would identify most of the distinguished guests; and what the album failed to reveal, the movie film of the wedding, packed in a tin can at the bottom of a bookshelf, would reveal. There was more than two thousand feet of home-movie film on the wedding, and he and Rosalie had enjoyed looking at it from time to time during the past eight years. The wedding event, the extravagance and splendor of it, had probably marked the high point of Joseph Bonanno's life, the pinnacle of his prestige; and a social historian of the underworld, should one ever exist, might describe the event as the "last of the great gangster weddings," coming before the Apalachin exposure and other vexations had put an end to such displays.

One of the things that had most fascinated Bill Bonanno about the film, after he had seen it three or four times, was what it revealed about the caste-consciousness of the mafiosi who had attended, and no doubt the FBI would be equally interested if it could review the film. By observing the way that a mafioso dressed, one could determine his rank within the organization. The lower-echelon men, Bonanno had noticed, all wore white dinner jackets to the wedding; while the middle-level men, the lieutenants and captains, wore light-blue dinner jackets. The top men, the dons, all were dressed in black tuxedoes; except, of course, the principal males in the wedding party, who wore cutaways.

On November 5, which was Bill Bonanno's thirty-second birthday, and was fifteen days after the elder Bonanno's disappearance, five of the Bonanno officers decided that they had had all the confinement they could stand—they needed a short vacation. Bill Bonanno agreed. It did not appear that their enemies planned an armed confrontation at this time, not with so many police on the alert, and Bonanno also welcomed a change of scenery. He had sent word to Rosalie through one of his men that he was alive. He had said no more than that, nor did Rosalie expect more. The question facing Bonanno now was where to go to find rest and relaxation and not attract attention. He and his men could not fly South because the airports were too well patrolled and, even with their disguises, they might be spotted. He also did not want to venture too far from New York because there was always the chance of some new development concerning his father. They would have to use their cars, traveling at night; and after a few hours of thought, Bonanno decided that they should visit the ski country of New England. None of the men had ever been on skis, nor did they intend to try. They merely wished to experience again the act of movement, to travel over open roads in the brisk outdoors, to clear their minds, recharge the batteries of their cars and walk their dogs away from the repressive environment of New York.

They left that evening within the first hour of darkness. Two men to a car, they planned to meet at a large motel near Albany. Bonanno's green Cadillac was parked a block away, under a lamplight. He approached it slowly and carefully, alert for any movement or sound around the car or along the dark street. Labruzzo followed several feet behind, holding the dog on a leash with his left hand and keeping his right hand free for his gun.

Lowering a suitcase to the ground, Bonanno walked around the car, which was covered with dust and a few fallen leaves. He examined the front fenders and the hood for fingerprints, as he always did before unlocking the door, in an attempt to detect the planting of bombs within the vehicle. Confident that the car had not been touched since he had left it, he got in and turned on the ignition. The car started up immediately, which did not surprise him, for he had always maintained it to perfection, changing the batteries and other engine parts long before they had ceased to function properly. Relaxing in the cold soft leather seats waiting for Labruzzo, he felt a renewed sense of appreciation for the car, its powerful engine idling quietly, its gleaming dashboard adorned with a stereo. It was a big comfortable car for a tall heavy man of his size, and he guessed that his weight had increased by eight or ten pounds during the last few weeks of tension and confinement. He was probably 235 pounds, and he felt it. Leaning toward the rear-view mirror, he saw that he bore little resemblance to his recent newspaper photographs. His face was heavier; and with his beard, his plain-glass horn-rimmed glasses and the hat that he wore as part of his disguise, he imagined that he looked like a jazz musician.

After Labruzzo had deposited the dog in the back seat, and the gun under the front seat, the two men began the slow ride through the side streets of Queens that Bonanno knew so well. Within a half hour they were rolling smoothly on the highway, saying very little as they listened to the stereo, the lights of the city behind them. Bonanno was delighted to be leaving New York. He had never liked the city very much, and recently he had come to hate it. He had often wondered why so many mafiosi, men with roots in the sunny agrarian lands of Southern Europe, had settled in this cold polluted jungle crowded with cops and nosy newsmen, with hazards of every conceivable nature.

The Mafia bosses in the South, or in the Far West, in places like Boulder, Colorado, undoubtedly lived a much better life than any of the five dons with organizations centered in New York City. The don in

Colorado probably owned a trucking business or a little nightclub and, with only ten or twelve men under his command, ran a few gambling parlors or a numbers racket on the side. He worked regular hours, probably played golf every afternoon, and had time in the evening for his family. His sons would graduate from college, becoming business executives or lawyers, and would know how to steal legally.

The five dons in New York each commanded forces of between 250 and 500 men, meaning that approximately two thousand mafiosi—40 percent of the national membership of five thousand—were in New York fighting the traffic and one another. The New York dons never felt secure no matter how much power they had. Why did they remain? Bonanno knew the answer, of course; New York was where the big money was. It was the great marketplace, the center of everything. Each day a million trucks came rolling into or out of New York—it was a hijacker's paradise, a town of tall shadows, sharp angles, and crooked people from top to bottom. Most New Yorkers, from the police to the prostitutes, were on the take or on the make. Even the average citizens seemed to enjoy breaking the law, or beating the system in some way. Part of the success of the numbers racket, which was the Mafia's most lucrative source of income, was that it was illegal. If the lawmakers would legitimize numbers betting, it would hurt business because it would deprive customers of that satisfactory sense of having beaten the system, of having outwitted the police and the august judiciary, with the mere placing of a bet. It was the same satisfactory sense that people got forty years ago when they dealt with their bootlegger, or were admitted into an all-night speakeasy.

New York was also a marvelous place in which to hide. One could get lost in the crowds of New York, could blend in with the blurring sights, movement, shadows and confusion. People tended to mind their own business in New York, to remain uninvolved with the affairs of their neighbors, and this was a great asset for men in hiding. Bonanno knew that one of his father's captains, a man named Joseph Morale, had been hiding from Federal authorities for twenty years, and was still in circulation, living most of the time at his home in a neighborhood of nondescript houses in Queens. Morale came and went at odd hours, never following a predictable routine, and his family had been trained in ways that would not expose him by word or act.

Bonanno's father had once concealed himself for more than a year in

Brooklyn, during the gangland discord of 1929 to 1930, a time when a rival boss had issued a "contract" for his death. Bill Bonanno was sure that if his father were alive now he could hide indefinitely in New York because he possessed the necessary discipline to do so. Discipline was the main requirement. Disguises and hideaways, false identification cards and loyal friends were important, but individual discipline was the essential factor, combining the capacity to change one's routine, to adjust to solitude, to remain alert without panicking, to avoid the places and people that had frequently been visited in the past. When his father had gone into hiding in 1929, a time when he had been actively courting Fay Labruzzo, he had suddenly and without explanation stopped appearing at her home. She had heard nothing from him for several months and assumed that their engagement had been terminated. Then one of her brothers-in-law noticed that the window shades of the building directly opposite the Labruzzo home, on Jefferson Street in Brooklyn, had been down for a long time; and later he saw the glimmer of rifle barrels poised behind the small opening at the bottom of the shades, obviously waiting for Bonanno to appear in front of the Labruzzo home.

Bill Bonanno was confident that, if he had to, he could hide in New York for a very long time. He believed that he had discipline, that he would not panic if the search parties were getting close, that he had a certain talent for elusiveness. Even now, driving at night on the New York State Thruway, obeying the speed limit, he was aware of every car that followed him, the arrangements of their headlights in his rearview mirror. Whenever he passed a car he observed its body style, the license plate, tried to get a look at the driver, and his alertness intensified whenever a car behind him gained speed to pass. He tried to maintain a certain distance between himself and the others, shifting lanes or reducing speed when necessary. Since he had carefully studied the road map prior to the trip, as he did before every trip, he knew the exits, the detours, the possible routes of escape.

Whenever he planned to remain in a single town or certain area for a few days, he familiarized himself not only with the streets but also with the hill formations and arrangements of trees along certain roads that might temporarily obscure his car as he drove it from the view of drivers behind him. He actually charted out zones of obscurity into which he would drive when he felt he was being followed, particularly places where the road dipped or curved and was joined by an alternate route.

Whenever he sensed that he was being tailed in Long Island, for example, he led his possible pursuers into Garden City, where he was intimately familiar with several short curving roads that linked with other roads, and he knew several places where the roads dipped, then rose, then dipped again, stretches where his car vanished from sight for several seconds if his followers were keeping at a subtle distance. He also knew about seven ways to get into and out of Garden City, and anyone who followed him into that city, be it Federal agents or unfriendly *amici*, was almost sure to lose him.

Another reason that Bonanno had confidence in his ability to hide was that loneliness did not bother him. He had adjusted to it as a young teenager in Arizona when he had lived alone in a motel room, later in his parents' home, each year between fall and winter while his parents were in New York—an arrangement made necessary by his eviction at the age of fifteen from his boarding-school dormitory because one day he had led a group of classmates, who were supposed to be visiting a museum, into a film house showing the controversial *Forever Amber*. He remembered how embittered he had become by the punishment, which permitted him to attend classes but had prohibited his remaining on campus at night. He had also been surprised by his father's lack of influence with the headmaster, who had accepted generous gifts from the Bonannos in the past, including large shipments of cheese for the school from the factory in Wisconsin, and also butter when it was scarce because of World War II rationing. His parents, remaining in New York because of his father's activities, could do nothing after the eviction but arrange for him to stay at the Luna Motel, which was close to a bus stop where Bill could get a ride to school.

In angry response to his punishment, Bill had withdrawn his horse from the school's stable. He had kept the animal in a yard behind the motel. The horse and a miniature Doberman pinscher, the same type of dog that was in his car now as he drove upstate, had been his main companions during those months his parents were away, and he had become very independent and self-reliant. Each morning he got himself up, made his own breakfast. He had spent many evenings alone in the motel room listening to the radio. He remembered the sound of the fast-talking Garry Moore on the Jimmy Durante show, and the reassuring voice of Dr. Christian. Occasionally at sunset he would take long rides on his horse through the Arizona desert, passing the ranches of the rich, the smoking mud huts of the Zuñi tribesmen, the dusty wranglers and bronco riders who nodded toward him as he passed.

He had first ridden a horse as a three-year-old boy in Long Island, riding on weekends with his father and the other men. Many of Bonanno's men were superb horsemen, having ridden as small boys in Sicily where horses and donkeys were the main means of transportation; and Bill had many photographs of himself galloping with the mafiosi on weekends through the woods in Long Island. His father had insisted from the beginning that he ride a full-sized horse, not a pony, and his pride in his equestrianism compensated to a degree for his lack of achievement as an athlete when he got to high school.

It was not his ear ailment so much as his parents' travel schedule that limited his participation in organized sports. He had wanted to join the football team at Tucson High School, but he was with his parents in New York when football practice began in August. In the winter and spring, when his parents were in Arizona, he spent considerable time with his father after school hours. His life had been one of extremes: he had either been entirely alone, or he had been encircled by his family and his father's friends. There had been times when he had wanted to escape the extremities, and not long after his eviction from the dormitory he had taken some money and run away. He had boarded a bus for New York, a five-day journey, and on arriving at the terminal on Forty-third Street off Broadway he had taken another bus upstate to the family farm in Middletown, which was very close to where he was driving at this moment on the New York State Thruway, and he was tempted now to pull off the main road and briefly revisit the farm that his father had since sold. He resisted the temptation, however, although he continued to think about his visit to the farm many years ago, remembering how upset the farmers had been when he had arrived, saying that his father had telephoned and had just flown to Tucson in an attempt to find him.

Within a few days the elder Bonanno had arrived at the farm, angry at first, but then his anger had subsided. He admitted that he had also run away at fifteen, in Sicily, and he thought that perhaps such experiences were part of a boy's growing up. He nevertheless talked his son into returning to school in Tucson, where a new yellow jeep would await him.

Once back in Arizona, Bill also arranged to visit a doctor. He had

had stomach pains sporadically during the year, and after a medical examination it had been determined that he had an ulcer.

. . .

By most people's definition, the trip made by Bonanno, Labruzzo, and the other men through New York State into New England would hardly qualify as a vacation: it consisted largely of driving hundreds of miles each day and remaining in motels at night, watching television and talking among themselves.

After Albany they drove through Bennington, Vermont, and continued on up to Burlington along Lake Champlain. They then headed east into New Hampshire, then south two days later into Massachusetts. The travel route was charted each morning by one of the men who was a native New Englander, and they met each night at predestined places before they registered, in pairs, at separate motels which were close to one another and had suites with kitchenettes.

They shopped for groceries at local stores and, after walking the dogs, gathered at night in Bonanno's suite where the cooking was done. Bonanno had brought with him in his attaché case various spices and herbs and also a paperback edition of James Beard's cookbook. Each night he cooked and the other men cleaned up afterward. He was impressed with the modernization of motels since his boyhood days at the Luna—in addition to the streamlined kitchenettes there were the ice-making machines, body vibrators installed in beds, wall-to-wall carpeting, color television, and cocktail lounges that provided room service.

The most relaxing part of the trip for Bonanno was the act of driving, moving for dozens of miles without pausing for a traffic jam or even a signal light, and observing the tranquility of small towns and imagining the peaceful existence of those who occupied them. Occasionally he passed cars driven by young people with skis strapped onto the roofs and college emblems stuck to the windows, and also the Greek letters of fraternities that he could identify, and he was constantly reminded of how far he had drifted from the campus life he had known a decade ago.

It had been a very gradual drifting, occurring so slowly over a period of years that he did not really know when he had crossed the border into his father's world. During most of his college career, which had begun in the summer of 1951 and had extended irregularly through 1956, he had lived a kind of dual existence. At certain times, particularly when his father seemed to be at odds with other bosses or to be hounded by Federal agents, he had felt both a desire and a responsibility to stand by his father, to lend verbal and emotional support even though his father had not requested it, saying instead that he wanted Bill to remain in school concentrating on his studies. And there were times when Bill's interests had seemed to be centered entirely around the campus—he attended classes punctually, joined student groups, supported the football team. He was gregarious and generous, was popular with his classmates; and he always had a car and a girl.

But as a student he had limited powers of concentration, seeming to lose interest in subjects that he could not quickly master. He had grown accustomed in high school to making the grade with a minimum of effort because of his superior education in boarding school, but in college this advantage did not exist and he was also distracted quite often by an increasing awareness of his father and by the many conflicts that he was recognizing in himself. While he did not want to inherit his father's problems, did not want to be identified with gangsterism and to suffer the social ostracism resultant from exposure in the press, he also did not want to separate himself from his father's circumstances, nor to feel apologetic or defensive about his name, particularly since he did not believe that his father was guilty of crimes against society, feeling sometimes that the reverse was true, society was using such men as Joseph Bonanno to pay for the widespread sins in the system. In any case, no matter how damaging the consequences might be to himself, he could not turn against his father, nor did he really want to. His emotional link with his father was very strong, exceeding the normal bond of filial fidelity—it was more intense, more unquestioning, there was a unity in the tension shared and a certain romanticism about the risks and dangers involved, and there was also a kind of religious overtone in the relationship, a combination of blind faith and fear, formality and love. The many long periods of separation had in a strange way drawn them closer, had made each visit an event, a time of reunion and rejoicing; and during their months apart Bill's youthful imagination and memory had often endowed his father with qualities approximating a deity, so impressive, absolute and almost foreign had the elder Bonanno been in person.

Joseph Bonanno was handsome in ways both strong and serene, having soft brown eyes, a finely etched face and a benign expression that was evident even in photographs taken by the police. Considering that police photographers and the tabloid cameramen were rarely flattering, and usually made all Mafia suspects appear to be grim and sinister, Bill thought it remarkable that his father had seemed gracious and composed in nearly every one of the hundreds of news photos and police posters that had been displayed in recent years, including the latest ones circulated since his disappearance. Never let anyone know how you feel, Joseph Bonanno had told his son, and Bill had tried to follow the advice, remembering an occasion years ago when he had accepted an invitation to appear on Alumni Day at his old boarding school and how, after he had delivered a pleasant little speech to the students expressing the hope that his own children might one day benefit from the school's fine principles, he had walked across the stage, smiling, and had shaken the hand of the headmaster who had evicted him from the campus.

During the drive through New England he remembered several incidents from his past that had seemed inconsequential when they had occurred, but now in retrospect they revealed the double life he had led as a boy, the private battles he had fought without knowing he was fighting. He knew then only that his life was dominated by a soft-spoken man in silk suits who arrived in Arizona each winter from New York to end the loneliness, speaking in oracles, offering ancient remedies for contemporary ailments. He remembered his father directing him into the desert sun each afternoon to sit on a chair and tilt his head in such a way as to expose his left ear to the heat, saying that it would stop the draining; and it had. He remembered a summer day in Long Island when his sister had badly cut her leg while climbing a fence, and how his father had carried her into the house, had placed her on a table, and had squeezed lemon juice into her leg, massaging it in a slow special way that had not only stopped the bleeding but, after the wound had healed, had left no scar. He recalled how his father had arranged with a judge to free him without penalty after he had been caught speeding without a license when he was thirteen; and he remembered being extricated from other situations, too, boyish pranks or minor crimes during his hot-rodding days in high school, which was when he had become curious and even intrigued by his father's world.

He had wondered how he would measure up to the men around his father. He had heard them sometimes speaking casually about the danger they faced, or the jails that might await them, and he wondered if he would have been so calm in such circumstances.

The idea of jail had both worried and fascinated him in those days, and he remembered as a high-school student how he had once been arrested. He and a group of boys had been at a football game, behaving boisterously throughout the afternoon. Their pushing, shouting, and tossing of paper cups had so irritated other spectators that the police had finally evicted them from the stadium and charged them with disorderly conduct. They had spent the night in jail, an experience that Bill had found interesting during the first hour, but then it had quickly palled. And yet he realized that his offensive behavior had been deliberate, he had really wanted to end up in jail, and he was also somewhat satisfied later that he had remained cool and controlled during confinement.

News of the incident had not reached his father, although his teachers had learned of it and been disappointed and surprised. Unlike some boys in the junior class, Bill Bonanno was not thought of as troublesome or rebellious. He was regarded as a student leader; he was president of the student anti-liquor club, an organizer of the blood drive, an editor on the magazine. He did not smoke cigarettes, having one day promised an elderly woman he had met in a café, a tubercular recuperating in Tucson, that he would avoid the habit. After asking for his pledge in writing on a paper napkin, she handed him a five-dollar bill, and he had kept his word along with the money and napkin from that day on.

But despite the appearance of propriety and leadership in high school, there were nights when he indulged his restlessness by traveling with a gang of Mexican youths who specialized in stealing Cadillac hubcaps and other auto accessories that could be resold to used-car dealers, junkyards, or individual motorists. Some gang members became involved in the summer of 1950 with an older group of gunrunners along the Mexican border, a risky and exciting operation that appealed to Bill Bonanno, but he could not pursue it because he had to go East with his parents in June.

He remembered that trip as a strange, tense journey of long silences and new insights into his father's way of life. He had expected that his father would let him drive much of the way through Arizona into

Texas and onward toward New York, as his father had done during previous June trips to New York for the summer; but on this occasion in 1950 his father would not relinquish the wheel, and, in addition to his mother and baby brother, there was one of his father's men in the car. The route his father followed was different from what had been familiar in the past; they drove through El Paso and Van Horn, avoiding the customary visit to Dallas, and then remained for two days in Brownsville, Texas, where other men had arrived to speak with his father. He remembered while stopping for the night in St. Louis that his mother and father had not registered together at the hotel; the elder Bonanno and his companion had taken one room, and Mrs. Bonanno and the two sons shared a suite elsewhere in the hotel. They left St. Louis in the middle of the night and drove before daybreak toward Wisconsin, not along the usual roads toward New York.

Through June and most of July they remained in Wisconsin, living in motels or cabins near the lakes north of Green Bay, not arriving in New York until the end of July. Then they settled in a house on the north shore of Long Island, living almost in seclusion except for the visits of men. It was a mournful summer in which conversations seemed leveled to a whisper, and dinner was served each night without the usual clattering of plates or rattling of silver. Bill had asked no questions. But he knew what was happening—his father and many of his father's friends were feeling the pressure of the Kefauver committee, and they were trying to avoid subpoenas that would summon them to testify before the Senate and the television cameras.

Although the main target of the committee was Frank Costello, whose appearance was marked by his ill temper under the hot lights as the cameras focused on his nervously tapping fingertips, there were other names mentioned in the press each day with which Bill Bonanno was personally familiar. Joseph Profaci was prominently cited on the Senate crime charts, and so was Joseph Magliocco. While Joseph Bonanno was also mentioned, he had not received great attention, and he had successfully avoided an appearance before the investigators. Nevertheless, Bonanno was deeply disturbed by the publicity he did get, it being the first time in years that he had been openly associated with organized crime. He was especially upset because the exposure had introduced his daughter to the charges against him, and Catherine, who was then sixteen, had broken down and cried for days. But the revelation did not diminish her affection for him. She, like Bill, was filled with compassion and actually felt closer to her father than she had before.

After that summer Bill had left New York to begin his final term at Tucson High. Borrowing a company car from the Bonanno cheese factory, and accompanied by a school friend, he drove quickly across the country, loving the buoyant sense of escape he felt behind the wheel, and he arrived in Arizona a week before classes began. Then he drove an additional thousand miles alone to San Antonio to visit a girl he was fond of, the sister of a classmate from his boarding-school days. Her father, an industrialist in Michigan, raised polo ponies, and Bill remembered riding them during the visit, galloping over the turf imagining the good life of men in white helmets and jodhpurs, swinging mallets through the sky.

But his final year in high school dragged on listlessly, the single memorable event being his father's graduation gift, a new Chevrolet Bel Air hardtop. He began at the University of Arizona that June, contemplating a degree in prelaw, but soon he switched to agricultural engineering, believing it would provide a useful background for the day when he would inherit part of his father's share in a large cotton farm north of Tucson. On reaching twenty-one, he would have in his own name not only land but certain income-producing properties that his father, a skillful real-estate speculator, had acquired since coming to Arizona. Bill looked forward to earning his own money, for his father had always been tight about allowances, an inconsistent trait in an otherwise generous man. It was typical of his father to buy him a new car but to provide so little spending money that Bill was usually out of gas.

As a result Bill had been compelled to take part-time jobs after school hours, which was what his father had wanted; the elder Bonanno abhorred idleness, and one of his favorite expressions was: The best way to kill time is to work it to death. Bill had begun working during his early teens, and during his college days he worked at night at a drive-in hamburger stand, where he met a pretty blonde waitress, a divorcée with whom he had his first sexual affair.

Prior to this time his experience had consisted largely of heavy petting with such girls as the one in San Antonio, and quick ejaculations into a town tart who had first seduced him in the projection room of the Catalina movie house in Tucson on a day no film was being shown. Although he had had opportunities with other girls, and could have used his parents' home, he had never taken full advantage of their many absences. He had been somewhat puritanical in those days, incapable of sex in his mother's linen, and he had not even held parties there with his young friends because there was the possibility that outsiders might snoop through his father's things.

The affair with the divorcée had been conducted at her apartment, continuing for more than a year without his parents' knowledge. While there had never been talk of marriage he was very possessive of her, and he had become infuriated when he heard that she had dated in his absence a jockey who was in Arizona for the racing season. The fear of losing her, the first girl he thought he had ever truly had, and the shocking realization that she could make love to him and then date other men, had filled him with fury and despair. For the first time in his life he recognized his capacity for violence.

He remembered waiting for her in the apartment, then seeing her walking up the path with two tiny men, both tailored to the toes in an expensive but flashy way, their small sun-tanned faces drawn tight across their cheekbones. As she opened the door, laughing at something one of them had said, Bill had stepped forward, towering over them, shouting. When one of the men yelled back, Bill had grabbed him and shook him, then began to slap him hard against the wall as the girl screamed and the other jockey ran.

Soon the police had arrived to arrest Bill for assault. Later, however, perhaps through his father's influence, the case against him was dismissed.

The end of the romance was part of a depressing year in general. He was doing poorly in college; the girl in San Antonio informed him that she was going steady with a Texas football star; and then his father suffered a heart attack, and left Tucson to recuperate in a quiet spot near La Jolla, California. Bill was again alone in the house through the winter and spring, and through another session of summer school.

He spent part of the summer at an ROTC camp, preparing for a commission in the Army. He had adapted easily to the routine of military discipline, and he was soon promoted to drill sergeant in the cadets' elite unit, the Pershing Rifles. On the firing range he was a superb marksman with a rifle or pistol, having had previous target practice at boarding school, and being on familiar terms with guns since his boyhood days, when he noticed them bulging from beneath the jackets of men who came to visit. But it was after leaving New York for Arizona that he had become most aware of guns, seeing them carried openly and casually by people in cars or on horseback, by ranchers, wranglers, and Indians, and he sometimes felt that he was on the set of a cowboy film. And he liked the feeling.

He also liked the clothes, becoming quickly accustomed to wearing boots, hip-hugging pants, and string ties, and his father had done the same in Arizona. So had some of his father's men during their extended visits, although the fatter ones had always looked uncomfortable and comical in these clothes, their Western buckles lost under their bellies. Nevertheless a kinship of sorts probably did exist between these men and the legendary American cowboy, Bill thought, impressed by the similarity between the tales of the old West and certain stories he had heard as a boy involving gun battles between mounted mafiosi in the hills of western Sicily. He had heard that his grandmother in Castellammare had sometimes packed a pistol in her skirts, a kind of Ma Barker, and the Sicilians of that region today still honor the memory of the bandit Giuliano, a leader of a gang of outlaws who shared what they had stolen with the poor.

Although Giuliano was a hero in western Sicily he might easily be regarded elsewhere as a common thief—it depended largely on one's point of view, and the same could be said when appraising the life of any man, the activities of any group, the policies of any nation. If Bill Bonanno had learned anything from reading the memoirs of great statesmen and generals it was that the line between what was right and wrong, moral or immoral, was often very thin indeed, with the final verdict being written by the victors. When he had gone to ROTC camp, and later into military service with the Army Reserve, he had been trained in the technique of legal killing. He had learned how to use a bayonet, how to fire an M-1 rifle, how to adjust the range finder of a cannon in a Patton tank. He had memorized the United States military code, which in principle was not so dissimilar from the Mafia's, emphasizing honor, obedience, and silence if captured. And if he had gone into combat and had killed several North Koreans or Chinese Communists he might have become a hero. But if he killed one of his father's enemies in a Mafia war, where buried in the issues were the same mixture of greed and self-righteousness found in all the wars of great nations, he could be charged with murder.

In the Mafia today were many American veterans of World War II, one being a decorated infantryman who became Joseph Bonanno's bodyguard. This veteran wore a metal plate in his forehead and had several scars on his body as a result of combat against the Germans. He had fought in the North African campaign and also participated in the invasion of Sicily in which the Americans employed local mafiosi as intelligence agents and underground organizers against the Nazi and Fascist forces. Many such agents were rewarded with lawful authority by the Allies after the war, a fact documented in many books about the Mafia that Bill Bonanno had read; some of them became the mayors of towns and officials in the regional government because of their strong anti-fascism and hatred of Mussolini. During the Fascist regime in Italy, Mussolini had sponsored a campaign of terror against the Mafia, torturing many Mafia suspects, and without a fair trial killing many more. When Mussolini himself had been captured and killed, Bill remembered the satisfied reaction of his father and his father's friends. His father had been forced out of Sicily during his days as a student radical because he had opposed certain Fascist policies, and as a result he had settled in the United States. Otherwise he might have remained in his native land, and Bill wondered what it would have been like if he, too, had been born and had remained in Castellammare. Perhaps life might have been better. Perhaps it would have been worse.

Although the trip through New England taken by Bill Bonanno, Frank Labruzzo, and the other men was pleasantly uneventful and restful, there gradually developed within Bonanno a slight nagging feeling that he could not explain. It was as if he had forgotten something, was ignoring an obligation, compromising a trust, was somehow failing to fulfill all that his father might have expected of him. Whatever it was, he reasoned that it must be relatively unimportant, otherwise he would have no difficulty in defining it; and yet it continued to bother him as he drove south along Massachusetts Bay, then headed west toward Concord.

It was getting dark. Soon he and Labruzzo would be stopping at a motel where they would be joined later by the other men for dinner. They had now been on the road for a week, and during that time there had been nothing in the newspapers or on the radio indicating that the situation had changed in New York. The gangs were apparently still remaining out of sight. There had been no message on Bonanno's answering service requiring an immediate response. The government's search for his father had revealed no clues. Some police officials believed that Joseph Bonanno was still hiding in the Catskills, others believed that he was dead. Bill did not know what to believe, and during the last few days he had managed not to think too much about it. Maybe that was what had been bothering him. He did not know.

After dinner he wandered off by himself to walk the dog along a narrow dirt road near the highway, leaving the men seated around the television set in his suite. They were watching a crime series called *The Untouchables*, which was based loosely on the Mafia and had angered many Italo-Americans around the nation because the scriptwriters tended to give Italian names to the gangster roles. But the real-life gangsters enjoyed watching the show, Bonanno knew, although they appreciated it on a different level than the producers had intended. The gangsters saw this show, along with such other ones as *The F.B.I.* series and *Perry Mason*, as broad comedy or satire. They laughed at lines that were not intended to be funny; they mocked the dim-witted caricatures of themselves; they hooted and jeered the characters representing the FBI or the police, turning television-watching into a kind of psychodrama. They mostly seemed to enjoy the Perry Mason series, whose murder mysteries they could usually solve before the second commercial, and whose courtroom scene at the end of each show—a scene in which a prime suspect always collapses under cross-examination and jumps to his feet proclaiming his guilt—they found ridiculously amusing.

Returning to the motel, uncomfortably cold and unaccustomed to Eastern climate after so many winters in Arizona, Bill Bonanno thought of Rosalie and the children, wishing that he could call them. If only Rosalie were reachable at a phone that was not tapped, he would call her at this moment; and as he thought about this he slowly became excited—he was clarifying what it was that had been bothering him.

He recalled a conversation with his father four months ago, in late July, immediately after the elder Bonanno had been evicted from Montreal and had returned to the United States. At that time Joseph Bonanno had recounted his legal hassle with the Canadian immigration authorities, the frustration of appearing all day in the Montreal courthouse and then not being able to reach Bill at night to talk freely on an untapped phone; and he said that should they ever again be separated for an extended period, they should have some system that would permit them to communicate. Joseph Bonanno had then devised a plan—a workable system, Bill had thought at the time, but during the hectic months that followed, culminating in his father's disappearance, Bill had forgotten all about his father's proposal. Now, on this November night in Massachusetts, it had come back to him.

The plan specified that, if they lost contact without explanation, Bill was to go to a particular telephone booth in Long Island on each Thursday evening, at eight o'clock sharp, until the elder Bonanno was able to call him there. The booth was located next to a diner on Old Country Road between Hicksville and Westbury, and Joseph Bonanno had kept a record of that number as he had of dozens of other booths that he had used in the past, at prearranged times, to speak with one of his men. This specific booth was selected for his son because it was not far from Bill's home, and because it had not been used so often in the past that it was likely to be under police surveillance. The booth was also chosen because there was a second telephone booth near it that could be used if the first was busy.

Excitedly, entering the motel, Bill announced to the other men that he was returning to New York early the next morning. He explained the reason, adding that the next day, November 12, was a Thursday. But the men thought it highly unlikely that the elder Bonanno would call; even if he were alive and unharmed, and had not forgotten his arrangement of four months ago, he would probably be too cautious or otherwise unable to make the call, they said. Bill, however, would not be discouraged. If his father were alive, he would make the call, Bill said. If he did not make it this Thursday, then he would make it next Thursday, or the Thursday after that, and Bill said he would be there every time, just in case, until he was convinced that his father was dead. He also pointed out, in a low tone that seemed almost self-accusatory, that when they had left New York a week ago, on the night of November 5, it had been a Thursday, and perhaps he had already missed one of his father's calls.

So it was agreed that they would return to New York. The other men were to go directly to their apartments, informing the subordinates that they were back in town, while Bonanno and Labruzzo would go on to Long Island.

They arrived in New York shortly before seven P.M., the distant skyline glowing softly in the early-evening light, the last of the commuter traffic moving swiftly out of the city. At a quarter to eight, Bonanno and Labruzzo arrived at the diner on Old Country Road. They turned into the parking lot, stopping near the booth. It was glass-paneled and trimmed in green aluminum, and it was empty. They sat in the car for a few minutes, the motor running, the headlights off. Then, at five before eight, Bonanno got out, walked into the booth, and stood waiting.

He was relieved that the coin slot was not covered with the familiar yellow sticker reading "out of order"; and after depositing a coin and getting the reassuring sound of a dial tone, he replaced the receiver. The condition of coin-box phones was of vital importance to him and the other men, and he knew how infuriated they had all been at one time or another by malfunctioning phones, and they had sworn vengeance on the petty thieves who tamper with outdoor phones. Whenever they discovered one that was jammed or broken into, they reported it to the telephone company, and later checked back at the booth to be certain that the repairs had been made and also to be sure that the number had not been changed. If it had been, they recorded the new number on a private list they kept in their cars—a list containing not only the telephone numbers and booth locations, but also an identifying number that distinguished one booth from another. These last numbers were memorized by the Bonanno men as faithfully as baseball fans memorized the numbers on the backs of players, and the system had greatly reduced the organization's communications problem in recent years—it had enabled the elder Bonanno, for example, to use his home telephone, which was tapped, to call his son's home, where the phone was also tapped, and to engage his son in a folksy conversation in Sicilian dialect into which he slipped two numbers that indicated he wished to speak privately with Bill: the first number identified the locale of the booth that Bill was to go to, the second established the hour that Bill was to be there. Then, before the appointed hour, Joseph Bonanno would leave his home and go to a booth, would dial his son at the other booth, and they would speak freely without worrying about being tapped.

This system was similar to what Joseph Bonanno had proposed in July, except Bill had been told then to go automatically to booth No. 27—the one near the diner—each Thursday at eight P.M. and to wait, as he was now waiting on this night in November. He felt chilly and cramped within the four glass walls that pressed him from all sides. He must go on a diet, he thought; he was becoming too large for phone booths. Raising his left arm, he looked at his watch, a diamond-studded gold one given him months ago by a few of his father's men. It was seven-fifty-nine.

The silence in the booth was becoming intense, reminding him of boyhood moments waiting in a confessional, fretful seconds before the stern priest slapped open the sliding screen. At eight o'clock his senses were so sharp and expectant that he could almost hear ringing sounds piercing deep within his mind's ear and, looking down at the green plastic instrument, he searched for the slightest sign of vibration. But it hung motionless, quiet in its cradle.

He looked through the glass doors, seeing the parked car with Labruzzo behind the wheel. Labruzzo sat perfectly still, but the dog was jumping in the back, paws against the closed window. Bonanno then heard sounds coming from behind him—three men were leaving the diner, talking and laughing, getting into a station wagon. They did not look in his direction. Soon they were gone. He waited. Finally, he looked at his watch.

It was eight-four. It was all over for tonight, he thought. If his father did not call on the dot, he would not call at all. He also knew that his father would not want him to linger and possibly attract attention. So he reluctantly pulled open the door of the booth and walked slowly toward the car. Labruzzo flashed on the headlights. They drove in silence back to the apartment in Queens.

The rest of the week, and the weeks that followed through November into December, were for the most part monotonous. Bonanno and Labruzzo resumed housekeeping in their hideaway. They ventured out at night, remaining indoors during the day. They spoke with the men, read the papers, listened to the radio, learned very little.

On Thursdays, however, their mood changed. Each Thursday was the high point of their week; it began in the morning with a sense of anticipation and it heightened during the late afternoon, building with each mile of the trip to the booth. The trip was taking on a strange almost mystical meaning for Bonanno and Labruzzo—it was becoming an act of faith, a test of fidelity; and the booth, too, a solitary glowing structure in the vacant darkness, was approached almost reverentially. They drove slowly up to it, neither man speaking. Then Bill, after getting out of the car, would stand in the bright enclosure for two minutes— from seven-fifty-nine to eight-one. Conceding the silence, he would step out, betraying no emotion as he walked to the car. There was always another Thursday ahead, another visit to be made to the telephone booth that might finally link them to the hidden world of Joseph Bonanno.

The longer the government search continued without a trace of his father or the discovery of a bullet-riddled body, the more encouraged Bill Bonanno became. It was now six weeks since the disappearance; and if the elder Bonanno had been killed, that fact would presumably have already been circulated through the underworld by his father's ecstatic rivals, or it would at least have been hinted at in Mafia gossip. But so far the speculation about Bonanno's death had been largely limited to the newspapers, whose information came from the government, which was no doubt becoming embarrassed by its inability to find Bonanno after so much searching.

The younger Bonanno was also now encouraged by his own efforts during his father's absence. Quickly recovering from the initial shock, he had assumed the responsibility of trying to hold the organization together by eluding his potential captors and by demonstrating always a sense of confidence and optimism. In spite of his youth, he believed that he was now accepted by most of the men as their interim leader, their attitude toward him having changed considerably from what it had been when he first joined the outfit in the mid-fifties as "J.B.'s kid," and when the respect shown him had been in deference to the name. Aware of that situation, his father had contemplated denying him a place in the "family" and having him join the organization headed by Albert Anastasia. Anastasia, a close friend of Joseph Profaci, had come to know Bill during the latter's summer vacations from college, occasionally taking him to the Copacabana, and he would have eagerly found a spot for him. It might have been very advantageous for Anastasia to have done so, for it might have fostered closer ties with both the Bonanno and Profaci groups and perhaps ultimately formed a tight three-family alliance that could have dominated the two larger gangs in New York, one headed by Vito Genovese, the other by Thomas Luchese.

But Joseph Bonanno finally decided that he wanted his son with him, sensing perhaps the Mafia hierarchy's growing dissatisfaction with Anastasia, an autocratic and ambitious man with a tendency to overstep his boundaries—a tendency that would cost him his life. So Bill Bonanno, having quit college without a degree, followed in his father's path, although he straddled two worlds for a while—operating legitimate businesses in Arizona, including a wholesale food market and real estate trading, while being affiliated with the Bonanno organization, whose small Southwestern branch was involved in bookmaking and other illegal gambling activities.

Bill did not enjoy his involvement with his father's world during these years; he had no objection to it on moral grounds, but rather resented his lowly status among his father's men. Whether Bill was in New York or Arizona, his father gave him little to do, and he invariably dismissed all of Bill's suggestions promptly and without deliberation. His father seemed to be constantly second-guessing him, questioning him, and Bill had resented it.

He remembered one occasion when he had fought back, losing his temper completely and screaming uncontrollably at his father; and he remembered the look of surprise and shock on his father's face, the speechless astonishment. The elder Bonanno had apparently never been shouted at before in such an unrestrained manner, and he did not know how to react, at least toward his own son. Bill had quickly tried to pass over the situation, saying, "Look, I was born to lead, not to follow." After a pause, his father had replied with quiet firmness: "Before you can lead, you must learn to follow."

After that, Bill had managed to control his temper in front of his father, and although he did not refrain from disagreeing in private when he felt justified, he learned to follow orders. When he was told to be at a certain place at a certain time, he was there at the precise moment, remaining until he was instructed to leave. He remembered one morning when he had driven his father to a drugstore and had been told to wait outside. He waited for one hour, then a second hour. Then he left the car and looked into the drugstore and saw his father seated at a booth talking with another man, drinking coffee. Bill returned to the car, continuing to wait. The afternoon passed, extending into early evening. Finally, twelve hours after his father had entered the drugstore, he walked out. He nodded toward Bill, but did not apologize or explain what had taken so long.

Now, years later, looking back on that incident and similar incidents, Bill realized how his father had tested his patience and discipline, seeing how he would respond to a condition that was so necessary and common in the organization and yet was so unnatural to most restless men—waiting. In Bill's case, however, waiting had been no problem. He had spent most of his life waiting, especially for his father, waiting as a young teenager in Arizona for his father's reappearances each winter, as expectantly and hopefully as he was waiting now. His past had prepared him for the present, he thought, and he believed that he was now truly disciplined, capable of withstanding the worst that might come along, and this possibility pleased him very much.

On Thursday evening, December 17, Bill Bonanno and Frank Labruzzo paid their weekly visit to the phone booth on Long Island. It was the sixth consecutive Thursday that they had gone there. In a week it would be Christmas Eve, and on the way to the booth the two men wondered aloud if the holiday truce would be observed by the various gangs this year as it had been in the past. Under normal circumstances, it would be—all organization members would temporarily forget their differences until after January 1; but since the Bonanno loyalists were technically suspended from the national union, neither Bill nor Frank Labruzzo knew for sure whether the holiday policy would now be followed with regard to their people. They would have to anticipate the worst, they decided, and so both men assumed that they would not be spending Christmas with their wives and children.

At seven-fifty-five P.M., they pulled into the parking lot near the diner and parked a few feet away from the booth. It was a very cold night, and Bill, turning off the radio, sat waiting in the car with the window partly open. The sky was dark and cloudy, the only reflection came from the big neon sign above the diner. There were three cars parked in front of the diner, and except for a few customers seated at the counter and an elderly couple at a table, it was empty. The food must be terrible, Bill thought, for the diner had never seemed busy during any of his visits, although he conceded the possibility that it had a late trade, maybe truck drivers, which might explain the large parking lot. Many people thought that places patronized by truckers must be serving good food, but Bill believed that the opposite was probably true. He had eaten at hundreds of roadside places during his many motor trips across the country, and most of the time he had observed the truckmen eating chicken soup and salted crackers, and he was willing to bet that most of them suffered from nervous stomachs and hemorrhoids.

He looked at his watch. It was exactly eight o'clock. He and Labruzzo sat silently as the seconds ticked away. He was about to conclude that it was another uneventful Thursday. Then, the telephone rang.

Bill slammed against the door, bounced out of the car, ran into the booth with such force that it shook. Labruzzo ran after him, pressing against the glass door that Bill had pulled shut.

Bill heard a woman's voice, very formal, sounding far away—it was the operator repeating the number, asking if it corresponded to the telephone number in the booth.

"Yes," Bill replied, feeling his heart pounding, "yes it is."

He heard muffled sounds from the other end, then silence for a second, then the sound of coins being dropped into the slot, quarters, six or seven quarters gonging—it was long distance.

"Hello, Bill?"

It was a male voice, not his father's, a voice he did not recognize.

"Yes, who is this?"

"Never mind," the man replied, "just listen to me. Your father's okay. You'll probably be seeing him in a few days."

"How do I know he's okay?" Bill demanded, suddenly aggressive.

"Where the hell do you think I got this number from?" The man was now irritated. Bill calmed down.

"Now look," the man continued, "don't make waves! Everything's okay. Just sit back, don't do anything, and don't worry about anything."

Before Bill could respond, the man had hung up.

• • •

The excitement, the ecstasy that Bill Bonanno felt was overwhelming, and during the drive back to Queens he heard the conversation again and again, and he repeated it to Labruzzo. Your father's okay, you'll probably be seeing him in a few days. Bill was so happy that he wanted to go to a bar and have a few drinks in celebration, but both he and Labruzzo agreed that despite the good news they should remain as careful and alert as they had been before. They would follow the advice of the man on the telephone, would sit back and wait; in a few days Joseph Bonanno would reappear to make the next move.

Although, in the interest of efficiency, Bill thought that some preparation for his father's return was necessary; he felt, for example, that his father's attorney, William P. Maloney, should be informed immediately of this latest development. Bill reasoned that Maloney would be his father's chief spokesman after the reappearance, an event that would undoubtedly cause a circus of confusion and complex legal maneuvering in the courthouse, and Maloney would have to plan the elder Bonanno's strategy before the latter's interrogation by the Federal grand jury. Bill also felt a touch of guilt with regard to Maloney, about whom he had been so suspicious after the incident on Park Avenue. The veteran lawyer had been forced to appear on five or six occasions since then before the grand jury to defend himself against government implications that he was somehow involved in the kidnapping incident, and Bill imagined that Maloney's reputation as a lawyer might have suffered as a result. So, on the following day, Bill Bonanno drove to a telephone booth and called Maloney's office.

"Hi, Mr. Maloney, this is Bill Bonanno," he said, cheerfully, picturing the old man jumping out of his chair.

"Hey," Maloney yelled, "where are you? Where's your dad?"

"Hold on," Bonanno said, "take it easy. Go to a phone outside your office, to one of the booths downstairs, and call me at this number." He gave Maloney the number. Within a few minutes the lawyer had called back, and Bonanno recounted all that he had been told the night before.

But Maloney was dissatisfied with the brevity of the details. He wanted more specific information. He wondered on what day the elder Bonanno would appear, where he would be staying, how he could be reached now and through whom? Bill said he did not know anything other than what he had already told, adding that as soon as he knew more he would contact Maloney at once. When Maloney persisted with more questions, Bonanno cut him off. He had to run, he said. He hung up.

He returned to the apartment. Labruzzo had arranged for certain men to be there that evening, having already informed them of the news. The pace was quickening, there was activity, anticipation, and Bill Bonanno was confident that soon a few things would be resolved, soon he and the other men might get some relief from the wretched routine of hiding. The reappearance of his father should stabilize the organization to a degree and lessen the uncertainty. His father had undoubtedly come to some terms with his captors, or he would not be alive, and so the next hurdle was the government. His father would appear before the Federal grand jury, and Bill and the other men who were sought would probably do the same. They would come out of hiding, would accept their subpoenas, and, after consultation with their lawyers, would present themselves in court. If their answers displeased the judge, they might be sentenced to jail for contempt, but at this juncture they had few alternatives. Their terms could be for a month, a year, or more; but it would not be intolerable so long as some stability had been reestablished within the organization, and perhaps their status had been restored in the national society. Hopefully they would not enter prison as underworld outcasts. Their existence behind bars was much more pleasant when they were known to be members in good standing; they were accorded a respect not only by the other prisoners, but also by the prison guards and certain other workers, men for whom favors could be done on the outside. The "man of respect" serving time also knew that during his confinement he need not worry about his wife and children; they were being looked after by organizational representatives, and if they required help they received it.

While Bill Bonanno sat in the living room of the apartment reading the afternoon papers, Labruzzo took a nap, undisturbed by the noise from the television. It was too early for the evening news, and neither man had paid much attention during the last few hours to the series of quiz shows, soap operas, or comedies that monopolized the screen.

Suddenly, there was an interruption of the program—the announcement of a special news bulletin. Bill Bonanno looked up from his newspaper, waited. He expected to hear that war was declared, Russian bombers were on the way. Instead he heard the announcer say: Mafia leader Joseph Bonanno, who was kidnapped and believed to have been killed by rival mobsters in October, is alive. Bonanno's attorney, William Power Maloney, made the announcement today. Maloney also said that his client would appear before the Federal grand jury investigating organized crime, at nine A.M. on Monday, and . . .

Bill Bonanno sat stunned. Labruzzo came running in to watch. Bonanno began to swear quietly. Maloney had not only called a press conference, but had also identified him as the source of the information. Bonanno buried his head in his hands. He felt heat racing through his body, his sweat rising and seeping through his shirt. He knew he had made a horrible mistake in talking to Maloney in the first place, then in not swearing him to secrecy. Now he did not know what was ahead for his father. He recalled the words of the man on the phone saying don't make waves . . . don't do anything. And, stupidly, he had done it. He had possibly ruined everything, for the announcement would make Page One all over the country, would drive the elder Bonanno deeper into hiding, and it would intensify on a grand scale the investigation, activating those agents who had been lulled into thinking that Joseph Bonanno was dead.

The television set displayed a picture of Maloney, then a picture of the Park Avenue apartment house, and suddenly Bill was sick of the whole episode—and, reaching for a heavy glass ashtray on a nearby table, he threw it hard at the set, hitting the screen squarely in the center. It exploded like a bomb. Thousands of tiny pieces of glass sprayed the room, tubes popped, wires curled and burned in varicolored flame, sparks flared in several directions—a remarkable little fireworks show of self-destruction was playing itself out within the twenty-one-inch screen, and Bonanno and Labruzzo watched with fascination until the interior of the set had nearly evaporated into a smoldering hole of jagged edges and fizzling filament.

"The Kidnapping of Joe Bonnano" was the first in a series of three segments excerpted by Esquire *in 1971 from Talese's book* Honor Thy Father, *which was reissued in 2009 by Harper Perennial.*

Charlie Manson's Home on the Range

The horse wrangler, tall and ruggedly handsome, placed his hands on the hips of a pretty girl wearing white bell-bottomed trousers and casually lifted her onto a hitching post near the stable; then, voluntarily, almost automatically, she spread her legs and he stood between her, moving slowly from side to side and up and down, stroking her long blonde hair while her arms and fingers caressed his back, not quickly or eagerly but quite passively, indolently, a mood harmonious with his own.

They continued their slow erotic slumber for several moments under the mid-morning sun, swaying silently and looking without expression into one another's eyes, seeming totally unaware of their own lack of privacy and the smell of horse manure near their feet and the thousands of flies buzzing around them and the automobile that had just come down the dusty road and was now parked, motor idling, with a man inside calling through an open window to where the wrangler stood between the girl.

He slowly turned his head toward the car but did not withdraw from the girl. He was about six feet four and wore a bone-like ornament around his neck, and he had a long angular face with a sandy beard and pale sharply focused blue eyes. He did not seem perturbed by the stranger in the automobile; he assumed that he was probably a reporter or detective, both having come in great numbers recently to this ranch in Southern California to speak with the proprietor, an old man named George Spahn, about a group of violent hippies that had lived on the ranch for a year but were now believed to have all moved away.

Spahn was not reluctant to talk about them, the wrangler knew, even though Spahn had never seen them, the old man being blind; and so when the man in the car asked for George Spahn, a little smile formed on the wrangler's face, knowing but enigmatic, and he pointed toward a shack at the end of a row of dilapidated empty wooden buildings. Then, as the car pulled away, he again began his slow movements with the girl delicately balanced on the hitching post.

Spahn's ranch is lost in desert brush and rocky hills, but it is not so much a ranch as it is the old Western movie set it once was. The row of empty buildings extending along the dirt road toward Spahn's shack—decaying structures with faded signs marking them as a saloon, a barbershop, a café, a jail, and a carriage house—all were constructed many years ago as Hollywood settings for cowboy brawls and Indian ambushes, and among the many actors who performed in them, or in front of them, were Tom Mix and Johnny Mack Brown, Hoot Gibson, Wallace Beery, and the Cisco Kid. In the carriage house is a coach that supposedly was used by Grace Kelly in *High Noon*, and scattered here and there, and slept in by the stray dogs and cats that run wild on this land, are old wagons and other props used in scenes in *Duel in the Sun*, *The Lone Ranger* television series, and *Bonanza*. Around the street set, on the edge of the clearing near the trees, are smaller broken-down shacks lived in by wranglers or itinerants who drift to this place periodically and work briefly at some odd job and then disappear. There is an atmosphere of impermanence and neglect about the place, the unwashed windows, the rotting wood, the hauling trucks parked on inclines because their batteries are low and need the momentum of a downhill start; and yet there is much that is natural and appealing about the place, not the ranch area itself but the land in back of where the old man lives, it being thick with trees and berry bushes and dipping toward a small creek and rising again toward the rocky foothills of the Santa Susanna Mountains. There are a few caves in the mountains that have been used from time to time as shelters by shy vagrants, and in the last few years hippies have sometimes been seen along the rocky ridges strumming guitars and singing songs. Now the whole area is quiet and still and, though it is only twenty miles northwest of downtown Beverly Hills, it is possible from certain heights to look for miles in any direction without seeing any sign of modern life.

Spahn came to this region in the 1930s in the first great migration of the automobile age, a time when it was said to be the dream of every Midwestern Model T salesman to move to sunny Southern California and live in a bungalow with a banana plant in the front yard. Except George Spahn had no such dream, nor was he a Midwestern Model T salesman. He was a fairly successful dairy farmer from Pennsylvania with a passion for horses, preferring them to cars and to most of the people that he knew. The fact that his father had been kicked to death by a horse, an accident that occurred in 1891 when the elder Spahn was delivering slaughtered livestock in a horse-drawn wagon near Philadelphia, did not instill in the son any fear of that animal; in fact, Spahn quit school after the third grade to work behind a horse on a milk wagon, and his close association with horses was to continue through the rest of his life, being interrupted by choice only once.

That was during his sixteenth year when, temporarily tired of rising at three A.M. for his daily milk route, he accepted a job as a carpenter's apprentice, living in the carpenter's home and becoming in time seduced by the carpenter's lusty nineteen-year-old daughter. She would entice him into the woods beyond the house on afternoons when her father was away, or into her bedroom at night after her father had gone to sleep; and even, one day, observing through her window two dogs copulating in the yard, she was suddenly overcome with desire and pulled Spahn to the floor on top of her—all this happening when he was sixteen, in 1906, a first sexual relationship that he can remember vividly and wistfully even now at the age of eighty-one.

Though never handsome, Spahn was a strong solidly built man in his youth with a plain yet personable manner. He had a hot temper at times, but he was never lazy. When he was in his middle twenties his milk business in Willow Grove, Pennsylvania, was large enough for him to operate five wagons and seven horses; and one of the men whom he employed, more out of kindness than anything else, was his stepfather, Tom Reah, whom he had once despised. Spahn could never understand what his strict German-Irish mother had ever seen in Reah, a raw-boned man with a large belly who, when drunk, could be vicious. When in this condition, Reah would sometimes assault young Spahn, beating him badly; although later Spahn fought back, once swearing at Reah: "You son of a bitch, I'm gonna kill you some day!" On another occasion he threw an ice ax at Reah's head, missing by inches.

Before Spahn was thirty he had obtained an eighty-six-acre farm near Lansdale, Pennsylvania, on which he kept thirty-five cows, several horses, and a lady housekeeper he had hired after placing an advertisement in a local newspaper. She had previously been married to a racing-car driver who had been killed, leaving her with one child. Spahn found her congenial and able, if not reminiscent of the carpenter's daughter; and at some later date that Spahn cannot remember, they were married. While it would not be an entirely happy or lasting marriage, they would remain together long enough to have ten children, nearly all of whom would be named after Spahn's horses. He named his first daughter, Alice, after a yellow-white pinto he had once owned; and his second daughter, Georgianna, was named in honor of a gelding called George. His third daughter, Mary, was named after a big bay mare; and when Spahn had a son, he named him George after himself *and* the aforementioned gelding. Next came Dolly, after a big sorrel mare; and Paul, after a freckled pinto; and so on down the line.

During the early 1930s, in the Depression, Spahn contemplated moving West. Animal feed was scarce in Pennsylvania, the milk was frequently spoiled by the inadequate refrigeration system on his farm, and he was becoming disenchanted with life in general. In an advertisement circulated by the Union Pacific Railroad, he had read about the virtues of Southern California, its predictable and mild climate, its lack of rain in summertime, its abundant feed for animals, and he was tempted. He first came alone by train to see Southern California for himself; then, satisfied, he returned home. He sold his farm and packed his family, his furniture, and his horse collars in a Packard sedan and a truck, and shipped his best horses separately by rail. He began the long voyage across the continent. He would not regret his decision.

Within a few years, giving up the milk business to concentrate on raising horses and operating a riding stable, he prospered. Within a decade, moving from Long Beach to South Los Angeles, and then to North Hollywood, he expanded his business to include children's pony rides, the rental of horses for parades and fairs, and the supplying of horses and wranglers for use in cowboy films. In one movie that featured a desert battle between Arabs and Ethiopians, Spahn himself became part of the cast, playing an Arab horseman and wearing a desert robe and white bloomers. In 1948, when one of the ranches used by the moviemakers was offered for sale, a ranch once owned by William S. Hart, a cowboy star of the silent screen, Spahn bought it. Spahn and his wife parted company at about this time, but there soon appeared at Spahn's side a new leading lady of the ranch, a onetime dog trainer and circus performer named Ruby Pearl.

She was a perky redhead of about thirty with lively blue eyes, a petite figure, and lots of nerve. She had been born on a farm in Sandstone, Minnesota, and had a desire to get into show business somehow, an ambition that was as confusing as it was shocking to her mother, a Christian preacher's daughter, and her father, a conscientious routine-oriented railroad man. After graduating from high school, where she had acted in school plays and had won first prize in the girls' hundred-yard dash and broad-jump competition in a county-wide track meet, she traveled to Minneapolis on her father's railroad pass, presumably to attend secretarial school and embark on a respectable career in that city. But one day, scanning the classified ads in the *Minneapolis Tribune*, she saw a job opportunity that appealed to her. She applied and got the job, that of being a cocktail waitress at Lindy's, a local club patronized by, among other distinguished figures, Al Capone.

When Capone and his men were in town they were invariably accompanied by very attractive girls in ermine or mink, and they were always given the large table at Lindy's in the back room where the drinks were served all night. Ruby Pearl liked serving the big table, not only because of the generous tips she received but because of the sense of excitement she felt in the Capone party's presence. But she had neither the desire nor the time to become further involved, devoting all her free hours and earnings to the dancing school she attended every day, learning ballet and adagio, tap-dancing, the rumba, and the tango. After Lindy's was raided by the police and closed down, Ruby Pearl supported herself as a bus girl in a cafeteria, pouring coffee and clearing dishes. Soon she caught the eye of the assistant manager, an engineering student at the University of Minnesota. He became her first lover and husband, and after his graduation he was hired by Lockheed in Burbank, California, and the newly married couple set up housekeeping in a motor court on the fringe of Hollywood.

On certain evenings, together with other young engineers from Lockheed and their wives, Ruby and her husband would go to the Brown Derby and Ciro's and various night spots where there was live entertainment and dancing. Ruby invariably became restless and tense on these occasions, seated around the table with the others, sipping her drink, and wishing that she was not with the dull wives of engineers but rather that she was in the spotlight on the stage, kicking up her heels.

Her marriage did not produce children, nor did she want any. She wanted to resume with her dancing, and she did, attending classes conducted by a sleek French-Indian adagio dancer who later gave Ruby a part in his touring trio that featured himself and his jealous girlfriend. Ruby also danced in a chorus of a Hollywood club for a while, as her marriage deteriorated and finally ended in divorce.

At about this time, approaching an age when she could no longer maintain a dancer's pace, she was introduced, by a man she had met, to a new career of training dogs to dance, sit, jump through hoops, and ride atop ponies. She had a natural facility for animal training, and within a few years she had perfected an act with three dogs and a pony that was booked at several community fairs in Southern California, in addition to a number of schools, circuses, and local television shows. At one community fair, in Thousand Oaks, Ruby met a man, a wrestler, who would become her next husband. He was a burly, strong, and tender man who had done quite well financially, and he also owned a restaurant on the side, a subject of interest to Ruby because of her days as a wait-ress. Not long afterward, Ruby met another man with whom she had much in common, a proprietor of a pony-riding ring for children and a movie ranch—George Spahn.

She had seen Spahn at a few of the parades for which he had provided horses, and on a few occasions she had helped with the handling of the horses, displaying her skill as a wrangler. After Spahn had obtained the movie ranch, Ruby applied for a job there and was hired. Spahn was happy to have her. His eyesight was not yet so poor that he was unaware of her fine figure and appeal, and he also welcomed the return of a woman's touch around the place, for it had been absent since the recent departure of his wife. There was not only the film business but also the riding stable that required extra help, particularly on weekends when there would sometimes be a long line of cars with people wanting to rent a horse and go riding through the woods for an hour or two. Ruby knew the horses well, knew the frisky ones from the slower ones, and she could tell pretty much by the way people walked up to the riding stable whether or not they possessed the coordination to safely mount and ride Spahn's better horses. Ruby Pearl was also important to Spahn because she could keep an eye on the young wranglers' manners with regard to the schoolgirls and other young women who often rented horses, although he had to admit that some of the women seemed deliberately dressed for a seduction scene when they came to the ranch—skintight chinos and no bras, their long hair loose and legs wide and bumping up and down as they capered through the woods—it was a risky business.

But Ruby Pearl kept order, and the more responsibility she took the more Spahn relied upon her. His children were now grown and married. Occasionally, Ruby would spend the night on the ranch, and as Spahn's sight worsened in the next few years she accompanied him on shopping trips off the ranch, held him close as they climbed steps, guided his hand as he signed checks, dialed telephone numbers for him, helped to prepare his meals. There were rumors in the nearby town, and among the ranch hands, that associated the pair romantically, and once her husband, the wrestler, complained about the time she was devoting to the ranch. But she quickly dismissed the subject, saying sharply, "I'm *needed* there."

In the last few years, however, Spahn gradually began to notice changes in Ruby Pearl. Slowly, as his sight failed completely and his imagination sharpened, he began to think that she was drifting away from the ranch and himself. He began to notice a difference in the way she held his arm as they walked—she seemed to be holding on more to the cloth of his sleeve than to his arm, and eventually it seemed that she was leading him around while holding *only* to the cloth. He began to miss, or to imagine he was missing, many of the things he once had, among them the presence of female voices on the ranch at night. Perhaps that is why, when the hippie girls arrived, even though they were often noisy and sang songs all night, he felt more alive than he had felt in a very long time.

He does not remember exactly when they first moved onto the ranch. He believes one group of hippie girls and boys arrived sometime in 1967, possibly having come down from San Francisco, and settled briefly in a roadside church several miles north of his ranch; and eventually, in their wanderings down the hill searching for food, they discovered the many empty shacks along the riding path in the woods. They lived in the shacks briefly, and Spahn did not object; but one morning there was a police raid in search of marijuana, and many of the young people were taken into custody. The police asked if Spahn wished to press charges, but he said he did not. The police nonetheless warned the hippies against trespassing, and for a long time it was again very quiet on the ranch at night.

Then one day a school bus carrying hippies arrived at the ranch and parked in the woods, and young girls approached Spahn's doorway, tapping lightly on the screen, and asked if they could stay for a few days. He was reluctant, but when they assured him that it would be only for a few days, adding that they had had automobile trouble, he acquiesced. The next morning Spahn became aware of the sound of weeds being clipped not far from his house, and he was told by one of the wranglers that the work was being done by a few long-haired girls and boys. Later, one of the girls offered to make the old man's lunch, to clean out the shack, to wash the windows. She had a sweet, gentle voice, and she was obviously an educated and very considerate young lady. Spahn was pleased.

In the days that followed, extending into weeks and months, Spahn became familiar with the sounds of the other girls' voices, equally gentle and eager to do whatever had to be done; he did not have to ask them for anything, they saw what had to be done, and they did it. Spahn also came to know the young man who seemed to be in charge of the group, another gentle voice who explained that he was a musician, a singer and poet, and that his name was Charlie Manson. Spahn liked Manson, too. Manson would visit his shack on quiet afternoons and talk for hours about deep philosophical questions, subjects that bewildered the old man but interested him, relieving the loneliness. Sometimes after Spahn had heard Manson walk out the door, and after he had sat in silence for a while, the old man might mutter something to himself—and Manson would reply. Manson seemed to breathe soundlessly, to walk with unbelievable silence over creaky floors. Spahn had heard the wranglers tell of how they would see Charlie Manson sitting quietly by himself in one part of the ranch, and then suddenly they would discover him somewhere else. He seemed to be here, there, everywhere, sitting under a tree softly strumming his guitar. The wranglers had described Manson as a rather small, dark-haired man in his middle thirties, and they could not understand the strong attraction that the six or eight women had for him. Obviously, they adored him. They made his clothes, sat at his feet while he ate, made love to him whenever he wished, did whatever he asked. He had asked that the girls look after the old man's needs, and a few of them would sometimes spend the night in his shack, rising early to make his breakfast. During the day they would paint portraits of

Spahn, using oil paint on small canvases that they had brought. Manson brought Spahn many presents, one of them being a large tapestry of a horse.

He also gave presents to Ruby Pearl—a camera, a silver serving set, tapestries—and once, when he said he was short of money, he sold her a two-hundred-dollar television set for fifty dollars. It was rare, however, that Manson admitted to needing money, although nobody on the ranch knew where he got the money that he had, having to speculate that he had been given it by his girls out of their checks from home, or had earned it from his music. Manson claimed to have written music for rock-and-roll recording artists, and sometimes he was visited at the ranch by members of the Beach Boys and also by Doris Day's son, Terry Melcher. All sorts of new people had been visiting the ranch since Manson's arrival, and one wrangler even claimed to have seen the pregnant movie actress Sharon Tate riding through the ranch one evening on a horse. But Spahn could not be sure.

Spahn could not be certain of anything after Manson had been there for a few months. Many new people, new sounds and elements, had intruded so quickly upon what had been familiar to the old blind man on the ranch that he could not distinguish the voices, the footsteps, the mannerisms as he once had; and without Ruby Pearl on the ranch each night, Spahn's view of reality was largely through the eyes of the hippies or the wranglers, and he did not know which of the two groups was the more bizarre, harebrained, hallucinatory. He knew that the wranglers were now associating with the hippies; he could hear them talking together during the day near the horse corral, and at night he thought he recognized wranglers' voices in the crowd that had gathered to hear Manson's music in the café of the old Western movie set. The hippies were wearing Western clothes and boots and were riding the horses, he had heard; and perhaps the motorcycle sounds he heard in the morning were being made by wranglers, he did not know. The atmosphere was now a blend of horse manure and marijuana, and most of the people seemed to speak in soft voices, wranglers as well as hippies, and this greatly irritated the old man. He yelled toward them, "Speak up, *speak up*, I want to hear, too!" They would speak up, but in tones still soft and placid; and Spahn often overheard them describing him as a "beautiful person."

None of Spahn's experience in life had prepared him for this; he was thoroughly confused by Manson and his followers, yet was pleasantly distracted by their presence and particularly fascinated by Manson's girls. They would do anything that Manson asked, anything, and their submissiveness was in sharp contrast to all the women that Spahn had ever known, beginning with his stern mother in Pennsylvania and extending through the carpenter's aggressive daughter, and the untimid housekeeper who became his wife, and the independent woman who was Ruby Pearl. Manson's girls, intellectually superior to all the women that George Spahn had known, were also more domestic: they liked to cook, to clean, to sew, to make love to Manson or to whomever he designated.

On occasions when Manson was in Spahn's shack, the old man tried to learn the secret of Manson's handling of women, but the latter would mostly laugh—"All you gotta do, George, is grab 'em by the hair, and kick 'em you know where"—and then Manson would be gone, his secret unexplained, and the girls would arrive, docile, delightful.

Abruptly, it ended.

Manson and his followers left the ranch in their bus one day, going as mysteriously as they had come, and for a while the old man's life reverted to what it had been. But then the police and detectives began to visit the ranch, inspecting the movie shacks where the hippies had lived, taking fingerprints and even digging large holes in the woodlands beyond the clearing in search of bodies. Then the reporters and television cameramen arrived, flashing light into Spahn's face that was so bright he could see it, and asking him questions about Charlie Manson and his "family" who were now charged with murdering Sharon Tate and several others. Spahn was stunned, disbelieving, but he told them what he knew. He sat in his shack for several hours with the press, slumped in a chair, holding a cane in one hand and a small dog in the other, wearing a soiled tan Stetson and dark sunglasses to protect his head and eyes from the flies and the light and the dirt and the flicking tails of his horses, and he answered the reporters' questions and posed for photographs. Hanging from the wall behind him, or resting on the mantel, were psychedelic portraits of him done by the girls, and on a nearby table was a guitar, and on another wall was the tapestry of a horse that Manson had given him.

For the next several days, with the television cameras on trucks focusing on the ranch, lighting up the rickety Hollywood sets, it was like old times for Spahn. Ruby Pearl was there to lead him around, although still holding him by the cloth of his sleeve, and his picture appeared on television and his words were quoted in the national press. He said that it was hard for him to believe that the girls had participated in the murders; if they had, he continued, they were undoubtedly under the influence of drugs.

As for Manson, Spahn said, there was no explanation—he had a hypnotic spell over the girls, they were his slaves. But Spahn was reluctant to say too much against Manson; and when the reporters asked why this was so, Spahn confessed that he was somewhat fearful of Manson, even though the latter was in jail. Manson might get out, Spahn suggested, or there might still be people on the ranch who were loyal to him.

The reporters did not press Spahn further. After they had finished with their questions, they wandered around the ranch taking photographs of the movie set and the soft-spoken wranglers and the girl who stood near the hitching post.

A Matter of Fantasy

She was completely nude, lying on her stomach in the desert sand, her legs spread wide, her long hair flowing in the wind, her head tilted back with her eyes closed. She seemed lost in private thoughts, remote from the world, reclining on this windswept dune in California near the Mexican border, adorned by nothing but her natural beauty. She wore no jewelry, no flowers in her hair; there were no footprints in the sand, nothing dated the day or spoiled the perfection of this photograph except the moist fingers of the seventeen-year-old schoolboy who held it and looked at it with adolescent longing and lust.

The photograph was in an art-camera magazine that he had just bought at a newsstand on the corner of Cermak Road in suburban Chicago. It was an early evening in 1957, cold and windy, but Harold Rubin could feel the warmth rising within him as he studied the photograph under the streetlamp near the curb behind the stand, oblivious to the sounds of traffic and the people passing on their way home.

He flipped through the pages to look at the other nude women, seeing to what degree he could respond to them. There had been times in the past when, after buying one of these magazines hastily, because they were sold under the counter and were therefore unavailable for adequate erotic preview, he had been greatly disappointed. Either the volleyball-playing nudists in *Sunshine & Health*, the only magazine showing pubic hair in the 1950s, were too hefty; or the semi-nude Bunnies in *Playboy* were too plastic; or the smiling show girls in *Modern Man* were trying too hard to entice; or the models in *Classic Photography* were merely objects of the camera, lost in artistic shadows.

While Harold Rubin usually could achieve some solitary fulfillment from these, they were soon relegated to the lower levels of the stacks of magazines that he kept at home in the closet of his bedroom. At the top of the pile were the more proven products, those women who projected a certain emotion or posed in a certain way that was immediately stimulating to him; and, more important, their effect was enduring. He could ignore them in the closet for weeks or months as he sought a new discovery elsewhere. But, failing to find it, he knew he could return home and revive a relationship with one of the favorites in his paper harem, achieving gratification that was certainly different from but not incompatible with the sex life he had with a girl he knew from Morton High School. One blended with the other somehow. When he was making love to her on the sofa when her parents were out, he was sometimes thinking of the more mature women in the magazines. At other times, when alone with his magazines, he might recall moments with his girlfriend, remembering what she looked like with her clothes off, what she felt like, what they did together.

Recently, however, perhaps because he was feeling restless and uncertain and was thinking of dropping out of school, leaving his girl and joining the Air Force, Harold Rubin was more deeply detached than usual from life in Chicago, was more into fantasy, particularly when in the presence of pictures of one special woman who, he had to admit, was becoming an obsession.

It was this woman whose picture he had just seen in the magazine he now held on the sidewalk, the nude on the sand dune. He had first noticed her months ago in a camera quarterly. She also had appeared in several men's publications, adventure magazines, and a nudist calendar. It was not only her beauty that had attracted him, the classic lines of her body or the wholesome features of her face, but the entire aura that accompanied each picture, a feeling of her being completely free with nature and herself as she walked along the seashore, or stood near a palm tree, or sat on a rocky cliff with waves splashing below. While in some pictures she seemed remote and ethereal, probably unobtainable, there was a pervasive reality about her, and he felt close to her. He also knew her name. It had appeared in a picture caption, and he was confident that it was her real name and not one of those pixie pseudonyms used by some playmates and pinups who concealed their true identity from the men they wished to titillate.

Her name was Diane Webber. Her home was along the beach at Malibu. It was said that she was a ballet dancer, which explained to Harold the disciplined body control she exhibited in several of her positions in front of the camera. In one picture in the magazine he now held, Diane Webber was almost acrobatic as she balanced herself gracefully above the sand on her outstretched arms with a leg extended high over her head, her toes pointed up into a cloudless sky. On the opposite page she was resting on her side, hips fully rounded, one thigh raised slightly and barely covering her pubis, her breasts revealed, the nipples erect.

Harold Rubin quickly closed the magazine. He slipped it between his school books and tucked them under his arm. It was getting late and he was soon due home for dinner. Turning, he noticed that the old cigar-smoking news vendor was looking at him, winking, but Harold ignored him. With his hands deep in the pockets of his black leather coat, Harold Rubin headed home, his long blond hair, worn in the duck's-ass style of Elvis Presley, brushing against his upraised collar. He decided to walk instead of taking the bus, because he wanted to avoid close contact with people, wanted no one to invade his privacy as he anxiously anticipated the hour at night when, after his parents had gone to sleep, he would be alone in his bedroom with Diane Webber.

He walked on Oak Park Avenue, then north to Twenty-first Street, passing bungalows and larger brick houses in this quiet residential community called Berwyn, a thirty-minute drive from downtown Chicago. The people here were conservative, hardworking and thrifty. A high percentage of them had parents or grandparents who had immigrated to this area from Central Europe earlier in the century, especially from the western region of Czechoslovakia called Bohemia. They still referred to themselves as Bohemians despite the fact that, much to their chagrin, the name was now more popularly associated in America with carefree, loose-living young people who wore sandals and read beatnik poetry.

Harold's paternal grandmother, whom he felt closer to than anyone in his family and visited regularly, had been born in Czechoslovakia, but not in the region of Bohemia. She had come from a small village in southern Czechoslovakia near the Danube and the old Hungarian capital of Bratislava. She had told Harold often of how she had arrived in

America at fourteen to work as a servant girl in a boardinghouse in one of those grim, teeming industrial towns along Lake Michigan that had attracted thousands of sturdy Slavic men to work in the steel mills, oil refineries, and other factories around East Chicago, Gary, and Hammond, Indiana. Living conditions were so overcrowded in those days, she said, that in the first boardinghouse where she worked there were four men from the day shift renting four beds at night and four other men from the night shift renting those same beds during the day.

These men were treated like animals and lived like animals, she said, and when they were not being exploited by their bosses in the factories they were trying to exploit the few working girls like herself who were unfortunate enough to be living in these towns at that time. The men in the boardinghouse were always grabbing at her, she said, banging on her locked door at night as she tried to sleep. When she related this to Harold during a recent visit, while he sat in the kitchen eating a sandwich she had made, he suddenly had a vision of what his grandmother must have looked like fifty years ago, a shy servant girl with fair complexion and blue eyes like his own, her long hair in a bun, her youthful body moving quickly around the house in a long drab dress, trying to elude the clutching fingers and strong arms of the burly men from the mill.

As Harold Rubin continued to walk home, his school books and the magazine held tightly under his arm, he remembered how sad yet fascinated he had been by his grandmother's reminiscing, and he understood why she spoke freely with him. He was the only person in the family who was genuinely interested in her, who took the time to be with her in the big brick house in which she was otherwise nearly always alone. Her husband, John Rubin, a former teamster who made a fortune in the trucking business, spent his days at the garage with his fleet of vehicles and his nights with a secretary who, if referred to at all by Harold's grandmother, was referred to as "the whore." The only child in this unhappy marriage, Harold's father, was completely dominated by *his* father, for whom he worked long hours in the garage; and Harold's grandmother did not feel sufficiently close to Harold's mother to share the frustration and bitterness she felt. So it was mainly Harold, sometimes accompanied by his younger brother, who interrupted the prevailing silence and boredom of the house. And as Harold became older and more curious, more remote from his parents and his own surroundings, he gradually became his grandmother's confidant, her ally in alienation.

From her he learned much about his father's boyhood, his grandfather's past, and why she had married such a tyrannical man. John Rubin had been born sixty-six years ago in Russia, the son of a Jewish peddler, and at the age of two he had immigrated with his parents to a city near Lake Michigan called Sobieski, named in honor of a seventeenth-century Polish king. After a minimum of schooling and unrelieved poverty, Rubin and other youths were arrested staging a holdup during which a policeman was shot. Released on probation, and after working at various jobs for a few years, Rubin one day visited his older married sister in Chicago and became attracted to the young Czechoslovakian girl then taking care of the baby.

On a subsequent visit he found her in the house alone, and after she had rejected his advances—as she had previously done with men when she had worked in the boardinghouse—he forced her into her bedroom and raped her. She was then sixteen. It had been her first sexual experience, and it would make her pregnant. Panicked, but having no close relatives or friends nearby to help, she was persuaded by her employers to marry John Rubin, or else he would go off to prison because of his prior criminal offense, and she would be no better off. They were married in October, 1912. Six months later they had a son, Harold's father.

The loveless marriage did not greatly improve with time, Harold's grandmother said, adding that her husband regularly beat his son, beat her when she interfered, and devoted himself mainly to the maintenance of his trucks. His lucrative career had begun when, after he had worked as a deliveryman on a horse and wagon for Spiegel Inc., a large mail-order house in Chicago, he convinced management to lend him enough money to invest in a truck and start his own motorized delivery service, thus eliminating Spiegel's need for several horses whose performance he said could not match his own. After buying one truck and fulfilling his promise, he bought a second truck, then a third. Within a decade John Rubin had a dozen trucks handling all of Spiegel's local cartage, as well as that of other companies.

Over the futile protests of his wife, his son was summoned as an adolescent into the garage to work as a driver's helper, and although John Rubin was amassing great personal wealth at this time and was generous with his bribes to local politicians and the police—"If you wanna slide, you gotta grease," he often said—he was a miser with the family budget, and he frequently accused his wife of stealing coins that he had left around the house. Later he began deliberately to leave money here and there in amounts that he precisely remembered, or he would arrange coins in a certain way on the bureau or elsewhere in the house in the hope that he could prove that his wife took some or at least touched them; but he never could.

These and other remembrances of Harold's grandmother, and similar observations that he made himself while in his grandfather's chilly presence, gave Harold considerable insight into his own father, a quiet and humorless man of forty-four resembling not in the slightest the photograph on the piano that was taken during World War II and showed him in a corporal's uniform looking relaxed and handsome, many miles from home. But the fact that Harold could understand his father did not make living with him any easier, and as Harold now approached East Avenue, the street on which he lived, he could feel the tension and apprehension, and he wondered what his father would choose to complain about today.

In the past, if there had not been complaints about Harold's school-work, then there had been about the length of Harold's hair, or Harold's late hours with his girl, or Harold's nudist magazines that his father had once seen spread out on the bed after Harold had carelessly left his door open.

"What's all this crap?" his father had asked, using a word far more delicate than his grandfather would have used. His grandfather's vocabulary was peppered with every imaginable profanity, delivered in tones of deep contempt, whereas his father's words were more restrained, lacking emotion.

"They're my magazines," Harold had answered.

"Well, get rid of them," his father had said.

"They're *mine!*" Harold suddenly shouted. His father had looked at him curiously, then began to shake his head slowly in disgust and left the room. They had not spoken for weeks after that incident, and tonight Harold did not want to repeat that confrontation. He hoped to get through dinner peacefully and quickly.

Before entering the house, he looked in the garage and saw that his father's car was there, a gleaming 1956 Lincoln that his father had bought new a year ago, trading in his pampered 1953 Cadillac. Harold climbed the steps to the back door, quietly entered the house. His mother, a matronly woman with a kindly face, was in the kitchen preparing dinner; he could hear the television on in the living room and saw his father sitting there reading the *Chicago American*. Smiling at his mother, Harold said hello in a voice loud enough that it would carry into the living room and perhaps count as a double greeting. There was no response from his father.

Harold's mother informed him that his brother was in bed with a cold and fever and would not be joining them for dinner. Harold, saying nothing, walked into his bedroom and closed the door softly. It was a nicely furnished room with a comfortable chair, a polished dark wood desk, and a large Viking oak bed. Books were neatly arranged on shelves, and hanging from the wall were replicas of Civil War swords and rifles that had been his father's and also a framed glass case in which were mounted several steel tools that Harold had made last year in a manual-arts class and which had won him a citation in a national contest sponsored by the Ford Motor Company. He had also won an art award from Wieboldt's department store for his oil painting of a clown, and his skill as a wood craftsman was most recently demonstrated in his construction of a wooden stand designed to hold a magazine in an open position and thus permit him to look at it with both of his hands free.

Taking off his coat and placing his school books on the desk, Harold opened the magazine to the photographs of the nude Diane Webber. He stood near the bed holding the magazine in his right hand and, with his eyes half closed, he gently brushed his left hand across the front of his trousers, softly touching his genitals. The response was immediate. He wished that he now had the time before dinner to undress and be fulfilled, or at least to go down the hall to the bathroom for quick relief over the sink, holding her photograph up to the medicine-cabinet mirror to see a reflection of himself exposed to her nude body, pretending a presence with her in the sun and sand, directing her dark lovely lowered eyes toward his tumescent organ and imagining that his soapy hand was part of her.

He had done this many times before, usually during the afternoons when it might have seemed surreptitious for him to close his bedroom door. But, despite the guaranteed privacy behind the locked door of the bathroom, Harold had to admit that he was never completely comfortable there, partly because he really preferred reclining on his bed to standing, and because there was insufficient room around the sink on which to lay down the magazine if he wished to use both hands. Also, and perhaps more important, if he was not careful the magazine might be stained by drops of water bouncing up from the sink, since he kept the faucet running to alert the family to his presence in the bathroom, and also because he occasionally needed additional water for lathering when the soap went dry on his fingers. While the water-stained photographs of nude women might not offend the aesthetics of most young men, this was not the case with Harold Rubin.

And finally there was a practical consideration involved in his desire to protect his magazines from damage: having read in newspapers this year about the more zealous anti-pornography drives around the nation, he could not be sure that he would always be able to buy new magazines featuring nudes, not even under the counter. Even *Sunshine & Health*, which had been in circulation for two decades and populated its pages with family pictures including grandparents and children, had been described as obscene this year at a California judiciary hearing. Art-camera magazines had also been cited as "smut" by some politicians and church groups, even though these publications had attempted to disassociate themselves from girly magazines by including under each nude picture such instructive captions as, *Taken with 2 1/4 x 3 1/4 Crown Graphic fitted with 101 mm Ektar, f/11, at 1/100 sec.* Harold had read that President Eisenhower's Postmaster General, Arthur Summerfield, was intent on keeping sexual literature and magazines out of the mails, and a New York publisher, Samuel Roth, had just been sentenced to five years in prison and a fine of $5,000 for violating the federal mail statute. Roth had previously been convicted for disseminating copies of *Lady Chatterley's Lover*, and his first arrest, in 1928, came after the police had raided his publishing company and seized the printing plate of *Ulysses*, which Roth had smuggled in from Paris.

Harold had read that a Brigitte Bardot film had been interfered with in Los Angeles, and he could only assume that in a city like Chicago, a workingman's town with a tough police force and considerable moral influence from the Catholic Church, sexual expression would be repressed even more, particularly during the administration of the new mayor, Richard J. Daley. Already Harold had noticed that the burlesque house on Wabash Avenue had been closed down, as had the one on State Street. If the trend continued, it might mean that his favorite newsstand on Cermak Road would be reduced to selling such magazines as *Good Housekeeping* and the *Saturday Evening Post*, a happenstance that he knew would provoke no protest from his parents.

In all the years that he had lived at home he had never heard his parents express a sexual thought, had never seen either of them in the nude, had never heard their bed creaking at night with love sounds. He assumed that they still did make love, but he could not be certain. While he did not know how active his grandfather was in his sixties with his mistress, his grandmother had recently confided in a typically bitter moment that they had not made love since 1936. He had been an unskilled lover anyway, his grandmother had quickly added, and as Harold had pondered that statement he wondered for the first time if his grandmother had secret lovers. He seriously doubted it, never having observed men visiting her home, or her often leaving it; but he did recall discovering to his surprise a year ago in her library a romantic sex novel. It had been covered in brown paper, and on the copyright page was the name of a French publishing house, and under it the date, 1909. While his grandmother had been taking a nap, Harold sat on the floor reading once then twice the one-hundred-three-page novel, enthralled by the tale and amazed by the explicit language. The story described the unhappy sex lives of several young women in Europe and the East who, after leaving their small towns and villages in despair, wandered into Morocco and became captives of a pasha who secluded them in a seraglio. One day, when the pasha was away, one of the women noticed through the window a handsome sea captain below and, luring him upstairs, made passionate love to him, as did the others in turn, pausing between acts to reveal to the captain the sordid details of their past that had eventually led them to this place. Harold had read the book during subsequent visits so often that he could practically recite certain passages . . . "Her soft arms were wound around me in response, and our lips met in a delicious and prolonged kiss, during which my shaft was imprisoned against her warm smooth belly. Then she raised herself on tiptoes, which brought its crest among the short thick hair where the belly terminated. With one hand I guided my shaft to the entrance, which welcomed it; with my other I held her plump buttocks toward me . . ."

Harold heard his mother calling him from the kitchen. It was time for dinner. He put the magazine with its photographs of Diane Webber under his pillow. He replied to his mother, waiting momentarily as his erection subsided. Then he opened his door and walked casually toward the kitchen.

His father was already seated at the table with a bowl of soup in front of him, reading the paper, while his mother stood at the stove talking airily, unaware of the minimal attention she was receiving. She was saying that while shopping in town today she had met one of her old friends from the Cook County tax assessor's office, which is where she had once worked, operating a Comptometer. Harold, who knew that she had left that job shortly before his birth seventeen years ago, never to work again outside the house, commented to his mother on the fine aroma of the cooking, and his father looked up from his paper and nodded without a smile.

As Harold sat down and began sipping the soup, his mother continued to talk, while slicing beef on a sideboard before bringing it to the table. She wore a housedress, little makeup, and smoked a filter-tipped cigarette. Both of Harold's parents were heavy smokers, smoking being their only pleasure insofar as he knew. Neither of them was fond of drinking whiskey, beer, or wine, and dinner was served with cream soda or root beer, purchased weekly by the case.

After his mother had seated herself, the telephone rang. His father, who always kept the phone within reach at the dinner table, frowned as he grabbed it. Someone was calling from the garage. It happened almost every night during dinner, and from his father's expression it might be assumed that he was receiving unwelcome news—perhaps a truck had broken down before making its delivery, or the Teamsters union was going out on strike; but Harold knew from living in the house that the grim, tight-lipped look of his father did not necessarily reflect what was being said on the telephone. It was an inextricable part of his father's nature to look sullenly upon the world, and Harold knew that even if this phone call had come from a television game show announcing that his father had just won a prize, his father would react with a frown.

Still, despite whatever genuine aggravation was inherent in managing the Rubin trucking business, his father got up diligently at five-thirty each morning to be the first on the job, and he spent his days dealing with problems ranging from the maintenance of one hundred forty-two trucks to the occasional pilferage of cargo, and he had to deal as well with the irascible old man, John Rubin, who personally wanted to control everything, even though the operation was now too big for him to do so.

Harold had recently heard that several of Rubin's drivers had been stopped by the police for driving without license plates, which had infuriated the old man, who ignored the fact that his stinginess had caused this: trying to save money, he had purchased only thirty-two sets of license plates for his hundred forty-two trucks, requiring that the men in the garage keep switching the plates from vehicle to vehicle or risk making deliveries without plates. Harold knew that sooner or later this scheme would result in a court case, and then his grandfather would try to bribe his way out of it and, even if he was lucky enough to do so, it would probably cost him more than if he had paid for the proper number of plates in the beginning.

Harold vowed that he would never work full time in the garage. He had tried working there during the summer but had soon quit because he could not tolerate the verbal abuse from his grandfather, who had often called him a "little bum," and also that of his father, who had remarked sourly one day, "You'll never amount to anything." This prediction had not bothered Harold because he knew that the price of appeasing these men was total subjugation, and he was determined that he would not repeat the mistake of his father in becoming subservient to an old man who had sired a son he had not wanted with a woman he had not loved.

After his father had hung up the telephone, he resumed eating, revealing nothing of what had been said. A cup of coffee was placed in front of him, heavy with cream as he liked it, and he lit up an Old Gold. Harold's mother mentioned not having seen their neighbors from across the street in several days, and Harold suggested that they might be away or vacation. She stood to clear the table, then went to check the fever of her younger son, who was still sleeping. Harold's father went into the living room, turned on the television set. Harold later joined him, sitting on the other side of the room. Harold could hear his mother doing the dishes in the kitchen and his father yawning as he listlessly watched television and completed the crossword puzzle in the newspaper. He then stood, yawned again, and said he was going to bed. It was shortly after nine o'clock. Within a half hour, Harold's mother had come into the living room to say good night, and soon Harold turned off the television and the house was soundless and still. He walked to his bedroom and closed the door, feeling a quiet exuberance and relief. He was finally alone.

He removed his clothes, hung them in the closet. He reached for the small bottle of hand lotion, Italian Balm, that he kept on the upper shelf of his closet and he placed it on the bedside table next to a box of Kleenex. He turned on the bedside lamp of low wattage, turned off the overhead light, and the room was bathed in a soft glow.

He could hear the wind whipping against the storm windows on this freezing Chicago night, and he shivered as he slipped between the cool sheets and pulled the blankets over him. He lay back for a few moments, getting warm, and then he reached for the magazine under his pillow and began to flip through it in a cursory way—he did not want to focus yet on the object of his obsession, Diane Webber, who awaited him on the sand dune on page nineteen, but preferred instead to make an initial pass through the entire fifty-two-page issue, which contained thirty-nine nude pictures of eleven different women, a visual aphrodisiac of blondes and brunettes, preliminary stimulants before the main event.

A lean, dark-eyed woman on page four attracted Harold, but the photographer had posed her awkwardly on the gnarled branch of a tree, and he felt her discomfort. The nude on page 6, sitting cross-legged on a studio floor next to an easel, had fine breasts but a bland expression on her face. Harold, still on his back with his knees slightly raised under the blankets, continued to turn the pages past various legs and breasts, hips and buttocks and hair, female fingers and arms reaching out, eyes looking away from him, eyes looking *at* him as he occasionally paused to lightly stroke his genitals with his left hand, tilting the magazine in his right hand to eliminate the slight glare on the glossy pages.

Proceeding through the magazine page after page, he came to the exquisite pictures of Diane Webber, but he quickly skipped over them, not wanting to tempt himself now. He moved on to the Mexican girl on page twenty-seven who sat demurely with a fisherman's net spread across her thighs; and then to the heavy-breasted blonde reclining on the floor next to a small marble statue of *Venus di Milo*, and on to a lithe, lovely blonde standing in the shadows *1/25 sec. at f:22* of what appeared to be an empty stage of a theater, her arms crossed under her chin and above her upturned breasts, which were gracefully revealed, and, in the very subtle stage lighting, Harold was quite certain that he could see her pubic hair, and he felt himself for the first time becoming aroused.

If he were not so enamored of Diane Webber, he knew he could be satisfied by this willowy young blonde, satisfied perhaps more than once, which to him was the true test of an erotic picture. In the stacks of magazines in his closet were dozens of nudes who had aroused him in the past to solitary peaks, some having done so three or four times; and some were capable of doing it again in the future as long as they remained unseen for a while, thereby regaining their sense of mystery.

And then there were those extremely rare pictures, those of Diane Webber, that could fulfill him constantly. He estimated that his collection contained fifty photographs of her, and within a moment he could locate every one of them in the two hundred magazines that he kept. He would merely have to glance at the cover and would know exactly where she was within, how she was standing, what was in the background, what her attitude seemed to be during that special split second when the camera had clicked. He could remember, too, first seeing these pictures, could reconstruct where and when he had bought them; he could practically mark a moment in his life from each of her poses, each being so real that he believed he knew her personally, she was part of him, and through her he had become more in touch with himself in several ways, not merely through acts which Victorian moralists had defined as self-abuse, but rather through self-acceptance, his understanding the naturalness of his desires, and of asserting his right to an idealized woman.

Not able to resist any longer, Harold turned the page to Diane Webber on the dune. He looked at her, lying on her stomach, her head held up into the wind, her eyes closed, the nipple of her left breast erect, her legs spread wide, the late-afternoon sun casting an exaggerated shadow of her curvaceous body along the smooth, white sand. Beyond her body was nothing but a sprawling empty desert—she seemed so alone, so approachable and available; Harold had merely to desire her, and she was his.

He pushed the blankets off his body, warm with excitement and anticipation. He reached under his bed for the wooden stand he had made in school, knowing that his manual-arts teacher would be astonished to learn what use would be made of it tonight. He placed the magazine on the stand in front of him, between his knees and widely spread legs. Raising his head, supporting it on two pillows, he reached for the bottle of Italian Balm, poured lotion into his palms and rubbed it between his hands momentarily to warm it. Then, softly, he began to touch his penis and testicles, feeling the quick growth to full erection. With his eyes half closed, he lay back and gazed at his glistening organ towering in front of the picture, casting a shadow across the desert.

Continuing to massage himself up and down, up and down, back and forth across his testicles, he focused sharply on Diane Webber's arched back, her rising buttocks, her full hips, the warm place between her legs; and he now imagined himself approaching her, bending down to her, and determinedly penetrating her from behind without a word of protest from her as he thrust upward, faster, faster, and upward, faster, and suddenly he could feel her pounding back against his thighs, her hips moving from side to side, he could hear her sighs of pleasure as he tightened his grip around her hips, faster, and then her loud cries as she came in a series of quick convulsions that he could feel as fully as he now felt her hand reaching back to hold his tight testicles exactly as he liked to have them held, softly, then more firmly as she sensed the throbbing, shuttering start of sperm flowing upward and gushing out in great spurts that he grabbed in both hands as he closed his eyes. He lay very quietly in bed for a few moments, letting his muscles relax and his legs go limp. Then he opened his eyes and saw her there, as lovely and desirable as ever.

Finally he sat up, wiped himself with two pieces of Kleenex, then two more because his hands still were sticky with sperm and lotion. He rolled the tissue into a ball and tossed it into the wastebasket, not concerned that his mother might recognize it in the morning when she emptied the baskets. His days at home were numbered. In a matter of a few weeks, he would be in the Air Force, and beyond that he had no plans.

He closed the magazine and placed it on the top of the pile in his closet. He put the wooden stand back under the bed. Then he climbed under the covers, feeling tired but calm, and turned out the light. If he was lucky, he thought, the Air Force might send him to a base in Southern California. And then, somehow, he would find her.

• • •

In 1928, the mother of Diane Webber won a beauty contest in Southern California, sponsored by the manufacturers of the Graham-Paige automobile, and one of the prizes was a small part in a silent film directed by Cecil B. De Mille in which she portrayed the coy and pretty teenage girl that in real life she was.

She had come to California from Montana to live with her father who, after the bitter breakup of his marriage, had quit the Billings Electric Company and found work as an electrician in Los Angeles with

Warner Bros. studios. She was much closer to her father than her mother, and she also wanted to escape the harshness of the rural Northwest where her parents had so often quarreled, where her grandmother had been married five times, and where her great-grandmother, while swimming in a river one day, was killed by an arrow shot into her back by an Indian. She had arrived in Southern California convinced that it would offer more fulfillment than the limited horizons of the great-sky country.

And it did, in most ways, even though she would never achieve stardom in the several films in which she appeared in the late 1920s and early 1930s. Her satisfaction came rather from a sense of serenity she felt in Los Angeles, a sunny detachment from the grim girlhood she had known in Montana. In Los Angeles she felt free to pursue her whims, to revive her early interest in religion, to walk in the streets without wearing a bra, eventually to marry a man who was almost thirty years older and then, seven years later, to take a second husband who was five years younger. Southern California's characteristic disregard of traditional values, its relatively rootless society, its mobility and lack of continuity—the very qualities that had been a painful burden in her family's past in Montana—were accepted easily by her in Los Angeles, partly because she was now sharing these newly accepted values with thousands of her own generation, pretty young women like herself who had left their unglamorous hometowns elsewhere in America and had migrated to California in search of some vaguely defined goal. And while very few of these women would succeed as actresses, or models, or dancers—more likely they would spend their best years working as cocktail waitresses, or receptionists, or salesclerks, or as unhappily married women in San Fernando Valley—nearly all of them remained in California, and they had children, children who were reared in the sun during the Depression, who played outdoor sports the year round during the 1940s, who matured in the period of great California prosperity that began with World War II (when American defense investments poured millions into West Coast aircraft plants and technological industries); and by the 1950s there had emerged in California a new generation that was distinguished for its good looks, its casual style in dress, its relaxed view of life with an emphasis on health, a special look that on Madison Avenue, throughout the nation and overseas was regarded as peculiarly American—the California Look. And among those who possessed this look in the 1950s, though her mother was among the last to recognize it, was Diane Webber.

Diane's problems with her mother began after her parents were divorced. Diane's father, twenty-seven years older than her mother, was a writer from Ogden, Utah, named Guy Empey. He was a short, stocky, imperious, adventurous man who had joined the United States Cavalry in 1911, and, because his country was late in becoming involved in World War I, he joined the British Army. He saw frontline action in Europe, earning battle scars that he would proudly wear on his face the rest of his life, and in 1917 he wrote a bestselling book about his experiences called *Over the Top*, which sold more than a million copies. It also became a film, which he directed and in which he played the lead.

Guy Empey wrote other books during the next decade, though none nearly as popular as the first, and by 1930 he was reduced to writing pulp fiction for magazines, often under pseudonyms. It was around this time, at a social gathering in Hollywood, that he met the small, spry, twenty-year-old actress from Montana whose short dark hair, large brown eyes, and infectious smile reminded him of the silent-screen star, Clara Bow. He quickly courted her with bouquets of flowers, took her for rides in his Cadillac touring car, and soon he had proposed marriage—and she accepted, although at forty-six he was as old as her father.

Unwisely, he moved his bride into the home he shared with his beloved mother and sister, to whom he had dedicated *Over the Top*. Both were cultured, sophisticated women from New York—his mother's uncle, Richard Henry Dana, had written *Two Years Before the Mast*; and his widowed sister, who had been married to a top executive with W. & J. Sloane, read the *New Yorker* each week and had filled the Los Angeles house with fine furnishings and a wonderful library that she had brought with her from across the country. These two women, and particularly Guy Empey's strong-willed mother, were not overly impressed with the little actress from Montana, and he was unable or unwilling to resolve a growing marital conflict that was only briefly interrupted in the summer of 1932 by the birth of their only child, who was named, after a song then very popular, Diane.

When Diane was two, her mother separated from her father; when she was five, after a brief reconciliation, her parents were divorced, and Diane spent the ensuing years dividing her time between two households. During the week she lived with her mother, who in 1939 married a handsome man of twenty-four who had worked as a photographer for the International News Service and had modeled in a cowboy outfit on billboards advertising Chesterfield cigarettes. At the time of the marriage he owned a small restaurant on Sunset Boulevard, and Diane's twenty-nine-year-old mother repressed whatever lingering movie ambitions she still had, as she joined her new husband and worked as a waitress.

On weekends Diane would ride the trolley from the Hollywood Hills over to Echo Park, where her grandmother would meet her and escort her to her father's house; there, with the music of Handel softly playing on the phonograph, she would dwell in the intellectual presence of her aunt and grandmother, who encouraged her to read widely, who took her to proper films, and who were forever using words that sent her searching through the dictionary. As the women took their daily afternoon naps, and as her father worked at his typewriter—with a minimum of success—Diane would sit alone in her room quietly reading everything from *Anthony Adverse* to the plays of Shakespeare, from the *Arabian Nights* to *Gray's Anatomy*, acquiring gradually a strong if erratic classical background as well as an intense sense of fantasy.

Her fantasies were formed more clearly one afternoon after she had been taken to the ballet *The Nutcracker*. From then on, in her dreams, Diane saw herself as a glamorous girl in tights, twirling alone onstage in a graceful pirouette. She began taking ballet lessons once a week after school, but this was a privilege that her mother granted on the basis of Diane's personal behavior and how well she performed various chores around the house. Her stepfather, with whom she felt uncomfortable, would often watch her as she practiced at home, would sometimes gently tease her as she held onto the mantle in the living room and pointed a leg high into the air. This sight did not please her mother who, having already objected to her young husband's attempt to display Varga pinups in the hallway, certainly was no less amused by the attention he now was giving to her budding twelve-year-old daughter. Late one afternoon, in a moment of petulance that shattered Diane, her mother remarked that it was most unlikely that Diane's beauty would ever match her own.

The situation at home quickly worsened for Diane later that year when her mother gave birth to a son; and, two years later, to a baby daughter. Although Diane was approaching her teens, was becoming curious about boys and dating, she was expected to return home after school each day to help care for the children. This routine had continued more or less until she had graduated from high school, whereupon she left home to live temporarily in the apartment of her mother's sister, earning money for her keep and dancing lessons by working as a gift-wrapper in the Saks department store on Wilshire Boulevard. Months later, not wishing to further intrude upon the privacy of her maternal aunt, who was then dating a married man who worked in the office of the Beverly Hills Hotel, Diane moved into the Hollywood Studio Club, where her mother had once lived, a residence for women in the movie industry. It was there that Diane learned of an audition for chorus dancers willing to work in a nightclub in San Francisco, and while this was a dubious opportunity for an aspiring ballet dancer, she had concluded that she was probably already too old, at eighteen, and far too undertrained, ever to master the delicate physical art that she performed with such perfection in her fantasies. So she appeared at the audition and passed the test. When she approached her mother to ask if she could accept the position, her mother replied, "Don't ask me. Make your own decision." Diane left for San Francisco not knowing whether her mother had granted her independence or was expressing indifference.

Diane earned eighty dollars a week for doing three shows a night, six nights a week, dancing in the chorus behind such headline talents as Sophie Tucker. She wore a modest costume that revealed only her bare midriff, but while changing backstage she became exposed for the first time to group nudity, and she could see how her body compared to those of other women. It compared very well, and she was therefore not surprised when a friend in the chorus suggested that Diane might earn extra money as a figure model, and she gave her the name of an art professor at Berkeley who had paid other dancers twenty dollars for a brief photographic session in the nude.

Timidly, Diane appeared at the professor's residence, but his detached, formal manner soon put her at ease. She removed her clothes and stood nude before him, watched him back away and heard the camera click. She heard it click again and again, and without any instructions from him she began to move like a ballet dancer, her arms slowly reaching, her body turning, twirling on her toes as she heard interior music and the camera click, and she was no longer aware of the professor's presence. She was aware only of her body as an inspired instrument that she artfully controlled, and with which she could rise beyond her limitations. Though nude, she did not feel naked; she felt internalized as she danced, private, alone, deeply involved with emotions that might be projected externally in her movements or expressions, but she did not know, she did not contemplate what effect she was having on the professor behind the camera. She could barely perceive his fuzzy gray figure in the distance. Diane had her glasses off, and she was quite myopic.

Returning to Los Angeles after completing the nightclub engagement, Diane took the initiative and telephoned various fashion photographers who were listed in the classified directory, asking for an appointment. She called such men as David Balfour and Keith Bernard, Peter Gowland and David Mills, William Graham and Ed Lange, among others. Nearly all were attracted to her and were impressed by the fact that a young woman of such wholesome appeal would so willingly pose in the nude—she was at least ten years ahead of her time; by 1953, when she turned twenty-one, her photographs began to be seen in nudist and camera magazines all over the country, and around the world.

But since these publications paid very little, she was constantly in need of a job when there were no dancing assignments available. Briefly, she operated the elevator in the May Company store on Wilshire and Fairfax, managing to put aside some money for her mother toward the parochial-school expenses of her half-brother. Diane next worked as a receptionist at KHJ-TV, where one day she heard from a fellow employee that the president had seen her picture in a nudist magazine and was making inquiries concerning her moral habits, but she was never confronted personally. Finally, in what would prove to be a job of personal significance, she found nighttime work as an IBM operator in a check-clearing house of the Bank of America in downtown Los Angeles. There were several young women operating the machines, and a tall quiet man who served as the supervisor.

From the first time she saw him, she liked the way he moved. He had a soft, sensuous stride, like that of a big cat, and she noticed his calves, his narrow hips, and strong buttocks. As she watched him proceed down the aisle, between the rows of shiny gray machines, she was not so concerned that he might suddenly turn around and catch her as that he might turn around and disappoint her—she had yet to see his face. Diane continued to watch him, amazed that she could now be doing this, peering intently through her glasses at the posterior of a man, a perfect stranger, appraising him in a purely physical way.

He turned around. She was relieved. He was handsome, almost too handsome. He had deep-set hazel eyes, a strong chin and mouth, and a nose that she thought might be a bit too turned up. As he headed back in her direction, looking at a stack of cards he held in his hand, she guessed that he was at least six feet and not more than three or four years older than she. She stood facing him as he approached, but he walked right past her without even noticing.

It was not in the nature of Joseph Webber to look at women in a way that was obvious or revealing. He had done so once, as a young boy in Mitchell, South Dakota, and the consequences had been as dark and tumultuous as the midsummer dust storms that regularly attacked that farming region, creating mounds of dirt so high that the cattle were able to climb the fences.

The storm resulting from Joseph Webber's childhood indiscretion occurred because he and a little girl in his first-grade class, with whom he had been exchanging glances earlier in the day, decided after school to satisfy their curiosity about one another's bodies in a place where they thought they would not be noticed. But they were, by an enraged teacher, who quickly reported the act to Joseph Webber's mother, who in turn beat him with such vengeance and expressions of disgust that he will never forget it. He was relieved some months after the incident when his father decided to leave that land of poverty and bad memories and to pack the Model A Ford with what few valuables the family had and move on to Southern California.

The family rented a little house in a section of Los Angeles now called Watts, and Joseph's father found work as a combination superintendent and janitor in a music-and-arts building. His mother, always a woman of religious conviction, became deeply involved with faith healing in Southern California, and sometimes on weekends Joseph would accompany her to the Christian Science church to hear services that were also attended by the author Guy Empey and his daughter.

In grade school and high school, Joseph was bright and well liked but also very shy. Not having a car in this city meant that he was socially immobile. He thought of a career in forestry, having taken summer jobs in the woods and liking the close contact with nature. But after graduation in 1946 he decided to join the paratroopers, which he thought might enhance his image as a man of decision.

Riding the train across the country with other young recruits bound for military training in Aberdeen, Maryland, Joseph Webber suddenly heard someone yell out that they were now passing a nudist camp.

Everybody jumped up to look, including Joseph, but all he could see through the train window was a green blur of trees racing by. He had missed it. And as the recruit who had made the announcement proceeded to dramatically describe the details to the others in the aisle, Joseph went back to his seat and sat thinking quietly. He was strangely excited by the image of men and women, all gathered in the nude, basking openly in the sun, surrounded by nature and isolated from the confinements of city life. It seemed to him so healthy and honest, somehow so liberating.

On training missions with the 11th Airborne Division, Joseph Webber jumped out of airplanes eleven times, but on the ground he did nothing that could be described as daring. Sent to join the American occupational forces in Japan, where the triumphant spirit following the military victory still overshadowed moral doubts about the bomb, Joseph felt no pride in conquest and merely did his job. Once, with other paratroopers, he went to an Oriental bathhouse, but the American officers had made sure that no women were in sight; and the ghoulish films about gonorrhea that Joseph had been shown nullified whatever curiosity he might have had about Oriental females.

He returned home from the service older but not much wiser. During his absence, his parents had separated; his mother was still deeply into religion, and his father was working in the busy Lockheed plant in Burbank. Because of the GI Bill, Joseph was able to continue his education, going first to Mexico City College, where he had a pleasant first sexual experience with a young woman; and then the following year he transferred to Occidental College in the Los Angeles suburbs, where a member of the faculty approached Joseph during his final school year and asked if he was interested in joining the CIA. With the newspaper headlines now featuring stories about the Cold War, and with alleged Communist agents having infiltrated the American government, the universities, and the Hollywood entertainment industry, the CIA seemed to Joseph to be as respectable a place as any for a former paratrooper. He sent in his application. But for reasons never explained, he was turned down.

It was also at this time, early in 1953, that Joseph got a job after class working in the clearinghouse of the Bank of America. The building was convenient to where he lived, and he found the atmosphere congenial. On his first night, he noticed a stunning blonde operating one of the IBM machines. He was drawn to her, but did nothing. Weeks passed before he became aware of the young brunette wearing glasses who had been watching him; and he might never have paid much notice if he had not been visited one night at work by an old friend from the 11th Airborne, who, while they were chatting during a coffee break, asked, "Who's the good-looking chick with the dark hair and the great body?"

Joseph pondered, and, after his friend had gone on to describe the bespectacled young woman who could only be Diane, he confessed to having little knowledge of her except that she seemed pleasant and, he felt sure, quite modest—a conclusion that he had just made on the basis of her clothes, so unrevealing that he had never wondered about the female figure within.

The following night, Joseph asked Diane for a date that weekend. They went to an art film and got along well, though Diane found him guarded and reserved, qualities she normally preferred in a man, though not in a man she found so attractive. On subsequent dates they discovered things they had in common—their love of the outdoors, swimming, hiking, communicating with nature. Then Diane discussed her experience as a nude model and, while Joseph listened in his characteristically unrevealing way, he could feel his excitement and mounting curiosity, remembering his thoughts on the troop train years ago as it raced past the nudist camp somewhere in Maryland. And now this very demure and modestly attired operator of an IBM machine was telling him quite plainly that she had posed for dozens of photographers entirely in the nude.

The couple dated often after that, and soon Joseph had seen for himself the body she possessed and how glamorous she appeared outdoors on beaches with her glasses off and her long hair blowing freely in the wind. Although they engaged in heavy petting and gratified one another sexually in several ways, they did not have intercourse during the first six months of their courtship. She had not yet made love to a man, she confided one night, and Joseph was not yet sure he wished to become involved to a point that might risk marital expectations—an attitude very common in the fifties. He also was aware that Diane's condition was a valuable commodity, the last word being precisely the one he used in explaining to her why they should wait, get to know one another for a while longer before risking for her the loss of what another man, her husband, might cherish.

And so the nude photographs of Diane Webber that, to Harold Rubin in Chicago, had seemed so virginal were, in fact, the photographs of a virgin.

· · ·

Much to his disappointment, Harold Rubin had not been assigned by the Air Force to a base in California. After a brief assignment in Texas, he was sent to Belleville, Illinois, near St. Louis, and then on to Minneapolis, which had winters even more miserable than Harold had known in Chicago. Despite the military's attempt to channel his energies toward noble attainments as a file clerk, Harold Rubin found time to remain in close contact with Diane Webber throughout 1957, purchasing various magazines in the towns adjacent to the bases; he soon became aware that he was not the only man in the United States Air Force who coveted her.

He had, in fact, already met several airmen who, after he had displayed one of her pictures, obviously knew as much about her as he did. They not only knew her name and certain biographical facts, but Harold could also tell from the look in their eyes that they probably did what he did at night under the blankets, though he was sure that they would never admit it. It was also possible, Harold thought, that half his generation was privately hooked on her, and perhaps even old married men had images of her while making love to their wives. But none would admit it. Men do not revel in such admissions.

Harold also sensed from a few recent photographs that Diane Webber was somehow changing physically. Though as stunning as ever, her hips seemed a bit fuller, her breasts seemed larger in some photographs than in those that he remembered from Chicago. In one picture that he had seen since joining the Air Force, he could swear that she was in the early stages of pregnancy. But one could not be sure when looking at the pictures, because sometimes poor printing quality distorted a model's figure, and there also was no way of knowing how old some of the pictures were. Most—but not all—of the nudist and camera magazines displayed a date on the cover, but there was no indication as to when the photographer had taken the picture; so a picture that Harold Rubin was seeing of Diane Webber in 1957 might have actually been taken three or four years before, a likelihood that did not detract from her mysterious quality, nor did it lessen his confusion.

Returning to Chicago following his discharge, and finding his father as remote as ever, Harold moved out of the house and rented his own apartment. Though he had no specific career in mind, he had sometimes thought, while perusing camera magazines, that he might like to try photography. He did not believe that he yet possessed the capacity in self-denial to function as a photographer of nudes, but he had long recognized his interest in art and design, and, noticing an advertisement in the newspaper calling for a Photostat operator in a studio, he answered it and got the job.

Harold's social life in Chicago began auspiciously one Saturday afternoon when, while browsing through an antique bookshop, he noticed an attractive older woman working behind the counter. She appeared to be about thirty, ten years older than himself. Having never dated anyone older than eighteen, and feeling suddenly courageous, he approached the woman and asked if she would go to a movie with him that night. She accepted with a smile; and after seeing the film she invited him home, asking if he cared to spend the night. The fact that she lived in Berwyn close to the home of Harold's parents and announced that she was the divorced daughter of a local judge merely added to the ecstasy of the occasion.

Harold lived with her for a year and will remember her always as his most inspired sexual partner. She taught him things that he had never imagined despite his having read a large percentage of the hardcore sex novels that had been published in recent years, and he was pleased with her satisfaction in him. He was also fond of her young children, who lived in the house, and who, after hearing their mother exclaim in the kitchen one morning, "Harold, you're the best medicine I've had," proceeded to call him Mr. Medicine.

On Saturday afternoons, Harold would mow the lawn around the house, walking bare-chested with his broad back itching from the scratches she had placed there the night before and the night before that. Soon their relationship was the scandal of Berwyn, with neither Harold's mother nor the judge being able to put an end to it, though both tried. One afternoon when the judge's daughter was having coffee in a place patronized by local politicians and business leaders, a man sought to embarrass her by asking in a loud voice, "Tell me, just what do you see in that punk Harold Rubin?" Without hesitating, she replied in an equally loud voice: "Harold Rubin is the best lay in the western suburbs."

In addition to the sexual gratification and confidence that Harold gained as the complimented lover of a mature woman, the affair also signified a turning point in his life. For the first time, in this small conservative community in which he had been reared, he was revealing a rebellious attitude that he had long felt but only now was willing to acknowledge openly.

As he walked behind the noisy lawn mower, displaying a tattoo on his left arm from his Air Force days and the love scratches on his back, he was declaring himself not only sexually but politically. Sex *was* political, he thought. Sex was used by the government as a way of regulating people. In the name of public morality, the government invaded the private rights of people by legislating what they could read, what films they could see, what they could *think*. Since no government had ever been able to prove that people who saw sex films or read sex books were then inspired to commit sex crimes—a rapist like his grandfather had probably never read a book of any kind in his entire life, Harold felt sure—the government tried to justify its anti-pornography laws on the theory that the public's exposure to pornography might promote lustful thoughts. And it was on this basis that the police raided certain sex films, that the FBI confiscated truckloads of sex magazines, and postal inspectors classified as unmailable certain magazines that Harold liked to look at.

If he wished to masturbate to these magazines in his bedroom, he believed that it was his right to do so. It should be of no concern to the government, or to the Catholic Church which, along with certain fundamentalist and orthodox religions, still considered masturbation a sin, if no longer a medical link to impotence or insanity. Signs of human insanity, he believed, were not to be found in sexual acts but in military acts, such as when soldiers dropped bombs on people they did not know, killing people with whom they had no personal quarrel. That seemed insane to Harold Rubin. But such behavior did not seem to concern the government moralists and religious leaders as much as did a photograph of a copulating couple.

But Harold was also aware that many people in America were now beginning to challenge these "moralists," a fact that was being documented almost daily in the press, and he sensed that a sexual revolution was simmering with the arrival of the sixties and that he was part of it—he and the judge's daughter, Diane Webber and Hugh Hefner, the news vendor on Cermak Road, and many thousands of anonymous people who in various ways were reacting against attempts to control their sex lives and the inspirations of their fantasies. Harassment by the police of sex-magazine distributors was continuing, however, and Harold had read that the December, 1959, issue of *Playboy* had been ordered off the stands in several northern California cities because a police chief in San Mateo thought that the photograph of an embracing couple was not in "good taste."

In Chicago, Mayor Daley's vice squad had arrested fifty-five news vendors for selling sex magazines, among them *Sunshine & Health* and *Modern Man*, but the national distributor of these publications refused to pay the fine. The case went before a jury, with the national distributor hiring as its attorney a Los Angeles lawyer named Stanley Fleishman, who had argued against censorship in front of the United States Supreme Court. The trial in Chicago was widely reported in the press, and Harold had read every word.

On the first day of the trial, the lawyer had noticed that in the front rows of the courtroom several women were sitting with their eyes lowered; they appeared to be knitting or to be manipulating something in their hands that he did not immediately recognize. On closer inspection, Fleishman saw that these women were all holding rosary beads and, in full view of the jury, were praying. The lawyer concluded that these women had been brought there by an organized church group, and, after protesting loudly to the judge, the women were ordered to the back rows.

The trial went on for several weeks, with witnesses for both sides expressing varying views on the question of morality and freedom. Given the influence of church groups and the Daley regime in Chicago, Harold was not optimistic about the conclusion of the trial. But to his pleasure and surprise, the jury of seven men and five women, after deliberating for almost six hours, voted to acquit the distributor of sex magazines. After the verdict had been announced, the judge seemed stunned, then slumped forward from the bench. He was rushed to a hospital. He had had a heart attack.

If there were signs of improvement in the city of Chicago, none had yet reached Harold Rubin's family, particularly the home of his grandmother. Though she was now sixty-five and suffering from a variety of ailments, she nonetheless became alive with rage at the mere thought of her husband, about whom she spoke endlessly during each of Harold's visits. His grandfather was now living almost full time with his mistress, was lavishing gifts upon her, was handing out bribes to visitors he met in the kitchen on certain afternoons; and yet, she went on, he denied her a housekeeper and complained at the cost of an occasional cleaning lady. He was the world's most selfish man, she said; he ignored her small needs while he had amassed millions—some of which, she confided, was kept in cardboard boxes in the basement. She revealed this in a way that left little doubt in Harold's mind that, if he took some of it, he would be doing her a favor—it would be small retribution for all the misery that she had been subjected to by the old miser who had raped her fifty years ago.

If a grandmother seeking revenge had ever found a willing accomplice, she had found one now in Harold Rubin. Going to the basement and helping himself to the first box he could find, he walked off with close to $60,000. Saying good-bye to his grandmother, Harold went directly to a Cadillac dealer and purchased a new black convertible. Without pausing at his apartment, he drove south through Indiana and Kentucky, deciding to take a quick vacation in Florida. Along the way be bought clothes and shaving equipment, registered in the best hotels he could find, and was a generous host to several women he met in bars and restaurants.

In Fort Lauderdale, he rented an expensive apartment, purchased a stereo, leased a red Cadillac convertible for the lady who shared his bed. He proceeded to give nightly parties for the new friends who surrounded him and indulged in every hedonistic adventure that money could buy— until early one morning, with hard raps on the door, the police arrived. After arresting him on charges of grand larceny, the police searched the apartment for what remained of the money. They found none of it, having failed to disassemble the air-conditioner and search the filter.

Back in Chicago, in the presence of his lawyer, the police, and his smoldering grandfather, Harold denied any involvement in the theft, as had his grandmother. The following day, after reading about the incident in the newspapers, the district director of Internal Revenue sought to learn whether Harold's grandfather had paid taxes on the money. This question petrified the old man, who now feared that Harold might be aware of the larger cache, which in turn could lead to an extensive IRS investigation of the whole trucking operation. John Rubin suddenly lost his enthusiasm for a conviction, and, lacking evidence, the case was dropped. Harold Rubin was free. Disowned, but free.

Regular employment, which had never been one of his consuming ambitions, eluded Harold Rubin during much of the 1960s. Not knowing exactly what to do in life, he contented himself by doing nothing much of the time. The job he held longest—two years, eight months—was the one for which he was the least qualified emotionally. It was that of a private investigator, a quasi cop, a watchdog on wrongdoers like himself; it was a perfect job for a hypocrite, he thought bitterly, as he took it, justifying his decision because he needed the money and had been told by the employment agency that nothing else was available. He thought that he would quit it in a matter of days or weeks, but he did not. He had lost much of his confidence and spirit since the judge's daughter had left him for an older man.

After that relationship Harold had become involved with a young, impressionable blonde who worked as a clerical assistant in a doctor's office, and he quickly asked her to marry him. She did, but soon her mother convinced her that it had been a mistake, and the marriage ended in less than a year. It was also during this period that Harold learned for the first time of Diane Webber's marriage and the fact that she had a son. This uninspiring news had appeared in a magazine he had seen in a cigar store in downtown Chicago, a special eighty-page issue that was devoted entirely to her; it contained more than one hundred photographs—including several with her husband and son—and extensive biographical material that listed facts and dates about her modeling career and her private life.

Harold bought the magazine and took it to his apartment. Flipping through it, he recognized many of her nude photographs from the past, except now he was feeling differently about them. She was still beautiful, and she could easily arouse him, if he would let her; but he did not want that now. He concentrated instead on reading the biographical text, the many pages of type from which he learned her date of birth—July 27, 1932—the names of her parents, the schools she had attended; and also included on these pages were several snapshots from the family album, one showing her as a round-faced baby wearing a white cotton dress and a fragile batiste bonnet, being held in the arms of her stylish 1930s mother, smiling with dark eyes shaded by a wide-brimmed felt hat, wearing a white linen dress with a V neck and a strand of graduated pearls. There were photographs of Diane as a teenager at Hollywood High, where she had appeared in operettas and had served as the school choreographer; and in the middle of the magazine were the nude photographs that Harold had first seen in 1956 and 1957, but now he realized that these had been taken years before that, when her surname had been Empey. After her marriage to Joseph Webber in 1955, the editors of the camera and nudist magazines that Harold used to buy on Cermak Road had begun using her married name with many nude photographs that had been taken years before her marriage, so that Harold had really been obsessed all those years by another man's wife.

Harold looked at the pictures of Joseph Webber in this special issue, reluctantly conceding his good looks. There were photographs of Diane and Joseph Webber swimming together, sailing together, walking together in nudist camps in Southern California. In some pictures the couple had posed with their son, John, who had been born in February of 1956; and as Harold read this magazine now, in the winter of 1965, he realized that the boy was already nine years old.

Harold put the magazine aside. It was depressing. He was sorry that he had bought this issue devoted to Diane Webber because the editors had made her mundane. In showing her wearing clothes or a bathing suit in several pictures, they had dated her with the fashion of the period, whereas Harold had always seen her as a timeless beauty. All the facts about her family background, her husband and son, all the statistics and the proof of her existence in everyday reality had, for Harold Rubin, made her less real. The magazine had spoiled a perfect relationship. It had domesticated a dream.

It was while in this state of mind, filled with self-doubt and loneliness, that Harold Rubin, twenty-five years old, became a private investigator. And during the next three years, while the national headlines were describing the exploits of a new generation that was challenging the established order, was protesting racial inequality and inspiring a social and sexual revolution that he had once briefly identified with, Harold spent his days wandering through department stores trying to spot shoplifters, working in factories observing workers that management thought were stealing equipment, tailing married people who were suspected by their mates of infidelity. It was suitable employment for a disillusioned man, a job whose purpose was to obtain evidence to confirm other people's deceptions, to destroy the illusions they were seeking to preserve. While the job catered to his curiosity about people, it also filled him at times with feelings of paranoia, an abhorrence of the petty management policies of many large companies, and doubts about the wisdom of marriage.

He rented a new apartment farther from the city, away from the political counterculture and the police who were now busily preparing to protect the site of the Democratic National Convention. He moved into a modern complex near O'Hare Airport, a tenant encircled by transience, and he sought ephemeral pleasure from the most ephemeral of females, the airline stewardesses. He dated one of them several times, and one night in the apartment after making love she agreed to let him photograph her in the nude. He used the camera that he carried with him in the street occasionally when following a married person who was presumed to be en route to a romantic rendezvous.

One afternoon while Harold was walking on the North Side of Chicago, he noticed a building on Belmont Avenue with a sign outside that read "The Studio." Entering it, he saw two young women sitting in a reception room and near them sat a middle-aged man behind a desk on which were displayed several Polaroid cameras. This was a nude-model studio, the man explained after Harold had asked; for twenty dollars, a model would pose in the nude for fifteen minutes in one of the back rooms, with the customer borrowing one of the Polaroids. Harold, who had never known of such a business before, was told that this was the only place of its kind in Chicago, although there were several like it in California and New York, some of which also offered body-painting and massage privileges.

Harold paid the money and selected a camera. He followed the model through a long dark corridor to a room in the rear. She was a tall redhead, not very pretty. She was chewing gum. She wore a mini-skirt, a flowered T-shirt, and no bra. In the corridor Harold could hear voices coming from behind the closed doors of several rooms. Business was thriving, he thought, and he was fascinated.

After she had closed the door behind him, and they had exchanged comments, she removed her clothes and stood casually against a white wall. When Harold's camera was ready, she proceeded to strike various poses: hands on hips, arms held behind her head, a view from the side, a view from the rear—it was a very perfunctory performance, and the sign on the wall warning customers against physical contact with the models was, in Harold's case, wholly unnecessary. It was not the model's looks that he objected to as much as her indifferent manner and her rasping voice. Nude women in magazines are better, he thought. They do not have rasping voices, and they do not chew gum.

Still, the existence of this business in Chicago intrigued him. He left knowing that he would probably return. But as he approached the building on his next visit, he saw a police car pulling away from the curb. When he entered the studio he heard the disgruntled owner telling the models that he was quitting—he had just received a second summons and the next might mean jail. Without hesitation, Harold stepped forward and introduced himself. Then, speaking privately to the man in the corner, Harold volunteered to manage the studio for a small salary and relieve the owner of legal concerns. Harold was enthusiastic and convincing. He suddenly knew that he belonged in this garish place that flaunted nudity and attracted opposition from the police.

He had finally found a controversial political issue that he could identify with personally, one that might release his repressed rebelliousness. Bored with his life as an investigator, he now wanted action in this age of activism that exploited in the media the brutal style of Mayor Daley's police at the recent Democratic convention, during which numerous demonstrators had been beaten with clubs and dozens had been arrested.

To be arrested now was a mark of distinction, he thought, and he had read that even Diane Webber had spent weeks in a federal courtroom in Iowa; a postal obscenity case had been brought against a California distributor of sex magazines, including one that showed Diane walking nude out of the surf with one leg raised just high enough to be revealing. The distributor's lawyer, Stanley Fleishman, who had once successfully defended sex magazines in Chicago, had lost this case in Sioux City to a jury composed of farmers' wives—the men selected for jury duty had all avoided it, saying that they had to harvest the crops—but Fleishman later won the case on an appeal.

Harold Rubin's appeal to the owner of the studio was equally successful, and, after resigning from his job as an investigator, he began a controversial career in the service and sale of sexual fantasy. Using his talents in carpentry and design, he redecorated the studio in a Gay Nineties motif, using Victorian posters, brass spittoons, old-style drugstore medicine bottles, and several other items that he had purchased cheaply in various local junk shops. He hired new models who were more attractive and attentive, one being a friend of the airline stewardess he had dated, others being college students or dropouts who were into the counterculture and were sexually liberated in ways that few young people had dared to be in the relatively prim 1950s, before the popularity of protest and birth-control pills.

As business increased, the police returned to threaten Harold Rubin. But he offered no bribes, saying only that he would take the case to court if arrested. Health and fire inspectors also visited the studio regularly and issued summonses for alleged violations, which Harold corrected if possible or otherwise ignored. When some models quit because they were unnerved by the harassment, he hired others through advertisements in newspapers or by approaching young women he saw in the streets. One day he misdialed a phone number and found himself conversing with a perky young woman who lived nearby on the North Side and who, after agreeing to meet him, accepted a job at the studio and quickly became the customers' most popular model.

She was a slender, blue-eyed brunette named Millie, and she was as adventurous as she was lovely. Soon she and Harold were living together.

On weekends during the summer of 1969, they would drive out to one of the forest preserves in Cook County where, in secluded places in the woods, Harold would take nude pictures of Millie, posing her in the exact way that he had seen Diane Webber in magazines years ago. Harold once made a sexual home movie with Millie and another studio model— both women were bisexual—and he answered ads in swingers' publications with Millie; they experienced group sex and acted out every fantasy either of them had ever had. Not since the judge's daughter had Harold found such an exciting partner, and in 1970 he and Millie decided to open up their own studio, using money that Harold had saved in addition to a substantial loan from a wealthy Chicago businessman who had been one of the studio's regular customers.

Harold did not merely want a model studio, he wanted a sexual supermarket that would offer a wide assortment of commodities and services for sale: erotic books and magazines, vibrators, dildos, and other sexual gadgets; and in the rear of the building, private massage rooms equipped to show X-rated video films. He intended to decorate the place like a church, in dark wood of Gothic design and with several ecclesiastical objects that he knew would not endear him to Mayor Daley or the police. But he did not care. Harold Rubin was now possessed by a feverish spirit of rebellion against all authority in Chicago. And, after renting an empty store on South Wabash Avenue, he proceeded to build his blasphemous emporium.

From a wrecking company that had demolished a Catholic church on the South Side, he obtained a delicately carved section of ornate window tracery, a few prayer benches and other ornamental objects including a six-hundred-pound dark Gothic confessional in which he planned to have Millie sit while greeting the arriving customers. He arranged to buy erotic books and magazines, sexual equipment and films from a Chicago distributor who would obtain most of the merchandise from California. In order to protect his stock from shoplifters, who, he assumed, would be as prevalent in his place as they had been in the stores he had patrolled as an investigator, Harold bought several small television monitors that he hid high along the walls behind the wooden Gothic fixtures.

As a safeguard against the police, Harold established his business as a private club that customers could join only after they had produced verifiable identification papers and had signed a document stating that they were not affiliated with any law enforcement agency intending to entrap him or deprive him of his constitutional rights to freedom of expression—a statement that customers were not only required to sign but also to read aloud in front of the confessional, unaware that their voices were being recorded by a hidden microphone, and their faces were being filmed by a camera peering through the folds of the purple velvet draperies that hung within the confessional.

Reasoning that his uncommon business required an uncommon name, one that would both attract attention and be easily remembered, Harold considered a name given him by an airline stewardess who lived in his building. One night he had appeared outside her apartment, drunk and noisy, wearing only a nineteenth-century Prussian spiked helmet, and carrying a medieval shield and a mace; the stewardess opened the door, and, after looking at him momentarily in astonishment, she said, "You know something, Harold, you're really *weird*." After that she had regularly referred to him as "Weird Harold," or just called him "Weird" for short, and he liked the name. Now in 1970 he decided that the name perfectly described his place—Weird Harold's.

He used it in his corporation papers, in the telephone directory, on his business cards; and in January of 1971, he used it on the announcements that he sent out to local newspapers and television stations inviting them to a press party before the opening. Weird Harold Rubin received extensive publicity then, and he continued to receive it in the years since then, as he became engaged in a series of skirmishes with the police because of his outlandish behavior and his alleged violation of the law. He was arrested for not having a massage license. He was twice convicted for selling obscene books, the second offense resulting in a $1,200 fine and a judicial order that he produce three thousand "non-dirty" paperback books to be given to the Cook County Jail. Early in 1973, he displayed in his front window a sign reading, DICK NIXON BEFORE HE DICKS US, which he was forced to remove. In 1974 he sent a masseuse to streak through city hall in his home community of Berwyn. In 1975, during a garbage strike in Berwyn, he was publicly accused of dumping a cubic yard of horse manure on the steps of the city hall, and, while he denied the charge, he liked the publicity.

His antics and obsessions, his endless confrontations with the law, eventually became too enervating for Millie, who, after marrying him and producing a son, abandoned Harold and moved to Florida. He became infuriated. He refused to give up the son he cherished, and he placed a public notice in *Screw*, the sex newspaper, announcing that he was no longer responsible for any debts incurred by his wife.

For a while, he cared for his son in the sex shop, letting the little boy pedal his tricycle among the customers who were waiting for a massage or were browsing through the erotic books and magazines displayed on the shelves—which Harold believed was an atmosphere more healthy for a child than the restrictive one imposed on him by his own puritanical upbringing. When his son became five, Harold drove him to kindergarten each morning and arranged for a nurse to care for the boy until Harold returned at night to the suburban apartment, which he shared with a masseuse.

The apartment was close to the home of his eighty-year-old grandmother, whom he visited regularly. While he often spoke with his mother, he had not spoken to his father in years. His grandfather died in 1974 at the age of eighty-eight, but neither Harold nor his grandmother attended the funeral.

Harold Rubin's apartment is decorated in the same 1890s style that characterized the first model studio he managed. On the walls are turn-of-the-century posters, an advertisement for Fatima cigarettes, and, neatly framed, ten shares of stock in the Stutz Motor Car Company. There are antiques in the living room, including several chairs and sofas older than his grandmother; a still-functioning Edison phonograph built in 1910, a wooden icebox, a Packard jukebox, an equally old Pulver chewing-gum machine, and other items resembling those advertised in the Spiegel mail-order catalog back when his grandfather had made deliveries by horse and wagon.

In his bedroom, Harold still keeps, carefully preserved, magazines with the nude photographs of Diane Webber. Though he looks at them less often than he did when he was younger, he knows each photograph in each issue; and his knowledge of her present life and age has not diminished her freshness for him. To this day, despite all that he has built in a business that is an extension of his boyhood bedroom, he acknowledges that he has never found in real life anyone who has fulfilled for him the desire that Diane Webber created.

. . .

Diane Webber is now forty-three years old. She lives on an exquisitely designed sailboat in Southern California with her husband of twenty years, both having decided to give up their apartment on Malibu Beach for the greater freedom of life on the sea.

Their son, John, who is nineteen, lives and works in a nudist colony in the hills southeast of Malibu, a colony called Elysium Fields, which is owned by a former photographer named Ed Lange, a tall, fifty-five-year-old man with an elegantly trimmed gray beard. Lange had been born in Chicago, but he left in the 1940s to come to California, where he became the most prolific photographer of nudes in America. It was he who took most of the pictures of Diane Webber which appeared in the 1950s and 1960s.

Diane Webber's father, the writer Guy Empey, died at seventy-nine in 1963 in a veterans' center in Wadsworth, Kansas, leaving his military papers and his medals to the men in the ward. Diane's mother, who is sixty-five, still works in the little restaurant on Sunset Boulevard with her second husband.

The restaurant is surrounded by studios—Columbia Pictures, Hollywood Film Enterprises, United Recording—and the many performers and technicians who patronize the restaurant call her Pat, which was her name on the silent screen, and not Marguerite, which was her name at birth in Montana. But on the walls of the restaurant are hung reproductions of drawings and paintings by Charles Russell of the Old West, of the Montana that she had eagerly left nearly a half century ago.

Diane rarely sees her mother, for the trips she takes away from the harbor and the sailboat are in another direction, toward the Valley, where she teaches classes in belly dancing almost daily at Everywoman's Village in Van Nuys, still displaying remarkable body control as she demonstrates a difficult movement to her pupils while her upraised hands click rhythmically with bell-bronze finger cymbals. On special occasions she performs before an audience, adding to her mystery as she adorns her alluring figure in a long, flowing scarf and a low hip-hugging brocaded skirt jingling with a belt of coins; and as the flutes, drums, and strings resound with Middle Eastern music, her body turns and undulates in a way that is unabashedly sexual.

On such occasions, her husband, who works as a technician on educational films, is often in the audience; and recently, after one of her exotic performances, a man who had known the Webbers for a while and was aware of the stimulating effect caused by her nude photographs asked her husband, the individual who knew her most intimately, what she was really like.

Joseph Webber pondered the question momentarily. He does nothing in haste. And then he softly replied, "She is everything you have ever imagined."

Frank Sinatra Has a Cold

Frank Sinatra, holding a glass of bourbon in one hand and a cigarette in the other, stood in a dark corner of the bar between two attractive but fading blondes who sat waiting for him to say something. But he said nothing; he had been silent during much of the evening, except now in this private club in Beverly Hills he seemed even more distant, staring out through the smoke and semidarkness into a large room beyond the bar where dozens of young couples sat huddled around small tables or twisted in the center of the floor to the clamorous clang of folk-rock music blaring from the stereo. The two blondes knew, as did Sinatra's four male friends who stood nearby, that it was a bad idea to force conversation upon him when he was in this mood of sullen silence, a mood that had hardly been uncommon during this first week of November, a month before his fiftieth birthday.

Sinatra had been working in a film that he now disliked, could not wait to finish; he was tired of all the publicity attached to his dating the twenty-year-old Mia Farrow, who was not in sight tonight; he was angry that a CBS television documentary of his life, to be shown in two weeks, was reportedly prying into his privacy, even speculating on his possible friendship with Mafia leaders; he was worried about his starring role in an hour-long NBC show entitled *Sinatra—A Man and His Music*, which would require that he sing eighteen songs with a voice that at this particular moment, just a few nights before the taping was to begin, was weak and sore and uncertain. Sinatra was ill. He was the victim of an ailment so common that most people would consider it trivial. But when it gets to Sinatra it can plunge him into a state of anguish, deep depression, panic, even rage. Frank Sinatra had a cold.

Sinatra with a cold is Picasso without paint, Ferrari without fuel—only worse. For the common cold robs Sinatra of that uninsurable jewel, his voice, cutting into the core of his confidence, and it affects not only his own psyche but also seems to cause a kind of psychosomatic nasal drip within dozens of people who work for him, drink with him, love him, depend on him for their own welfare and stability. A Sinatra with a cold can, in a small way, send vibrations through the entertainment industry and beyond as surely as a president of the United States, suddenly sick, can shake the national economy.

For Frank Sinatra was now involved with many things involving many people—his own film company, his record company, his private airline, his missile-parts firm, his real-estate holdings across the nation, his personal staff of seventy-five—which are only a portion of the power he is and has come to represent. He seemed now to be also the embodiment of the fully emancipated male, perhaps the only one in America, the man who can do anything he wants, anything, can do it because he has money, the energy, and no apparent guilt. In an age when the very young seem to be taking over, protesting and picketing and demanding change, Frank Sinatra survives as a national phenomenon, one of the few prewar products to withstand the test of time. He is the champ who made the big comeback, the man who had everything, lost it, then got it back, letting nothing stand in his way, doing what few men can do: he uprooted his life, left his family, broke with everything that was familiar, learning in the process that one way to hold a woman is not to hold her. Now he has the affection of Nancy and Ava and Mia, the fine female produce of three generations, and still has the adoration of his children, the freedom of a bachelor, he does not feel old, he makes old men feel young, makes them think that if Frank Sinatra can do it, it can be done; not that they could do it, but it is still nice for other men to know, at fifty, that it can be done.

But now, standing at this bar in Beverly Hills, Sinatra had a cold, and he continued to drink quietly and he seemed miles away in his private world, not even reacting when suddenly the stereo in the other room switched to a Sinatra song, "In the Wee Small Hours of the Morning."

It is a lovely ballad that he first recorded ten years ago, and it now inspired many young couples who had been sitting, tired of twisting, to get up and move slowly around the dance floor, holding one another very close. Sinatra's intonation, precisely clipped, yet full and flowing, gave a deeper meaning to the simple lyrics—"In the wee small hours of the morning/while the whole wide world is fast asleep/you lie awake, and think about the girl . . ."—it was like so many of his classics, a song that evoked loneliness and sensuality, and when blended with the dim light and the alcohol and nicotine and late-night needs, it became a kind of airy aphrodisiac. Undoubtedly the words from this song, and others like it, had put millions in the mood, it was music to make love by, and doubtless much love had been made by it all over America at night in cars, while the batteries burned down, in cottages by the lake, on beaches during balmy summer evenings, in secluded parks and exclusive penthouses and furnished rooms, in cabin cruisers and cabs and cabanas—in all places where Sinatra's songs could be heard were these words that warmed women, wooed and won them, snipped the final thread of inhibition and gratified the male egos of ungrateful lovers; two generations of men had been the beneficiaries of such ballads, for which they were eternally in his debt, for which they may eternally hate him. Nevertheless here he was, the man himself, in the early hours of the morning in Beverly Hills, out of range.

The two blondes, who seemed to be in their middle thirties, were preened and polished, their matured bodies softly molded within tight dark suits. They sat, legs crossed, perched on the high bar stools. They listened to the music. Then one of them pulled out a Kent and Sinatra quickly placed his gold lighter under it and she held his hand, looked at his fingers: they were nubby and raw, and the pinkies protruded, being so stiff from arthritis that he could barely bend them. He was, as usual, immaculately dressed. He wore an oxford-gray suit with a vest, a suit conservatively cut on the outside but trimmed with flamboyant silk within; his shoes, British, seemed to be shined even on the bottom of the soles. He also wore, as everybody seemed to know, a remarkably convincing black hairpiece, one of sixty that he owns, most of them under the care of an inconspicuous little gray-haired lady who, holding his hair in a tiny satchel, follows him around whenever he performs. She earns four hundred dollars a week. The most distinguishing thing about Sinatra's face are his eyes, clear blue and alert, eyes that within seconds can go cold with anger, or glow with affection, or, as now, reflect a vague detachment that keeps his friends silent and distant.

Leo Durocher, one of Sinatra's closest friends, was now shooting pool in the small room behind the bar. Standing near the door was Jim Mahoney, Sinatra's press agent, a somewhat chunky young man with a square jaw and narrow eyes who would resemble a tough Irish plain-clothesman if it were not for the expensive continental suits he wears and his exquisite shoes often adorned with polished buckles. Also nearby was a big, broad-shouldered two-hundred-pound actor named Brad Dexter who seemed always to be thrusting out his chest so that his gut would not show.

Brad Dexter has appeared in several films and television shows, displaying fine talent as a character actor, but in Beverly Hills he is equally known for the role he played in Hawaii two years ago when he swam a few hundred yards and risked his life to save Sinatra from drowning in a riptide. Since then Dexter has been one of Sinatra's constant companions and has been made a producer in Sinatra's film company. He occupies a plush office near Sinatra's executive suite. He is endlessly searching for literary properties that might be converted into new starring roles for Sinatra. Whenever he is among strangers with Sinatra he worries because he knows that Sinatra brings out the best and worst in people—some men will become aggressive, some women will become seductive, others will stand around skeptically appraising him, the scene will be somehow intoxicated by his mere presence, and maybe Sinatra himself, if feeling as badly as he was tonight, might become intolerant or tense, and then: headlines. So Brad Dexter tries to antici-pate danger and warn Sinatra in advance. He confesses to feeling very protective of Sinatra, admitting in a recent moment of self-revelation: "I'd kill for him."

While this statement may seem outlandishly dramatic, particularly when taken out of context, it nonetheless expresses a fierce fidelity that is quite common within Sinatra's special circle. It is a characteristic that Sinatra, without admission, seems to prefer: All the Way; All or Nothing at All. This is the Sicilian in Sinatra; he permits his friends, if they wish to remain that, none of the easy Anglo-Saxon outs. But if they remain loyal, then there is nothing Sinatra will not do in turn—fabulous gifts, personal kindnesses, encouragement when they're down, adulation when they're up. They are wise to remember, however, one thing. He is Sinatra. The boss. Il Padrone.

I had seen something of this Sicilian side of Sinatra last summer at

Jilly's saloon in New York, which was the only other time I'd gotten a close view of him prior to this night in this California club. Jilly's, which is on West Fifty-second Street in Manhattan, is where Sinatra drinks whenever he is in New York, and there is a special chair reserved for him in the back room against the wall that nobody else may use. When he is occupying it, seated behind a long table flanked by his closest New York friends—who include the saloonkeeper, Jilly Rizzo, and Jilly's azure-haired wife, Honey, who is known as the "Blue Jew"—a rather strange ritualistic scene develops. That night dozens of people, some of them casual friends of Sinatra's, some mere acquaintances, some neither, appeared outside of Jilly's saloon. They approached it like a shrine. They had come to pay respect. They were from New York, Brooklyn, Atlantic City, Hoboken. They were old actors, young actors, former prizefighters, tired trumpet players, politicians, a boy with a cane. There was a fat lady who said she remembered Sinatra when he used to throw the Jersey Observer onto her front porch in 1933. There were middle-aged couples who said they had heard Sinatra sing at the Rustic Cabin in 1938 and "We knew then that he really had it!" Or they had heard him when he was with Harry James's band in 1939, or with Tommy Dorsey in 1941 ("Yeah, that's the song, 'I'll Never Smile Again'—he sang it one night in this dump near Newark and we danced . . ."); or they remembered that time at the Paramount with the swooners, and him with those bow ties, The Voice; and one woman remembered that awful boy she knew then—Alexander Dorogokupetz, an eighteen-year-old heckler who had thrown a tomato at Sinatra and the bobby-soxers in the balcony had tried to flail him to death. Whatever became of Alexander Dorogokupetz? The lady did not know.

And they remembered when Sinatra was a failure and sang trash like "Mairzy Doats," and they remembered his comeback and on this night they were all standing outside Jilly's saloon, dozens of them, but they could not get in. So some of them left. But most of them stayed, hoping that soon they might be able to push or wedge their way into Jilly's between the elbows and backsides of the men drinking three-deep at the bar, and they might be able to peek through and see him sitting back there. This is all they really wanted; they wanted to see him. And for a few moments they gazed in silence through the smoke and they stared. Then they turned, fought their way out of the bar, went home.

Some of Sinatra's close friends, all of whom are known to the men guarding Jilly's door, do manage to get an escort into the back room. But once they are there they, too, must fend for themselves. On the particular evening, Frank Gifford, the former football player, got only seven yards in three tries. Others who had somehow been close enough to shake Sinatra's hand did not shake it; instead they just touched him on the shoulder or sleeve, or they merely stood close enough for him to see them and, after he'd given them a wink of recognition or a wave or a nod or called out their names (he had a fantastic memory for first names), they would then turn and leave. They had checked in. They had paid their respects. And as I watched this ritualistic scene, I got the impression that Frank Sinatra was dwelling simultaneously in two worlds that were not contemporary.

On the one hand he is the swinger—as he is when talking and joking with Sammy Davis, Jr., Richard Conte, Liza Minelli, Bernice Massi, or any of the other show-business people who get to sit at the table; on the other, as when he is nodding or waving to his paisanos who are close to him (Al Silvani, a boxing manager who works with Sinatra's film company; Dominic Di Bona, his wardrobe man; Ed Pucci, a three-hundred-pound former football lineman who is his aide-de-camp), Frank Sinatra is Il Padrone. Or better still, he is what in traditional Sicily have long been called *uomini rispettati*—men of respect: men who are both majestic and humble, men who are loved by all and are very generous by nature, men whose hands are kissed as they walk from village to village, men who would personally go out of their way to redress a wrong.

Frank Sinatra does things personally. At Christmas time, he will personally pick dozens of presents for his close friends and family, remembering the type of jewelry they like, their favorite colors, the sizes of their shirts and dresses. When a musician friend's house was destroyed and his wife was killed in a Los Angeles mud slide a little more than a year ago, Sinatra personally came to his aid, finding the musician a new home, paying whatever hospital bills were left unpaid by the insurance, then personally supervising the furnishing of the new home down to the replacing of the silverware, the linen, the purchase of new clothing.

The same Sinatra who did this can, within the same hour, explode in a towering rage of intolerance should a small thing be incorrectly done for him by one of his paisanos. For example, when one of his men brought him a frankfurter with catsup on it, which Sinatra apparently abhors, he angrily threw the bottle at the man, splattering catsup all over him. Most of the men who work around Sinatra are big. But this never seems to intimidate Sinatra nor curb his impetuous behavior with them when he is mad. They will never take a swing back at him. He is Il Padrone.

At other times, aiming to please, his men will overreact to his desires: when he casually observed that his big orange desert jeep in Palm Springs seemed in need of a new painting, the word was swiftly passed down through the channels, becoming ever more urgent as it went, until finally it was a command that the jeep be painted now, immediately, yesterday. To accomplish this would require the hiring of a special crew of painters to work all night, at overtime rates; which, in turn, meant that the order had to be bucked back up the line for further approval. When it finally got back to Sinatra's desk, he did not know what it was all about; after he had figured it out he confessed, with a tired look on his face, that he did not care when the hell they painted the jeep.

Yet it would have been unwise for anyone to anticipate his reaction, for he is a wholly unpredictable man of many moods and great dimension, a man who responds instantaneously to instinct—suddenly, dramatically, wildly he responds, and nobody can predict what will follow. A young lady named Jane Hoag, a reporter at *Life*'s Los Angeles bureau who had attended the same school as Sinatra's daughter, Nancy, had once been invited to a party at Mrs. Sinatra's California home at which Frank Sinatra, who maintains very cordial relations with his former wife, acted as host. Early in the party Miss Hoag, while leaning against a table, accidentally with her elbow knocked over one of a pair of alabaster birds to the floor, smashing it to pieces. Suddenly, Miss Hoag recalled, Sinatra's daughter cried, "Oh, that was one of my mother's favorite . . ."—but before she could complete the sentence, Sinatra glared at her, cutting her off, and while forty other guests in the room all stared in silence, Sinatra walked over, quickly with his finger flicked the other alabaster bird off the table, smashing it to pieces, and then put an arm gently around Jane Hoag and said, in a way that put her completely at ease, "That's okay, kid."

Now Sinatra said a few words to the blondes. Then he turned from the bar and began to walk toward the poolroom. One of Sinatra's other men friends moved in to keep the girls company. Brad Dexter, who had been standing in the corner talking to some other people, now followed Sinatra.

The room cracked with the clack of billiard balls. There were about a dozen spectators in the room, most of them young men who were watching Leo Durocher shoot against two other aspiring hustlers who were not very good. This private drinking club has among its membership many actors, directors, writers, models, nearly all of them a good deal younger than Sinatra or Durocher and much more casual in the way they dress for the evening. Many of the young women, their long hair flowing loosely below their shoulders, wore tight, fanny-fitting Jax pants and very expensive sweaters; and a few of the young men wore blue or green velour shirts with high collars and narrow tight pants, and Italian loafers.

It was obvious from the way Sinatra looked at these people in the poolroom that they were not his style, but he leaned back against a high stool that was against the wall, holding his drink in his right hand, and said nothing, just watched Durocher slam the billiard balls back and forth. The younger men in the room, accustomed to seeing Sinatra at this club, treated him without deference, although they said nothing offensive. They were a cool young group, very California-cool and casual, and one of the coolest seemed to be a little guy, very quick of movement, who had a sharp profile, pale blue eyes, blondish hair, and squared eyeglasses. He wore a pair of brown corduroy slacks, a green shaggy-dog Shetland sweater, a tan suede jacket, and Game Warden boots, for which he had recently paid sixty dollars.

Frank Sinatra, leaning against the stool, sniffling a bit from his cold, could not take his eyes off the Game Warden boots. Once, after gazing at them for a few moments, he turned away; but now he was focused on them again. The owner of the boots, who was just standing in them watching the pool game, was named Harlan Ellison, a writer who had just completed work on a screenplay, *The Oscar*.

Finally Sinatra could not contain himself.

"Hey," he yelled in his slightly harsh voice that still had a soft, sharp edge. "Those Italian boots?"

"No," Ellison said.

"Spanish?"

"No."

"Are they English boots?"

"Look, I donno, man," Ellison shot back, frowning at Sinatra, then turning away again.

Now the poolroom was suddenly silent. Leo Durocher who had been poised behind his cue stick and was bent low just froze in that position for a second. Nobody moved. Then Sinatra moved away from the stool and walked with that slow, arrogant swagger of his toward Ellison, the hard tap of Sinatra's shoes the only sound in the room. Then, looking down at Ellison with a slightly raised eyebrow and a tricky little smile, Sinatra asked: "You expecting a storm?"

Harlan Ellison moved a step to the side. "Look, is there any reason why you're talking to me?"

"I don't like the way you're dressed," Sinatra said.

"Hate to shake you up," Ellison said, "but I dress to suit myself."

Now there was some rumbling in the room, and somebody said, "Com'on, Harlan, let's get out of here," and Leo Durocher made his pool shot and said, "Yeah, com'on."

But Ellison stood his ground.

Sinatra said, "What do you do?"

"I'm a plumber," Ellison said.

"No, no, he's not," another young man quickly yelled from across the table. "He wrote *The Oscar*."

"Oh, yeah," Sinatra said, "well I've seen it, and it's a piece of crap."

"That's strange," Ellison said, "because they haven't even released it yet."

"Well, I've seen it," Sinatra repeated, "and it's a piece of crap."

Now Brad Dexter, very anxious, very big opposite the small figure of Ellison, said, "Com'on, kid, I don't want you in this room."

"Hey," Sinatra interrupted Dexter, "can't you see I'm talking to this guy?"

Dexter was confused. Then his whole attitude changed, and his voice went soft and he said to Ellison, almost with a plea, "Why do you persist in tormenting me?"

The whole scene was becoming ridiculous, and it seemed that Sinatra was only half-serious, perhaps just reacting out of sheer boredom or inner despair; at any rate, after a few more exchanges Harlan Ellison left the room. By this time the word had gotten out to those on the dance floor about the Sinatra-Ellison exchange, and somebody went to look for the manager of the club. But somebody else said that the manager had already heard about it—and had quickly gone out the door, hopped in his car and drove home. So the assistant manager went into the poolroom.

"I don't want anybody in here without coats and ties," Sinatra snapped.

The assistant manager nodded, and walked back to his office.

It was the morning after. It was the beginning of another nervous day for Sinatra's press agent, Jim Mahoney. Mahoney had a headache, and he was worried but not over the Sinatra-Ellison incident of the night before. At the time Mahoney had been with his wife at a table in the other room, and possibly he had not even been aware of the little drama. The whole thing had lasted only about three minutes. And three minutes after it was over, Frank Sinatra had probably forgotten about it for the rest of his life—as Ellison will probably remember it for the rest of his life: he had had, as hundreds of others before him, at an unexpected moment between darkness and dawn, a scene with Sinatra.

It was just as well that Mahoney had not been in the poolroom; he had enough on his mind today. He was worried about Sinatra's cold and worried about the controversial CBS documentary that, despite Sinatra's protests and withdrawal of permission, would be shown on television in less than two weeks. The newspapers this morning were full of hints that Sinatra might sue the network, and Mahoney's phones were ringing without pause, and now he was plugged into New York talking to the *Daily News*'s Kay Gardella, saying: "that's right, Kay . . . they made a gentleman's agreement to not ask certain questions about Frank's private life, and then Cronkite went right ahead: 'Frank, tell me about those associations.' That question, Kay—out! That question should never have been asked . . ."

As he spoke, Mahoney leaned back in his leather chair, his head shaking slowly. He is a powerfully built man of thirty-seven; he has a round, ruddy face, a heavy jaw, and narrow pale eyes, and he might appear pugnacious if he did not speak with such clear, soft sincerity and if he were not so meticulous about his clothes. His suits and shoes are superbly tailored, which was one of the first things Sinatra noticed about him, and in his spacious office opposite the bar is a red-muff electrical shoe polisher and a pair of brown wooden shoulders on a stand over which Mahoney can drape his jackets. Near the bar is an autographed photograph of President Kennedy and a few pictures of Frank Sinatra, but there are none of Sinatra in any other rooms in Mahoney's public-relations agency; there once was a large photograph of him hanging in the reception room but this apparently bruised the egos of some of

Mahoney's other movie-star clients and, since Sinatra never shows up at the agency anyway, the photograph was removed.

Still, Sinatra seems ever present, and if Mahoney did not have legitimate worries about Sinatra, as he did today, he could invent them—and, as worry aids, he surrounds himself with little mementos of moments in the past when he did worry. In his shaving kit there is a two-year-old box of sleeping tablets dispensed by a Reno druggist—the date on the bottle marks the kidnapping of Frank Sinatra, Jr. There is on a table in Mahoney's office a mounted wood reproduction of Frank Sinatra's ransom note written on the aforementioned occasion. One of Mahoney's mannerisms, when he is sitting at his desk worrying, is to tinker with the tiny toy train he keeps in front of him—the train is a souvenir from the Sinatra film *Von Ryan's Express*; it is to men who are close to Sinatra what the PT-109 tie clasps are to men who were close to Kennedy—and Mahoney then proceeds to roll the little train back and forth on the six inches of track; back and forth, back and forth, click-clack-click-clack. It is his Queeg-thing.

Now Mahoney quickly put aside the little train. His secretary told him there was a very important call on the line. Mahoney picked it up, and his voice was even softer and more sincere than before. "Yes, Frank," he said. "Right . . . right . . . yes, Frank . . ."

When Mahoney put down the phone, quietly, he announced that Frank Sinatra had left in his private jet to spend the weekend at his home in Palm Springs, which is a sixteen-minute flight from his home in Los Angeles. Mahoney was now worried again. The Lear jet that Sinatra's pilot would be flying was identical, Mahoney said, to the one that had just crashed in another part of California.

On the following Monday, a cloudy and unseasonably cool California day, more than one hundred people gathered inside a white television studio, an enormous room dominated by a white stage, white walls, and with dozens of lights and lamps dangling: it rather resembled a gigantic operating room. In this room, within an hour or so, NBC was scheduled to begin taping a one-hour show that would be televised in color on the night of November 24 and would highlight, as much as it could in the limited time, the twenty-five-year career of Frank Sinatra as a public entertainer. It would not attempt to probe, as the forthcoming CBS Sinatra documentary allegedly would, that area of Sinatra's life that he regards as private. The NBC show would be mainly an hour of Sinatra singing some of the hits that carried him from Hoboken to Hollywood, a show that would be interrupted only now and then by a few film clips and commercials for Budweiser beer. Prior to his cold, Sinatra had been very excited about this show; he saw here an opportunity to appeal not only to those nostalgic, but also to communicate his talent to some rock-and-rollers—in a sense, he was battling the Beatles. The press releases being prepared by Mahoney's agency stressed this, reading: "If you happen to be tired of kid singers wearing mops of hair thick enough to hide a crate of melons . . . it should be refreshing, to consider the entertainment value of a video special titled *Sinatra—A Man and His Music.*"

But now in this NBC studio in Los Angeles, there was an atmosphere of anticipation and tension because of the uncertainty of the Sinatra voice. The forty-three musicians in Nelson Riddle's orchestra had already arrived and some were up on the white platform warming up. Dwight Hemion, a youthful sandy-haired director who had won praise for his television special on Barbra Streisand, was seated in the glass-enclosed control booth that overlooked the orchestra and stage. The camera crews, technical teams, security guards, Budweiser ad men were also standing between the floor lamps and cameras, waiting, as were a dozen or so ladies who worked as secretaries in other parts of the building but had sneaked away so they could watch this.

A few minutes before eleven o'clock, word spread quickly through the long corridor into the big studio that Sinatra was spotted walking through the parking lot and was on his way, and was looking fine. There seemed great relief among the group that was gathered; but when the lean, sharply dressed figure of the man got closer, and closer, they saw to their dismay that it was not Frank Sinatra. It was his double. Johnny Delgado.

Delgado walks like Sinatra, has Sinatra's build, and from certain facial angles does resemble Sinatra. But he seems a rather shy individual. Fifteen years ago, early in his acting career, Delgado applied for a role in *From Here to Eternity*. He was hired, finding out later that he was to be Sinatra's double. In Sinatra's latest film, *Assault on a Queen*, a story in which Sinatra and some fellow conspirators attempt to hijack the *Queen Mary*, Johnny Delgado doubles for Sinatra in some water scenes; and now, in this NBC studio, his job was to stand under the hot television lights marking Sinatra's spots on the stage for the camera crews.

Five minutes later, the real Frank Sinatra walked in. His face was pale, his blue eyes seemed a bit watery. He had been unable to rid himself of the cold, but he was going to try to sing anyway because the schedule was tight and thousands of dollars were involved at this moment in the assembling of the orchestra and crews and the rental of the studio. But when Sinatra, on his way to his small rehearsal room to warm up his voice, looked into the studio and saw that the stage and orchestra's platform were not close together, as he had specifically requested, his lips tightened and he was obviously very upset. A few moments later, from his rehearsal room, could be heard the pounding of his fist against the top of the piano and the voice of his accompanist, Bill Miller, saying, softly, "Try not to upset yourself, Frank."

Later Jim Mahoney and another man walked in, and there was talk of Dorothy Kilgallen's death in New York earlier that morning. She had been an ardent foe of Sinatra for years, and he became equally uncomplimentary about her in his nightclub act, and now, though she was dead, he did not compromise his feelings. "Dorothy Kilgallen's dead," he repeated, walking out of the room toward the studio. "Well, guess I got to change my whole act."

When he strolled into the studio the musicians all picked up their instruments and stiffened in their seats. Sinatra cleared his throat a few times and then, after rehearsing a few ballads with the orchestra, he sang "Don't Worry About Me" to his satisfaction and, being uncertain of how long his voice could last, suddenly became impatient.

"Why don't we tape this mother?" he called out, looking up toward the glass booth where the director, Dwight Hemion, and his staff were sitting. Their heads seemed to be down, focusing on the control board.

"Why don't we tape this mother?" Sinatra repeated.

The production stage manager, who stands near the camera wearing a headset, repeated Sinatra's words exactly into his line to the control room: "Why don't we tape this mother?"

Hemion did not answer. Possibly his switch was off. It was hard to know because of the obscuring reflections the lights made against the glass booth.

"Why don't we put on a coat and tie," said Sinatra, then wearing a high-necked yellow pullover, "and tape this . . ."

Suddenly Hemion's voice came over the sound amplifier, very calmly: "Okay, Frank, would you mind going back over . . ."

"Yes, I would mind going back," Sinatra snapped.

The silence from Hemion's end, which lasted a second or two, was then again interrupted by Sinatra saying, "When we stop doing things around here the way we did them in 1950, maybe we . . ." and Sinatra continued to tear into Hemion, condemning as well the lack of modern techniques in putting such shows together; then, possibly not wanting to use his voice unnecessarily, he stopped. And Dwight Hemion, very patient, so patient and calm that one would assume he had not heard anything that Sinatra had just said, outlined the opening part of the show. And Sinatra a few minutes later was reading his opening remarks, words that would follow "Without a Song," off the large idiot-cards being held near the camera. Then, this done, he prepared to do the same thing on camera.

"Frank Sinatra Show, Act 1, page ten, Take 1," called a man with a clapboard, jumping in front of the camera—clap—then jumping away again.

"Did you ever stop to think," Sinatra began, "what the world would be like without a song? . . . It would be a pretty dreary place . . . Gives you something to think about, doesn't it? . . ."

Sinatra stopped.

"Excuse me," he said, adding, "Boy, I need a drink."

They tried it again.

"Frank Sinatra Show, Act 1, page ten, Take 2," yelled the jumping guy with the clapboard.

"Did you ever stop to think what the world would be like without a song? . . ." Frank Sinatra read it through this time without stopping. Then he rehearsed a few more songs, once or twice interrupting the orchestra when a certain instrumental sound was not quite what he wanted. It was hard to tell how well his voice was going to hold up, for this was early in the show; up to this point, however, everybody in the room seemed pleased, particularly when he sang an old sentimental favorite written more than twenty years ago by Jimmy Van Heusen and Phil Silvers—"Nancy," inspired by the first of Sinatra's three children when she was just a few years old.

> If I don't see her each day
> I miss her . . .
> Gee what a thrill
> Each time I kiss her

As Sinatra sang these words, though he has sung them hundreds and hundreds of times in the past, it was suddenly obvious to everybody in the studio that something quite special must be going on inside the man, because something quite special was coming out. He was singing now, cold or no cold, with power and warmth, he was letting himself go, the public arrogance was gone, the private side was in this song about the girl who, it is said, understands him better than anybody else, and is the only person in front of whom he can be unashamedly himself.

Nancy is twenty-five. She lives alone, her marriage to singer Tommy Sands having ended in divorce. Her home is in a Los Angeles suburb and she is now making her third film and is recording for her father's record company. She sees him every day; or, if not, he telephones, no matter if it be from Europe or Asia. When Sinatra's singing first became popular on radio, stimulating the swooners, Nancy would listen at home and cry. When Sinatra's first marriage broke up in 1951 and he left home, Nancy was the only child old enough to remember him as a father. She also saw him with Ava Gardner, Juliet Prowse, Mia Farrow, many others, has gone on double dates with him . . .

> She takes the winter
> And makes it summer . . .
> Summer could take
> Some lessons from her

Nancy now also sees him visiting at home with his first wife, the former Nancy Barbato, a plasterer's daughter from Jersey City whom he married in 1939 when he was earning twenty-five dollars a week singing at the Rustic Cabin near Hoboken.

The first Mrs. Sinatra, a striking woman who has never remarried ("When you've been married to Frank Sinatra . . ." she once explained to a friend), lives in a magnificent home in Los Angeles with her younger daughter, Tina, who is seventeen. There is no bitterness, only great respect and affection between Sinatra and his first wife, and he has long been welcome in her home and has even been known to wander in at odd hours, stoke the fire, lie on the sofa, and fall asleep. Frank Sinatra can fall asleep anywhere, something he learned when he used to ride bumpy roads with band buses; he also learned at that time, when sitting in a tuxedo, how to pinch the trouser creases in the back and tuck the jacket under and out, and fall asleep perfectly pressed. But he does not ride buses anymore, and his daughter Nancy, who in her younger days felt rejected when he slept on the sofa instead of giving attention to her, later realized that the sofa was one of the few places left in the world where Frank Sinatra could get any privacy, where his famous face would neither be stared at nor cause an abnormal reaction in others. She realized, too, that things normal have always eluded her father: his childhood was one of loneliness and a drive toward attention, and since attaining it he has never again been certain of solitude. Upon looking out the window of a home he once owned in Hasbrouck Heights, New Jersey, he would occasionally see the faces of teenagers peeking in; and in 1944, after moving to California and buying a home behind a ten-foot fence on Lake Toluca, he discovered that the only way to escape the telephone and other intrusions was to board his paddle boat with a few friends, a card table and a case of beer, and stay afloat all afternoon. But he has tried, insofar as it has been possible, to be like everyone else, Nancy says. He wept on her wedding day, he is very sentimental and sensitive . . .

"What the hell are you doing up there, Dwight?"

Silence from the control booth.

"Got a party or something going on up there, Dwight?"

Sinatra stood on the stage, arms folded, glaring up across the cameras toward Hemion. Sinatra had sung "Nancy" with probably all he had in his voice on this day. The next few numbers contained raspy notes, and twice his voice completely cracked. But now Hemion was in the control booth out of communication; then he was down in the studio walking over to where Sinatra stood. A few minutes later they both left the studio and were on the way up to the control booth. The tape was replayed for Sinatra. He watched only about five minutes of it before he started to shake his head. Then he said to Hemion: "Forget it, just forget it. You're wasting your time. What you got there," Sinatra said, nodding to the singing image of himself on the television screen, "is a man with a cold." Then he left the control booth, ordering that the whole day's performance be scrubbed and future taping postponed until he had recovered.

Soon the word spread like an emotional epidemic down through Sinatra's staff, then fanned out through Hollywood, then was heard across the nation in Jilly's saloon, and also on the other side of the Hudson River in the homes of Frank Sinatra's parents and his other relatives and friends in New Jersey.

When Frank Sinatra spoke with his father on the telephone and said
he was feeling awful, the elder Sinatra reported that he was also feeling
awful: that his left arm and fist were so stiff with a circulatory condition
he could barely use them, adding that the ailment might be the result of
having thrown too many left hooks during his days as a bantamweight
almost fifty years ago.

Martin Sinatra, a ruddy and tattooed little blue-eyed Sicilian born
in Catania, boxed under the name of "Marty O'Brien." In those days, in
those places, with the Irish running the lower reaches of city life, it was
not uncommon for Italians to wind up with such names. Most of the
Italians and Sicilians who migrated to America just prior to the 1900s
were poor and uneducated, were excluded from the building-trades
unions dominated by the Irish, and were somewhat intimidated by the
Irish police, Irish priests, Irish politicians.

One notable exception was Frank Sinatra's mother, Dolly, a large
and very ambitious woman who was brought to this country at two
months of age by her mother and father, a lithographer from Genoa. In
later years Dolly Sinatra, possessing a round red face and blue eyes, was
often mistaken for being Irish, and surprised many at the speed with
which she swung her heavy handbag at anyone uttering "Wop."

By playing skillful politics with North Jersey's Democratic machine,
Dolly Sinatra was to become, in her heyday, a kind of Catherine de
Medici of Hoboken's third ward. She could always be counted upon to
deliver six hundred votes at election time from her Italian neighborhood,
and this was her base of power. When she told one of the politicians that
she wanted her husband to be appointed to the Hoboken Fire
Department, and was told, "But, Dolly, we don't have an opening," she
snapped, "Make an opening."

They did. Years later she requested that her husband be made a
captain, and one day she got a call from one of the political bosses that
began, "Dolly, congratulations!"

"For what?"

"Captain Sinatra."

"Oh, you finally made him one—thank you very much."

Then she called the Hoboken Fire Department.

"Let me speak to Captain Sinatra," she said. The fireman called
Martin Sinatra to the phone, saying, "Marty, I think your wife has gone
nuts." When he got on the line, Dolly greeted him:

"Congratulations, Captain Sinatra!"

Dolly's only child, christened Francis Albert Sinatra, was born and nearly died on December 12, 1915. It was a difficult birth, and during his first moment on earth he received marks he will carry till death—the scars on the left side of his neck being the result of a doctor's clumsy forceps, and Sinatra has chosen not to obscure them with surgery.

After he was six months old, he was reared mainly by his grandmother. His mother had a full-time job as a chocolate dipper with a large firm and was so proficient at it that the firm once offered to send her to the Paris office to train others. While some people in Hoboken remember Frank Sinatra as a lonely child, one who spent many hours on the porch gazing into space, Sinatra was never a slum kid, never in jail, always well-dressed. He had so many pants that some people in Hoboken called him "Slacksey O'Brien."

Dolly Sinatra was not the sort of Italian mother who could be appeased merely by a child's obedience and good appetite. She made many demands on her son, was always very strict. She dreamed of his becoming an aviation engineer. When she discovered Bing Crosby pictures hanging on his bedroom walls one evening, and learned that her son wished to become a singer too, she became infuriated and threw a shoe at him. Later, finding she could not talk him out of it—"he takes after me"—she encouraged his singing.

Many Italo-American boys of his generation were then shooting for the same star—they were strong with song, weak with words, not a big novelist among them: no O'Hara, no Bellow, no Cheever, nor Shaw; yet they could communicate bel canto. This was more in their tradition, no need for a diploma; they could, with a song, someday see their names in lights ... Perry Como ... Frankie Laine ... Tony Bennett ... Vic Damone ... but none could see it better than Frank Sinatra.

Though he sang through much of the night at the Rustic Cabin, he was up the next day singing without a fee on New York radio to get more attention. Later he got a job singing with Harry James's band, and it was there in August of 1939 that Sinatra had his first recording hit—"All or Nothing at All." He became very fond of Harry James and the men in the band, but when he received an offer from Tommy Dorsey, who in those days had probably the best band in the country, Sinatra took it; the job paid $125 a week, and Dorsey knew how to feature a vocalist. Yet Sinatra was very depressed at leaving James's band, and the final night with them was so memorable that, twenty years later, Sinatra could recall the details to a friend: "the bus pulled out with the rest of the boys at about half-past midnight. I'd said good-bye to them all, and it was snowing, I remember. There was nobody around and I stood alone with my suitcase in the snow and watched the taillights disappear. Then the tears started and I tried to run after the bus. There was such spirit and enthusiasm in that band, I hated leaving it."

But he did—as he would leave other warm places, too, in search of something more, never wasting time, trying to do it all in one generation, fighting under his own name, defending underdogs, terrorizing top dogs. He threw a punch at a musician who said something anti-Semitic, espoused the Negro cause two decades before it became fashionable. He also threw a tray of glasses at Buddy Rich when he played the drums too loud.

Sinatra gave away $50,000 worth of gold cigarette lighters before he was thirty, was living an immigrant's wildest dream of America. He arrived suddenly on the scene when DiMaggio was silent, when paisanos were mournful, were quietly defensive about Hitler in their homeland. Sinatra became, in time, a kind of one-man Anti-Defamation League for Italians in America, the sort of organization that would be unlikely for them because, as the theory goes, they rarely agreed on anything, being extreme individualists: fine as soloists, but not so good in a choir; fine as heroes, but not so good in a parade.

When many Italian names were used in describing gangsters on a television show, *The Untouchables*, Sinatra was loud in his disapproval. Sinatra and many thousands of other Italo-Americans were resentful as well when a small-time hoodlum, Joseph Valachi, was brought by Bobby Kennedy into prominence as a Mafia expert, when indeed, from Valachi's testimony on television, he seemed to know less than most waiters on Mulberry Street. Many Italians in Sinatra's circle also regard Bobby Kennedy as something of an Irish cop, more dignified than those in Dolly's day, but no less intimidating. Together with Peter Lawford, Bobby Kennedy is said to have suddenly gotten "cocky" with Sinatra after John Kennedy's election, forgetting the contribution Sinatra had made in both fundraising and in influencing many anti-Irish Italian votes. Lawford and Bobby Kennedy are both suspected of having influenced the late President's decision to stay as a house guest with Bing Crosby instead of Sinatra, as originally planned, a social setback Sinatra may never forget. Peter Lawford has since been drummed out of Sinatra's "summit" in Las Vegas.

"Yes, my son is like me," Dolly Sinatra says, proudly. "You cross him, he never forgets." And while she concedes his power, she quickly points out, "He can't make his mother do anything she doesn't want to do," adding, "Even today, he wears the same brand of underwear I used to buy him."

Today Dolly Sinatra is seventy-one years old, a year or two younger than Martin, and all day long people are knocking on the back door of her large home asking her advice, seeking her influence. When she is not seeing people and not cooking in the kitchen, she is looking after her husband, a silent but stubborn man, and telling him to keep his sore left arm resting on the sponge she has placed on the armrest of a soft chair. "Oh, he went to some terrific fires, this guy did," Dolly said to a visitor, nodding with admiration toward her husband in the chair.

Though Dolly Sinatra has eighty-seven godchildren in Hoboken, and still goes to that city during political campaigns, she now lives with her husband in a beautiful sixteen-room house in Fort Lee, New Jersey. This home was a gift from their son on their fiftieth wedding anniversary three years ago. The home is tastefully furnished and is filled with a remarkable juxtaposition of the pious and the worldly—photographs of Pope John and Ava Gardner, of Pope Paul and Dean Martin; several statues of saints and holy water, a chair autographed by Sammy Davis Jr. and bottles of bourbon. In Mrs. Sinatra's jewelry box is a magnificent strand of pearls she had just received from Ava Gardner, whom she liked tremendously as a daughter-in-law and still keeps in touch with and talks about; and hung on the wall is a letter addressed to Dolly and Martin: "The sands of time have turned to gold, yet love continues to unfold like the petals of a rose, in God's garden of life . . . may God love you thru all eternity. I thank Him, I thank you for the being of one. Your loving son, Francis."

Mrs. Sinatra talks to her son on the telephone about once a week, and recently he suggested that, when visiting Manhattan, she make use of his apartment on East Seventy-second Street on the East River. This is an expensive neighborhood of New York even though there is a small factory on the block, but this latter fact was seized upon by Dolly Sinatra as a means of getting back at her son for some unflattering descriptions of his childhood in Hoboken.

"What—you want me to stay in your apartment, in that dump?" she asked. "You think I'm going to spend the night in that awful neighborhood?"

Frank Sinatra got the point, and said, "Excuse me, Mrs. Fort Lee."

After spending the week in Palm Springs, his cold much better, Frank Sinatra returned to Los Angeles, a lovely city of sun and sex, a Spanish discovery of Mexican misery, a star land of little men and little women sliding in and out of convertibles in tense tight pants.

Sinatra returned in time to see the long-awaited CBS documentary with his family. At about nine P.M. he drove to the home of his former wife, Nancy, and had dinner with her and their two daughters. Their son, whom they rarely see these days, was out of town.

Frank, Jr., who is twenty-two, was touring with a band and moving cross country toward a New York engagement at Basin Street East with the Pied Pipers, with whom Frank Sinatra sang when he was with Dorsey's band in the 1940s. Today Frank Sinatra, Jr., whom his father says he named after Franklin D. Roosevelt, lives mostly in hotels, dines each evening in his nightclub dressing room, and sings until two A.M., accepting graciously, because he has no choice, the inevitable comparisons. His voice is smooth and pleasant, and improving with work, and while he is very respectful of his father, he discusses him with objectivity and in an occasional tone of subdued cockiness.

Concurrent with his father's early fame, Frank, Jr. said, was the creation of a "press-release Sinatra" designed to "set him apart from the common man, separate him from the realities: it was suddenly Sinatra, the electric magnate, Sinatra who is supernormal, not superhuman but supernormal. And here," Frank, Jr. continued, "is the great fallacy, the great bullshit, for Frank Sinatra is normal, is the guy whom you'd meet on a street corner. But this other thing, the supernormal guise, has affected Frank Sinatra as much as anybody who watches one of his television shows, or reads a magazine article about him . . .

"Frank Sinatra's life in the beginning was so normal," he said, "that nobody would have guessed in 1934 that this little Italian kid with the curly hair would become the giant, the monster, the great living legend . . . He met my mother one summer on the beach. She was Nancy Barbato, daughter of Mike Barbato, a Jersey City plasterer. And she meets the fireman's son, Frank, one summer day on the beach at Long Branch, New Jersey. Both are Italian, both Roman Catholic, both lower-middle-class summer sweethearts—it is like a million bad movies starring Frankie Avalon . . .

"They have three children. The first child, Nancy, was the most normal of Frank Sinatra's children. Nancy was a cheerleader, went to summer camp, drove a Chevrolet, had the easiest kind of development centered around the home and family. Next is me. My life with the family is very, very normal up until September of 1958 when, in complete contrast to the rearing of both girls, I am put into a college-preparatory school. I am now away from the inner family circle, and my position within has never been remade to this day . . . The third child, Tina. And to be dead honest, I really couldn't say what her life is like."

The CBS show, narrated by Walter Cronkite, began at ten P.M. A minute before that, the Sinatra family, having finished dinner, turned their chairs around and faced the camera, united for whatever disaster might follow. Sinatra's men in other parts of town, in other parts of the nation, were doing the same thing. Sinatra's lawyer, Milton A. Rudin, smoking a cigar, was watching with a keen eye, an alert legal mind. Other sets were watched by Brad Dexter, Jim Mahoney, Ed Pucci; Sinatra's makeup man, "Shotgun" Britton; his New York representative, Henri Gine; his haberdasher, Richard Carroll; his insurance broker, John Lillie; his valet, George Jacobs, a handsome Negro who, when entertaining girls in his apartment, plays records by Ray Charles.

And like so much of Hollywood's fear, the apprehension about the CBS show all proved to be without foundation. It was a highly flattering hour that did not deeply probe, as rumors suggested it would, into Sinatra's love life, or the Mafia, or other areas of his private province. While the documentary was not authorized, wrote Jack Gould in the next day's *New York Times*, "it could have been."

Immediately after the show, the telephones began to ring throughout the Sinatra system conveying words of joy and relief—and from New York came Jilly's telegram: WE RULE THE WORLD!

The next day, standing in the corridor of the NBC building where he was about to resume taping his show, Sinatra was discussing the CBS show with several of his friends, and he said, "Oh, it was a gas."

"Yeah, Frank, a helluva show."

"But I think Jack Gould was right in the *Times* today," Sinatra said. "There should have been more on the man, not so much on the music . . ."

They nodded, nobody mentioning the past hysteria in the Sinatra world when it seemed CBS was zeroing in on the man; they just nodded and two of them laughed about Sinatra's apparently having gotten the word "bird" on the show—this being a favorite Sinatra word. He often inquires of his cronies, "How's your bird?"; and when he nearly drowned in Hawaii, he later explained, "Just got a little water on my bird"; and under a large photograph of him holding a whisky bottle, a photo that hangs in the home of an actor friend named Dick Bakalyan, the inscription reads: "Drink, Dickie! It's good for your bird." In the song, "Come Fly with Me," Sinatra sometimes alters the lyrics—"just say the words and we'll take our birds down to Acapulco Bay."

Ten minutes later Sinatra, following the orchestra, walked into the NBC studio, which did not resemble in the slightest the scene here of eight days ago. On this occasion Sinatra was in fine voice, he cracked jokes between numbers, nothing could upset him. Once, while he was singing "How Can I Ignore the Girl Next Door," standing on the stage next to a tree, a television camera mounted on a vehicle came rolling in too close and plowed against the tree.

"Kee-rist!" yelled one of the technical assistants.

But Sinatra seemed hardly to notice it.

"We've had a slight accident," he said, calmly. Then he began the song all over from the beginning.

When the show was over, Sinatra watched the rerun on the monitor in the control room. He was very pleased, shaking hands with Dwight Hemion and his assistants. Then the whisky bottles were opened in Sinatra's dressing room. Pat Lawford was there, and so were Andy Williams and a dozen others. The telegrams and telephone calls continued to be received from all over the country with praise for the CBS show. There was even a call, Mahoney said, from the CBS producer, Don Hewitt, with whom Sinatra had been so angry a few days before. And Sinatra was still angry, feeling that CBS had betrayed him, though the show itself was not objectionable.

"Shall I drop a line to Hewitt?" Mahoney asked.

"Can you send a fist through the mail?" Sinatra asked.

He has everything, he cannot sleep, he gives nice gifts, he is not happy, but he would not trade, even for happiness, what he is . . .

He is a piece of our past—but only we have aged, he hasn't . . . we are dogged by domesticity, he isn't . . . we have compunctions, he doesn't . . . it is our fault, not his . . .

He controls the menus of every Italian restaurant in Los Angeles; if you want North Italian cooking, fly to Milan . . .

Men follow him, imitate him, fight to be near him . . . there is something of the locker room, the barracks about him . . . bird . . . bird . . .

He believes you must play it big, wide, expansively—the more open you are, the more you take in, your dimensions deepen, you grow, you become more what you are—bigger, richer . . .

"He is better than anybody else, or at least they think he is, and he has to live up to it." —Nancy Sinatra Jr.

"He is calm on the outside—inwardly a million things are happening to him." —Dick Bakalyan

"He has an insatiable desire to live every moment to its fullest because, I guess, he feels that right around the corner is extinction." —Brad Dexter

"All I ever got out of any of my marriages was the two years Artie Shaw financed on an analyst's couch." —Ava Gardner

"We weren't mother and son—we were buddies." —Dolly Sinatra

"I'm for anything that gets you through the night, be it prayer, tranquilizers or a bottle of Jack Daniel's." —Frank Sinatra

Frank Sinatra was tired of all the talk, the gossip, the theory—tired of reading quotes about himself, of hearing what people were saying about him all over town. It had been a tedious three weeks, he said, and now he just wanted to get away, go to Las Vegas, let off some steam. So he hopped in his jet, soared over the California hills across the Nevada flats, then over miles and miles of desert to the Sands and the Clay-Patterson fight.

On the eve of the fight he stayed up all night and slept through most of the afternoon, though his recorded voice could be heard singing in the lobby of the Sands, in the gambling casino, even in the toilets, being interrupted every few bars however by the paging public address: "Telephone call for Mr. Ron Fish, Mr. Ron Fish . . . with a ribbon of gold in her hair . . . Telephone call for Mr. Herbert Rothstein, Mr. Herbert Rothstein . . . memories of a time so bright, keep me sleepless through dark endless nights."

Standing around in the lobby of the Sands and other hotels up and down the strip on this afternoon before the fight were the usual prefight prophets: the gamblers, the old champs, the little cigar butts from Eighth Avenue, the sportswriters who knock the big fights all year but would never miss one, the novelists who seem always to be identifying with one boxer or another, the local prostitutes assisted by some talent in from Los Angeles, and also a young brunette in a wrinkled black cocktail dress who was at the bell captain's desk crying, "But I want to speak to Mr. Sinatra."

"He's not here," the bell captain said.

"Won't you put me through to his room?"

"There are no messages going through, Miss," he said, and then she turned, unsteadily, seeming close to tears, and walked through the lobby into the big noisy casino crowded with men interested only in money.

Shortly before seven P.M., Jack Entratter, a big gray-haired man who operates the Sands, walked into the gambling room to tell some men around the blackjack table that Sinatra was getting dressed. He also said that he'd been unable to get front-row seats for everybody, and so some of the men—including Leo Durocher, who had a date, and Joey Bishop, who was accompanied by his wife—would not be able to fit in Frank Sinatra's row but would have to take seats in the third row. When Entratter walked over to tell this to Joey Bishop, Bishop's face fell. He did not seem angry; he merely looked at Entratter with an empty silence, seeming somewhat stunned.

"Joey, I'm sorry," Entratter said when the silence persisted, "but we couldn't get more than six together in the front row."

Bishop still said nothing. But when they all appeared at the fight, Joey Bishop was in the front row, his wife in the third.

The fight, called a holy war between Muslims and Christians, was preceded by the introduction of three balding ex-champions, Rocky Marciano, Joe Louis, Sonny Liston—and then there was "The Star-Spangled Banner" sung by another man from out of the past, Eddie Fisher. It had been more than fourteen years ago, but Sinatra could still remember every detail: Eddie Fisher was then the new king of the baritones, with Billy Eckstine and Guy Mitchell right with him, and Sinatra had been long counted out. One day he remembered walking into a broadcasting studio past dozens of Eddie Fisher fans waiting outside the hall, and when they saw Sinatra they began to jeer, "Frankie, Frankie, I'm swooning, I'm swooning." This was also the time when he was selling only about thirty thousand records a year, when he was dreadfully miscast as a funny man on his television show, and when he recorded such disasters as "Mama Will Bark," with Dagmar.

"I growled and barked on the record," Sinatra said, still horrified by the thought. "The only good it did me was with the dogs."

His voice and his artistic judgment were incredibly bad in 1952, but even more responsible for his decline, say his friends, was his pursuit of Ava Gardner. She was the big movie queen then, one of the most beautiful women in the world. Sinatra's daughter Nancy recalls seeing Ava swimming one day in her father's pool, then climbing out of the water with that fabulous body, walking slowly to the fire, leaning over it for a few moments, and then it suddenly seemed that her long dark hair was all dry, miraculously and effortlessly back in place.

With most women Sinatra dates, his friends say, he never knows whether they want him for what he can do for them now—or will do for them later. With Ava Gardner, it was different. He could do nothing for her later. She was on top. If Sinatra learned anything from his experience with her, he possibly learned that when a proud man is down a woman cannot help. Particularly a woman on top.

Nevertheless, despite a tired voice, some deep emotion seeped into his singing during this time. One particular song that is well remembered even now is "I'm a Fool to Want You," and a friend who was in the studio when Sinatra recorded it recalled: "Frank was really worked up that night. He did the song in one take, then turned around and walked out of the studio and that was that . . ."

Sinatra's manager at that time, a former song plugger named Hank Sanicola, said, "Ava loved Frank, but not the way he loved her. He needs a great deal of love. He wants it twenty-four hours a day, he must have people around—Frank is that kind of guy." Ava Gardner, Sanicola said, "was very insecure. She feared she could not really hold a man . . . twice he went chasing her to Africa, wasting his own career . . ."

"Ava didn't want Frank's men hanging around all the time," another friend said, "and this got him mad. With Nancy he used to be able to bring the whole band home with him, and Nancy, the good Italian wife, would never complain—she'd just make everybody a plate of spaghetti."

In 1953, after almost two years of marriage, Sinatra and Ava Gardner were divorced. Sinatra's mother reportedly arranged a reconciliation, but if Ava was willing, Frank Sinatra was not. He was seen with other women. The balance had shifted. Somewhere during this period Sinatra seemed to change from the kid singer, the boy actor in the sailor suit, to a man. Even before he had won the Oscar in 1953 for his role in *From*

Here to Eternity, some flashes of his old talent were coming through—in his recording of "The Birth of the Blues," in his Riviera-nightclub appearance that jazz critics enthusiastically praised; and there was also a trend now toward LPs and away from the quick three-minute deal, and Sinatra's concert style would have capitalized on this with or without an Oscar.

In 1954, totally committed to his talent once more, Frank Sinatra was selected Metronome's "Singer of the Year," and later he won the UPI disc-jockey poll, unseating Eddie Fisher—who now, in Las Vegas, having sung "The Star-Spangled Banner," climbed out of the ring, and the fight began.

Floyd Patterson chased Clay around the ring in the first round, but was unable to reach him, and from then on he was Clay's toy, the bout ending in a technical knockout in the twelfth round. A half hour later, nearly everybody had forgotten about the fight and was back at the gambling tables or lining up to buy tickets for the Dean Martin-Sinatra-Bishop nightclub routine on the stage of the Sands. This routine, which includes Sammy Davis, Jr. when he is in town, consists of a few songs and much cutting up, all of it very informal, very special, and rather ethnic—Martin, a drink in hand, asking Bishop: "Did you ever see a Jew jitsu?"; and Bishop, playing a Jewish waiter, warning the two Italians to watch out "because I got my own group—the Matzia."

Then after the last show at the Sands, the Sinatra crowd, which now numbered about twenty—and included Jilly, who had flown in from New York; Jimmy Cannon, Sinatra's favorite sports columnist; Harold Gibbons, a Teamster official expected to take over if Hoffa goes to jail—all got into a line of cars and headed for another club. It was three o'clock. The night was young.

They stopped at the Sahara, taking a long table near the back, and listened to a baldheaded little comedian named Don Rickles, who is probably more caustic than any comic in the country. His humor is so rude, in such bad taste, that it offends no one—it is too offensive to be offensive. Spotting Eddie Fisher among the audience, Rickles proceeded to ridicule him as a lover, saying it was no wonder that he could not handle Elizabeth Taylor; and when two businessmen in the audience acknowledged that they were Egyptian, Rickles cut into them for their country's policy toward Israel; and he strongly suggested that the woman seated at one table with her husband was actually a hooker.

When the Sinatra crowd walked in, Don Rickles could not be more delighted. Pointing to Jilly, Rickles yelled: "How's it feel to be Frank's tractor? . . . Yeah, Jilly keeps walking in front of Frank clearing the way." Then, nodding to Durocher, Rickles said, "Stand up Leo, show Frank how you slide." Then he focused on Sinatra, not failing to mention Mia Farrow, nor that he was wearing a toupee, nor to say that Sinatra was washed up as a singer, and when Sinatra laughed, everybody laughed, and Rickles pointed toward Bishop: "Joey Bishop keeps checking with Frank to see what's funny."

Then, after Rickles told some Jewish jokes, Dean Martin stood up and yelled, "Hey, you're always talking about the Jews, never about the Italians," and Rickles cut him off with, "What do we need the Italians for—all they do is keep the flies off our fish."

Sinatra laughed, they all laughed, and Rickles went on this way for nearly an hour until Sinatra, standing up, said, "All right, com'on, get this thing over with. I gotta go."

"Shaddup and sit down!" Rickles snapped. "I've had to listen to you sing . . ."

"Who do you think you're talking to?" Sinatra yelled back.

"Dick Haymes," Rickles replied, and Sinatra laughed again, and then Dean Martin, pouring a bottle of whisky over his head, entirely drenching his tuxedo, pounded the table.

"Who would ever believe that staggering would make a star?" Rickles said, but Martin called out, "Hey, I wanna make a speech."

"Shaddup."

"No, Don, I wanna tell ya," Dean Martin persisted, "that I think you're a great performer."

"Well, thank you, Dean," Rickles said, seeming pleased.

"But don't go by me," Martin said, plopping down into his seat, "I'm drunk."

"I'll buy that," Rickles said.

By four A.M. Frank Sinatra led the group out of the Sahara, some of them carrying their glasses of whisky with them, sipping it along the sidewalk and in the cars; then, returning to the Sands, they walked into the gambling casino. It was still packed with people, the roulette wheels spinning, the crapshooters screaming in the far corner.

Frank Sinatra, holding a shot glass of bourbon in his left hand, walked through the crowd. He, unlike some of his friends, was perfectly pressed, his tuxedo tie precisely pointed, his shoes unsmudged. He never seems to lose his dignity, never lets his guard completely down no matter how much he has drunk, nor how long he has been up. He never sways when he walks, like Dean Martin, nor does he ever dance in the aisles or jump up on tables, like Sammy Davis.

A part of Sinatra, no matter where he is, is never there. There is always a part of him, though sometimes a small part, that remains Il Padrone. Even now, resting his shot glass on the blackjack table, facing the dealer, Sinatra stood a bit back from the table, not leaning against it. He reached under his tuxedo jacket into his trouser pocket and came up with a thick but clean wad of bills. Gently he peeled off a one-hundred-dollar bill and placed it on the green-felt table. The dealer dealt him two cards. Sinatra called for a third card, overbid, lost the hundred.

Without a change of expression, Sinatra put down a second hundred-dollar bill. He lost that. Then he put down a third, and lost that. Then he placed two one-hundred-dollar bills on the table and lost those. Finally, putting his sixth hundred-dollar bill on the table, and losing it, Sinatra moved away from the table, nodding to the man, and announcing, "Good dealer."

The crowd that had gathered around him now opened up to let him through. But a woman stepped in front of him, handing him a piece of paper to autograph. He signed it and then he said, "Thank you."

In the rear of the Sands' large dining room was a long table reserved for Sinatra. The dining room was fairly empty at this hour, with perhaps two dozen other people in the room, including a table of four unescorted young ladies sitting near Sinatra. On the other side of the room, at another long table, sat seven men shoulder-to-shoulder against the wall, two of them wearing dark glasses, all of them eating quietly, speaking hardly a word, just sitting and eating and missing nothing.

The Sinatra party, after getting settled and having a few more drinks, ordered something to eat. The table was about the same size as the one reserved for Sinatra whenever he is at Jilly's in New York; and the people seated around this table in Las Vegas were many of the same people who are often seen with Sinatra at Jilly's or at a restaurant in California, or in Italy, or in New Jersey, or wherever Sinatra happens to be. When Sinatra sits to dine, his trusted friends are close; and no matter where he is, no matter how elegant the place may be, there is something of the neighborhood showing because Sinatra, no matter how far he has come, is still something of the boy from the neighborhood—only now he can take his neighborhood with him.

In some ways, this quasi-family affair at a reserved table in a public place is the closest thing Sinatra now has to home life. Perhaps, having had a home and left it, this approximation is as close as he cares to come; although this does not seem precisely so because he speaks with such warmth about his family, keeps in close touch with his first wife, and insists that she make no decision without first consulting him. He is always eager to place his furniture or other mementos of himself in her home or his daughter Nancy's, and he also is on amiable terms with Ava Gardner. When he was in Italy making *Von Ryan's Express*, they spent some time together, being pursued wherever they went by the paparazzi. It was reported then that the paparazzi had made Sinatra a collective offer of $16,000 if he would pose with Ava Gardner; Sinatra was said to have made a counter offer of $32,000 if he could break one paparazzi arm and leg.

While Sinatra is often delighted that he can be in his home completely without people, enabling him to read and think without interruption, there are occasions when he finds himself alone at night, and not by choice. He may have dialed a half-dozen women, and for one reason or another they are all unavailable. So he will call his valet, George Jacobs.

"I'll be coming home for dinner tonight, George."

"How many will there be?"

"Just myself," Sinatra will say. "I want something light, I'm not very hungry."

George Jacobs is a twice-divorced man of thirty-six who resembles Billy Eckstine. He has traveled all over the world with Sinatra and is devoted to him. Jacobs lives in a comfortable bachelor's apartment off Sunset Boulevard around the corner from Whisky a Go Go, and he is known around town for the assortment of frisky California girls he has as friends—a few of whom, he concedes, were possibly drawn to him initially because of his closeness to Frank Sinatra.

When Sinatra arrives, Jacobs will serve him dinner in the dining room. Then Sinatra will tell Jacobs that he is free to go home. If Sinatra, on such evenings, should ask Jacobs to stay longer, or to play a few hands of poker, he would be happy to do so. But Sinatra never does.

This was his second night in Las Vegas, and Frank Sinatra sat with friends in the Sands' dining room until nearly eight A.M. He slept through much of the day, then flew back to Los Angeles, and on the following morning he was driving his little golf cart through the Paramount Pictures movie lot. He was scheduled to complete two final scenes with the sultry blonde actress, Virna Lisi, in the film *Assault on a Queen.* As he maneuvered the little vehicle up the road between the big studio buildings, he spotted Steve Rossi who, with his comedy partner, Marty Allen, was making a film in an adjoining studio with Nancy Sinatra.

"Hey, Dag," he yelled to Rossi, "stop kissing Nancy."

"It's part of the film, Frank," Rossi said, turning as he walked.

"In the garage?"

"It's my Dago blood, Frank."

"Well, cool it," Sinatra said, winking, then cutting his golf cart around a corner and parking it outside a big drab building within which the scenes for *Assault* would be filmed.

"Where's the fat director?" Sinatra called out, striding into the studio that was crowded with dozens of technical assistants and actors all gathered around cameras. The director, Jack Donohue, a large man who has worked with Sinatra through twenty-two years on one production or other, has had headaches with this film. The script had been chopped, the actors seemed restless, and Sinatra had become bored. But now there were only two scenes left—a short one to be filmed in the pool, and a longer and passionate one featuring Sinatra and Virna Lisi to be shot on a simulated beach.

The pool scene, which dramatizes a situation where Sinatra and his hijackers fail in their attempt to sack the *Queen Mary*, went quickly and well. After Sinatra had been kept in the water shoulder-high for a few minutes, he said, "Let's move it, fellows—it's cold in this water, and I've just gotten over one cold."

So the camera crews moved in closer, Virna Lisi splashed next to Sinatra in the water, and Jack Donohue yelled to his assistants operating the fans, "Get the waves going," and another man gave the command, "Agitate!" and Sinatra broke out in song. "Agitate in rhythm," then quieted down just before the cameras started to roll.

Frank Sinatra was on the beach in the next situation, supposedly gazing up at the stars, and Virna Lisi was to approach him, toss one of her shoes near him to announce her presence, then sit near him and prepare for a passionate session. Just before beginning, Miss Lisi made a practice toss of her shoe toward the prone figure of Sinatra sprawled on the beach. As she tossed her shoe, Sinatra called out, "Hit me in my bird and I'm going home."

Virna Lisi, who understands little English and certainly none of Sinatra's special vocabulary, looked confused, but everybody behind the camera laughed. She threw the shoe toward him. It twirled in the air, landed on his stomach.

"Well, that's about three inches too high," he announced. She again was puzzled by the laughter behind the camera.

Then Jack Donohue had them rehearse their lines, and Sinatra, still very charged from the Las Vegas trip, and anxious to get the cameras rolling, said, "Let's try one." Donohue, not certain that Sinatra and Lisi knew their lines well enough, nevertheless said okay, and an assistant with a clapboard called, "419, Take 1," and Virna Lisi approached with the shoe, tossed it at Frank lying on the beach. It fell short of his thigh, and Sinatra's right eye raised almost imperceptibly, but the crew got the message, smiled.

"What do the stars tell you tonight?" Miss Lisi said, delivering her first line, and sitting next to Sinatra on the beach.

"The stars tell me tonight I'm an idiot," Sinatra said, "a gold-plated idiot to get mixed up in this thing . . ."

"Cut," Donohue said. There were some microphone shadows on the sand, and Virna Lisi was not sitting in the proper place near Sinatra.

"419, Take 2," the clapboard man called.

Miss Lisi again approached, threw the shoe at him, this time falling short—Sinatra exhaling only slightly—and she said, "What do the stars tell you tonight?"

"The stars tell me I'm an idiot, a gold-plated idiot to get mixed up in this thing . . ." Then, according to the script, Sinatra was to continue, "Do you know what we're getting into? The minute we step on the deck of the *Queen Mary*, we've just tattooed ourselves," but Sinatra, who often improvises on lines, recited them: "Do you know what we're getting into? The minute we step on the deck of that mother's-ass ship . . ."

"No, no," Donohue interrupted, shaking his head, "I don't think that's right."

The cameras stopped, some people laughed, and Sinatra looked up from his position in the sand as if he had been unfairly interrupted.

"I don't see why that can't work . . ." he began, but Richard Conte, standing behind the camera, yelled, "It won't play in London."

Donohue pushed his hand through his thinning gray hair and said, but not really in anger, "You know, that scene was pretty good until somebody blew the line . . ."

"Yeah," agreed the cameraman, Billy Daniels, his head popping out from around the camera, "it was a pretty good piece . . ."

"Watch your language," Sinatra cut in. Then Sinatra, who has a genius for figuring out ways of not reshooting scenes, suggested a way in which the film could be used and the "mother" line could be recorded later. This met with approval. Then the cameras were rolling again, Virna Lisi was leaning toward Sinatra in the sand, and then he pulled her down close to him. The camera now moved in for a close-up of their faces, ticking away for a few long seconds, but Sinatra and Lisi did not stop kissing, they just lay together in the sand wrapped in one another's arms, and then Virna Lisi's left leg just slightly began to rise a bit, and everybody in the studio now watched in silence, not saying anything until Donohue finally called out:

"If you ever get through, let me know. I'm running out of film."

Then Miss Lisi got up, straightened out her white dress, brushed back her blonde hair and touched her lipstick, which was smeared. Sinatra got up, a little smile on his lips, and headed for his dressing room.

Passing an older man who stood near a camera, Sinatra asked, "How's your Bell & Howell?"

The older man smiled.

"It's fine, Frank."

"Good."

In his dressing room Sinatra was met by an automobile designer who had the plans for Sinatra's new custom-built model to replace the $25,000 Ghia he has been driving for the last few years. He also was awaited by his secretary, Tom Conroy, who had a bag full of fan mail, including a letter from New York's mayor John Lindsay; and by Bill Miller, Sinatra's pianist, who would rehearse some of the songs that would be recorded later in the evening for Sinatra's newest album, *Moonlight Sinatra*.

While Sinatra does not mind hamming it up a bit on a movie set, he is extremely serious about his recording sessions; as he explained to a British writer, Robin Douglas-Home: "Once you're on that record singing, it's you and you alone. If it's bad and gets you criticized, it's you who's to blame—no one else. If it's good, it's also you. With a film it's never like that; there are producers and scriptwriters, and hundreds of men in offices and the thing is taken right out of your hands. With a record, you're it . . ."

> But now the days are short
> I'm in the autumn of the year
> And now I think of my life
> As vintage wine
> From fine old kegs

It no longer matters what song he is singing, or who wrote the words—they are all his words, his sentiments, they are chapters from the lyrical novel of his life.

> Life is a beautiful thing
> As long as I hold the string

When Frank Sinatra drives to the studio, he seems to dance out of the car across the sidewalk into the front door; then, snapping his fingers, he is standing in front of the orchestra in an intimate, airtight room, and soon he is dominating every man, every instrument, every sound wave. Some of the musicians have accompanied him for twenty-five years, have gotten old hearing him sing "You Make Me Feel So Young."

When his voice is on, as it was tonight, Sinatra is in ecstasy, the room becomes electric, there is an excitement that spreads through the orchestra and is felt in the control booth where a dozen men, Sinatra's friends, wave at him from behind the glass. One of the men is the Dodgers' pitcher, Don Drysdale ("Hey, Big D," Sinatra calls out, "hey, baby!"); another is the professional golfer Bo Wininger; there are also numbers of pretty women standing in the booth behind the engineers, women who smile at Sinatra and softly move their bodies to the mellow mood of his music:

> Will this be moon love
> Nothing but moon love
> Will you be gone when the dawn
> Comes stealing through

After he is finished, the record is played back on tape, and Nancy Sinatra, who has just walked in, joins her father near the front of the orchestra to hear the playback. They listen silently, all eyes on them, the king, the princess; and when the music ends there is applause from the control booth, Nancy smiles, and her father snaps his fingers and says, kicking a foot, "Ooba-deeba-boobe-do!"

Then Sinatra calls to one of his men. "Hey, Sarge, think I can have a half a cup of coffee?"

Sarge Weiss, who had been listening to the music, slowly gets up.

"Didn't mean to wake ya, Sarge," Sinatra says, smiling.

Then Weiss brings the coffee, and Sinatra looks at it, smells it, then announces, "I thought he'd be nice to me, but it's really coffee . . ."

There are more smiles, and then the orchestra prepares for the next number. And one hour later, it is over.

The musicians put their instruments into their cases, grab their coats, and begin to file out, saying good-night to Sinatra. He knows them all by name, knows much about them personally, from their bachelor days, through their divorces, through their ups and downs, as they know him. When a French-horn player, a short Italian named Vincent DeRosa, who has played with Sinatra since the Lucky Strike "Hit Parade" days on radio, strolled by, Sinatra reached out to hold him for a second.

"Vicenzo," Sinatra said, "how's your little girl?"

"She's fine, Frank."

"Oh, she's not a little girl anymore," Sinatra corrected himself, "she's a big girl now."

"Yes, she goes to college now. USC."

"That's great."

"She's also got a little talent, I think, Frank, as a singer."

Sinatra was silent for a moment, then said, "Yes, but it's very good for her to get her education first, Vicenzo."

Vincent DeRosa nodded.

"Yes, Frank," he said, and then he said, "Well, good-night, Frank."

"Good-night, Vicenzo."

After the musicians had all gone, Sinatra left the recording room and joined his friends in the corridor. He was going to go out and do some drinking with Drysdale, Wininger, and a few other friends, but first he walked to the other end of the corridor to say good-night to Nancy, who was getting her coat and was planning to drive home in her own car.

After Sinatra had kissed her on the cheek, he hurried to join his friends at the door. But before Nancy could leave the studio, one of Sinatra's men, Al Silvani, a former prizefight manager, joined her.

"Are you ready to leave yet, Nancy?"

"Oh, thanks, Al," she said, "but I'll be all right."

"Pope's orders," Silvani said, holding his hands up, palms out.

Only after Nancy had pointed to two of her friends who would escort her home, and only after Silvani recognized them as friends, would he leave.

The rest of the month was bright and balmy. The record session had gone magnificently, the film was finished, the television shows were out of the way, and now Sinatra was in his Ghia driving out to his office to begin coordinating his latest projects. He had an engagement at the Sands, a new spy film called *The Naked Runner* to be shot in England, and a couple more albums to do in the immediate months ahead. And within a week he would be fifty years old . . .

> Life is a beautiful thing
> As long as I hold the string
> I'd be a silly so-and-so
> If I should ever let go

Frank Sinatra stopped his car. The light was red. Pedestrians passed quickly across his windshield but, as usual, one did not. It was a girl in her twenties. She remained at the curb staring at him. Through the corner of his left eye he could see her, and he knew, because it happens almost every day, that she was thinking, It looks like him, but is it?

Just before the light turned green, Sinatra turned toward her, looked directly into her eyes waiting for the reaction he knew would come. It came and he smiled. She smiled and he was gone.

On Writing "Frank Sinatra Has a Cold"

As one who was identified in the 1960s with the popularization of a literary genre best known as the New Journalism—an innovation of uncertain origin that appeared prominently in *Esquire*, *Harper's*, the *New Yorker*, and other magazines, and was practiced by such writers as Norman Mailer and Lillian Ross, John McPhee, Tom Wolfe, and the late Truman Capote—I now find myself cheerlessly conceding that those impressive pieces of the past (exhaustively researched, creatively organized, distinct in style and attitude) are now increasingly rare, victimized in part by the reluctance of today's magazine editors to subsidize the escalating financial cost of such efforts, and diminished also by the inclination of so many younger magazine writers to save time and energy by conducting interviews with the use of that expedient but somewhat benumbing literary device, the tape recorder.

I myself have been interviewed by writers carrying recorders, and as I sit answering their questions, I see them half-listening, nodding pleasantly, and relaxing in the knowledge that the little wheels are rolling. But what they are getting from me (and I assume from other people they talk to) is not the insight that comes from deep probing and perceptive analysis and old-fashioned legwork; it is rather the first-draft drift of my mind, a once-over-lightly dialogue that—while perhaps symptomatic of a society permeated by fast-food computerized bottom-line impersonalized workmanship—too frequently reduces the once-artful craft of magazine writing to the level of talk radio on paper.

Far from decrying this trend, most editors tacitly approve it, because a taped interview that is faithfully transcribed can protect the periodical from those interviewees who might later claim that they had been damagingly misquoted—accusations that, in these times of impulsive litigation and soaring legal fees, cause much anxiety, and sometimes timidity, among even the most independent and courageous of editors.

Another reason editors are accepting of the tape recorder is that it enables them to obtain publishable articles from the influx of facile freelancers at pay rates below what would be expected and deserved by writers of more deliberation and commitment. With one or two interviews and a few hours of tape, a relatively inexperienced journalist today can produce a three-thousand-word article that relies heavily on direct quotation and (depending largely on the promotional value of the subject at the newsstand) will gain a writer's fee of anywhere from approximately $500 to slightly more than $2,000—which is fair payment, considering the time and skill involved, but it is less than what was being paid for articles of similar length and topicality when I began writing for some of these same magazines more than a quarter of a century ago.

In those days, however, the contemporary writers I admired usually devoted weeks and months to research and organization, writing and rewriting, before our articles were considered worthy of occupying the magazine space that today is filled by many of our successors in one tenth the time. And in the past, too, magazines seemed more liberal than now about research expenses.

During the winter of 1965 I recall being sent to Los Angeles by *Esquire* for an interview with Frank Sinatra, which the singer's publicist had arranged earlier with the magazine's editor. But after I had checked into the Beverly Wilshire, had reserved a rental car in the hotel garage, and had spent the evening of my arrival in a spacious room digesting a thick pack of background material on Sinatra, along with an equally thick steak accompanied by a fine bottle of California burgundy, I received a call from Sinatra's office saying that my scheduled interview the next afternoon would not take place.

Mr. Sinatra was very upset by the latest headlines in the press about his alleged Mafia connections, the caller explained, adding that Sinatra was also suffering from a head cold that threatened to postpone a recording date later in the week at a studio where I had hoped to observe the singer at work. Perhaps when Mr. Sinatra was feeling better, the caller went on, and perhaps if I would also submit my interview to the Sinatra office prior to its publication in *Esquire*, an interview could be rescheduled.

After commiserating about Sinatra's cold and the news items about the Mafia, I politely explained that I was obliged to honor my editor's right to being the first judge of my work; but I did ask if I might telephone the Sinatra office later in the week on the chance that his health and spirits might then be so improved that he would grant me a brief visit. I could call, Sinatra's representative said, but he could promise nothing.

For the rest of the week, after apprising Harold Hayes, the *Esquire* editor, of the situation, I arranged to interview a few actors and musicians, studio executives and record producers, restaurant owners and female acquaintances who had known Sinatra in one way or another through the years. From most of these people I got something: a tiny nugget of information here, a bit of color there, small pieces for a large mosaic that I hoped would reflect the man who for decades had commanded a spotlight and had cast long shadows across the fickle industry of entertainment and the American consciousness.

As I proceeded with my interviews—taking people out each day to lunch and dinner while amassing expenses that, including my hotel room and car, exceeded $1,300 after the first week—I rarely, if ever, removed a pen and pad from my pocket, and I certainly would not have considered using a tape recorder had I owned one. To have done so would have possibly inhibited these individuals' candor, or would have otherwise altered the relaxed, trusting, and forthcoming atmosphere that I believe was encouraged by my seemingly less assiduous research manner and the promise that, however retentive I considered my memory to be, I would not identifiably attribute or quote anything told me without first checking back with the source for confirmation and clarification.

Quoting people verbatim, to be sure, has rarely blended well with my narrative style of writing or with my wish to observe and describe people actively engaged in ordinary but revealing situations rather than to confine them to a room and present them in the passive posture of a monologist. Since my earliest days in journalism, I was far less interested in the exact words that came out of people's mouths than in the essence of their meaning. More important than what people say is what they think, even though the latter may initially be difficult for them to articulate and may require much pondering and reworking within the interviewee's mind—which is what I gently try to prod and stimulate as I query, interrelate, and identify with my subjects as I personally accompany them whenever possible, be it on their errands, their appointments, their aimless peregrinations before dinner or after work. Wherever it is, I try physically to be there in my role as a curious confidant, a trustworthy fellow traveler searching into their interior, seeking to discover, clarify, and finally to describe in words (my words) what they personify and how they think.

There are times, however, when I do take notes. Occasionally there is a remark that one hears—a turn of phrase, a special word, a personal revelation conveyed in an inimitable style—that should be put on paper at once lest part of it be forgotten. That is when I may take out a notepad and say, "That's wonderful! Let me get that down just as you said it"; and the person, usually flattered, not only repeats it but expands up on it. On such occasions there can emerge a heightened spirit of cooperation, almost of collaboration, as the person interviewed recognizes that he has contributed something that the writer appreciates to the point of wanting to preserve it in print.

At other times I make notes unobserved by the interviewee—such as during those interruptions in our talks when the person has temporarily left the room, thus allowing me moments in which to jot down what I believe to be the relevant parts of our conversation. I also occasionally make notes immediately after the interview is completed, when things are still very fresh in mind. Then, later in the evening, before I go to bed, I sit at my typewriter and describe in detail (sometimes filling four or five pages, single-spaced) my recollections of what I had seen and heard that day—a chronicle to which I constantly add pages with each passing day of the entire period of research.

This chronicle is kept in an ever-expanding series of cardboard folders containing such data as the places where I and my sources had breakfast, lunch, and dinner (restaurant receipts enclosed to document my expenses); the exact time, length, locale, and subject matter of every interview; together with the agreed-upon conditions of each meeting (i.e., am I free to identify the source, or am I obliged to contact that individual later for clarification and/or clearance?). And the pages of the chronicle also include my personal impressions of the people I interviewed, their mannerisms and physical description, my assessment of their credibility, and much about my private feelings and concerns as I work my way through each day—an intimate addendum that now, after nearly thirty years of habit, is of use to a somewhat autobiographical book I am writing; but the original intent of such admissive writing was self-clarification, reaffirming my own voice on paper after hours of concentrated listening to others, and also, not infrequently, the venting of some of the frustration I felt when my research appeared to be going badly, as it certainly did in the winter of 1965 when I was unable to meet face to face with Frank Sinatra.

After trying without success to reschedule the Sinatra interview during my second week in Los Angeles (I was told that he still had a cold), I continued to meet with people who were variously employed in some of Sinatra's many business enterprises—his record company, his film company, his real estate operation, his missile parts firm, his airplane hangar—and I also saw people who were more personally associated with the singer, such as his overshadowed son, his favorite haberdasher in Beverly Hills, one of his bodyguards (an ex-pro lineman), and a little gray-haired lady who traveled with Sinatra around the country on concert tours, carrying in a satchel his sixty hairpieces.

From such people I collected an assortment of facts and comments, but what I gained at first from these interviews was no particular insight or eloquent summation of Sinatra's stature; it was rather the awareness that so many of these people, who lived and worked in so many separate places, were united in the knowledge that Frank Sinatra had a cold. When I would allude to this in conversation, citing it as the reason my interview with him was being postponed, they would nod and say yes, they were aware of his cold, and they also knew from their contacts within Sinatra's inner circle that he was a most difficult man to be around when his throat was sore and his nose was running. Some of the musicians and studio technicians were delayed from working in his recording studio because of the cold, while others among his personal staff of seventy-five were not only sensitive to the effects of his ailment but they revealed examples of how volatile and short-tempered he had been all week because he was unable to meet his singing standards. And one evening in my hotel, I wrote in the chronicle:

> It is a few nights before Sinatra's recording session, but his voice is weak, sore and uncertain. Sinatra is ill. He is a victim of an ailment so common that most people would consider it trivial. But when it

gets to Sinatra it can plunge him into a state of anguish, deep depression, panic, even rage. Frank Sinatra has a cold.

Sinatra with a cold is Picasso without paint, Ferrari without fuel—only worse. For the common cold robs Sinatra of that uninsurable jewel, his voice, cutting into the core of his confidence, and it affects not only his own psyche but also seems to cause a kind of psychosomatic nasal drip within dozens of people who work for him, drink with him, love him, depend on him for their own welfare and stability.

A Sinatra with a cold can, in a small way, send vibrations through the entertainment industry and beyond as surely as a President of the United States, suddenly sick, can shake the national economy.

The next morning I received a call from Frank Sinatra's public relations director.

"I hear you're all over town seeing Frank's friends, taking Frank's friends to dinner," he began, almost accusingly.

"I'm working," I said. "How's Frank's cold?" (We were suddenly on a familiar basis.)

"Much better, but he still won't talk to you. But you can come with me tomorrow afternoon to a television taping if you'd like. Frank's going to try to tape part of his NBC special . . . Be outside your hotel at three. I'll pick you up."

I suspected that Sinatra's publicist wanted to keep a closer eye on me, but I was nonetheless pleased to be invited to the taping of the first segment of the one-hour special that NBC-TV was scheduled to air in two weeks, entitled *Sinatra—A Man and His Music*.

On the following afternoon, promptly and politely, I was picked up in a Mercedes convertible driven by Sinatra's dapper publicist, a square-jawed man with reddish hair and a deep tan who wore a three-piece gabardine suit that I favorably commented upon soon after getting in the car—prompting him to acknowledge, with a certain satisfaction, that he had obtained it at a special price from Frank's favorite haberdasher. As we drove, our conversation remained amiably centered around such subjects as clothes, sports, and the weather until we arrived at the NBC building and pulled into a white concrete parking lot in which there were about thirty other Mercedes convertibles as well as a number of limousines in which were slumped black-capped drivers trying to sleep.

Entering the building, I followed the publicist through a corridor into an enormous studio dominated by a white stage and white walls and dozens of lamps and lights dangling everywhere I looked. The place resembled a gigantic operating room. Gathered in one corner of the room behind the stage, awaiting the appearance of Sinatra, were about one hundred people—camera crews, technical advisers, Budweiser admen, attractive young women, Sinatra's bodyguards and hangers-on, and also the director of the show, a sandy-haired, cordial man named Dwight Hemion, whom I had known from New York because we had daughters who were preschool playmates. As I stood chatting with Hemion, and overhearing conversations all around me, and listening to the forty-three musicians, sitting in tuxedos on the bandstand, warming up their instruments, my mind was racing with ideas and impressions; and I would have liked to have taken out my notepad for a second or two. But I knew better.

And yet after two hours in the studio—during which time Sinatra's publicist never left my side, even when I went to the bathroom—I was able to recall later that night precise details about what I had seen and heard at the taping; and in my hotel I wrote in the chronicle:

Franks finally arrived on stage, wearing a high-necked yellow pullover, and even from my distant vantage point his face looked pale, his eyes seemed watery. He cleared his throat a few times. Then the musicians, who had been sitting stiffly and silently in their seats ever since Frank had joined them on the platform, began to play the opening song, "Don't Worry About Me." Then Frank sang through the whole song—a rehearsal prior to taping—and his voice sounded fine to me, and it apparently sounded fine to him, too, because after the rehearsal he suddenly wanted to get it on tape.

He looked up toward the director, Dwight Hemion, who sat in the glass-enclosed control booth overlooking the stage, and he yelled: "Why don't we tape this mother?"

Some people laughed in the background, and Frank stood there tapping a foot, waiting for some response from Hemion.

"Why don't we tape this mother?" Sinatra repeated, louder, but Hemion just sat up there with his headset around his ears, flanked by other men also wearing headsets, staring down at a table of knobs or something. Frank stood fidgeting on the white stage, glaring up at the booth, and finally the production stage manager— a man who stood to the left of Sinatra, and also wore a headset— repeated Frank's words exactly into his line to the control room: "Why don't we tape this mother?"

Maybe Hemion's switch was off up there, I don't know, and it was hard to see Hemion's face because of the obscuring reflections the lights made against the glass booth. But by this time Sinatra is clutching and stretching his yellow pullover out of shape and screaming up at Hemion: "Why don't we put on a coat and tie, and tape this . . ."

"Okay, Frank," Hemion cut in calmly, having apparently not been plugged into Sinatra's tantrum, "would you mind going back over . . ."

"Yes I *would* mind going back!" Sinatra snapped. "When we stop doing things around here the way we did them in 1959 maybe we . . ."

. . . Although Dwight Hemion later managed to calm Sinatra down, and in time to successfully tape the first song and a few others, Sinatra's voice became increasingly raspy as the show progressed—and on two occasions it cracked completely, causing Sinatra such anguish that in a fitful moment he decided to scrub the whole day's session. "Forget it, just forget it!" he told Hemion. "You're wasting your time. What you got there," he continued, nodding to the singing image of himself on the TV monitor, "is a man with a cold."

There was hardly a sound heard in the studio for a moment or two, except for the clacking heels of Sinatra as he left the stage and disappeared. Then the musicians put aside their instruments, and everybody else slowly turned toward the exit . . . In the car, coming back to the hotel, Frank's publicist said they'd try to retape the show within the week, he'd let me know when. He also said that in a few weeks he was going to Las Vegas for the Patterson-Clay heavyweight fight (Frank & friends would be there to watch it), and if I wanted to go he'd book me a room at the Sands and we could fly together. Sure, I said . . . but to myself I'm thinking: how long will *Esquire* continue to pay my expenses? By the end of the week, I'll

have spent more than $3,000, have not yet talked to Sinatra, and, at
the rate we're going, it's possible I never will . . .

Before going to bed that night, I telephoned Harold Hayes in New
York, briefed him on all that was happening and not happening, and
expressed concern about the expenses.

"Don't worry about the expenses as long as you're getting something
out there," he said. "Are you getting something?"

"I'm getting something," I said, "but I don't exactly know what
it is."

"Then stay there until you find out."

I stayed another three weeks, ran up expenses close to $5,000,
returned to New York, and then took another six weeks to organize and
write a fifty-five-page article that was largely drawn from a two-hundred-
page chronicle that represented interviews with more than one hundred
people and described Sinatra in such places as a bar in Beverly Hills
(where he got into a fight), a casino in Las Vegas (where he lost a small
fortune at blackjack), and the NBC studio in Burbank (where, after
recovering from the cold, he retaped the show and sang beautifully).

The *Esquire* editors titled the piece "Frank Sinatra Has a Cold," and
it appeared in the April 1966 issue. It remains in print today in a Dell
paperback collection of mine called *Fame and Obscurity*. While I was
never given the opportunity to sit down and speak alone with Frank
Sinatra, this fact is perhaps one of the strengths of the article. What
could he or *would* he have said (being among the most guarded of public
figures) that would have revealed him better than an observing writer
watching him in action, seeing him in stressful situations, listening and
lingering along the sidelines of his life?

This method of lingering and careful listening and describing scenes
that offer insight into the individual's character and personality—a
method that a generation ago came to be called the New Journalism—
was, at its best, really fortified by the "Old Journalism's" principles of
tireless legwork and fidelity to factual accuracy. As time-consuming and
financially costly as it was, it was this research that marked my Sinatra
piece and dozens of other magazine articles that I published during the
1960s—and there were other writers during this period who were doing
even more research than I was, particularly at the *New Yorker*, one of
the few publications that could afford, and today still chooses to afford,

the high cost of sending writers out on the road and allowing them whatever time it takes to write with depth and understanding about people and places. Among the writers of my generation at the *New Yorker* who personify this dedication to roadwork are Calvin Trillin and the aforementioned John McPhee; and the most recent example of it at *Esquire* was the piece about the former baseball star Ted Williams, written by Richard Ben Cramer, an old-fashioned legman of thirty-six whose keen capacity to *listen* has obviously not been dulled or otherwise corrupted by the plastic ear of a tape recorder.

But such examples in magazines are, as I mentioned earlier, becoming more and more rare in the 1980s, especially among freelancers. The best of the nonfiction writers today—those unaffiliated with such unsolvent institutions as the *New Yorker*—are either having their research expenditures underwritten by the book industry (and are excerpting parts of their books in magazines), or they are bestselling writers who can afford to do a well-researched magazine piece if they fancy the subject, or they are writers whose financial support comes mainly from faculty salaries and foundation grants. And what this latter group of writers are publishing today, mainly in modestly remunerative literary periodicals, are pieces that tell us more about themselves than about other people. They are opinioned pieces of intellectual or cultural content, or articles that are decidedly reflective and personal, and not dependent on costly time and travel. They are works researched out of a writer's own recollections. They are close to a writer's heart and place of dwelling. The road has become too expensive. The writer is home.

The Homeless Woman with
Two Homes

She was a petite and attractive woman in her early forties, with delicate bones, blue eyes, and short curly blonde hair; and although it was the coldest autumn afternoon in New York so far, she wore a light cotton frock and sandals, and her face retained the glow of a deep summer tan. I stood waiting next to her on a crowded corner at Lexington Avenue and Fifty-ninth Street, dividing my attention between her fine features and the fact that she was carrying over her shoulders two bulky bags, one plastic and one cloth, containing blankets and other items associated with people who sleep and beg in the streets.

The light changed. I crossed the street and continued on my way uptown. Bag ladies with appealing faces are not uncommon sights in New York. I have seen one such woman, an angular brunette in her late twenties, who, with the aid of a hairstylist and a change of wardrobe, could have blended in with those advertising scenarios by Ralph Lauren. I have seen many men, too, whose polite manner of solicitation and unshabby appearance have led me to wonder why they are where they are—panhandling in subways, curled up at night near subway gratings or within the doorways of boutiques and department stores.

By focusing on the outward appearance of such people, I do not mean to divert attention from their genuine plight, or to establish any distinction between them and the other unfortunate men and women who dwell, perhaps more convincingly, in the shadows of street life. On the contrary, I am suggesting that urban destitution and despair are now spreading to the degree that identifying their victims visually is often impossible. Increasingly, the victims in our streets are looking like the rest of us.

Still, a formidable language barrier separates us—along with some skepticism on our part as to who are the truly needy, and who are merely masqueraders pandering to our sympathies. And what of the small blonde woman with whom I had stood moments before at the corner of Fifty-ninth Street and Lexington Avenue?

Now on Sixty-second Street, I turned around. I spotted her in the crowd a half-block behind me. I had never approached a destitute person so directly, but at this moment I did not hesitate.

"Can I help you?" I asked, prompting her to stop and look up. Her inquiring blue eyes examined me, but whatever conclusion she came to she kept to herself.

"Are you a homeless person?" I continued, hoping this awkward question conveyed more compassion than curiosity.

She shifted the weight of the bags on her shoulders and waited for the noisy bus to pass the curb toward its stop near the southwest corner.

"Yes," she said in a cultivated voice barely audible above the street sounds.

"How long have you been homeless?"

"Five months, or more," she said.

"And where do you sleep and eat?"

"There's a women's shelter downtown, but I usually sleep in the park or the streets."

"Aren't you worried about the danger?"

She did not reply.

"Don't you have any family or friends?"

"Yes," she said, after a pause. Then after a longer pause, she added, "I also have three children."

There was another bus now, and the commotion of pedestrians passing between us and around us, for we were blocking the narrow side-walk that extended from the Korean market to the yellow-leafed tree rising out of a patch of curbside dirt littered with candy wrappings and bottle caps.

"How old are your children?"

"Eleven, ten, and eight."

"Who takes care of them?"

"My mother," she said. "And also my husband. He has a back

problem from his job and is home a lot." She explained that her husband, a mechanic on oil trucks who usually earns more than $50,000 a year, and her mother (employed as an accountant in Manhattan) share the domestic chores within a "high-rancher" house in Queens. The homeless woman said that she and her husband bought the Queens residence for $85,000 when they married twelve years ago, but that it is worth an estimated four times that now. She and her husband also own a weekend house in the Pocono Mountains with six acres and a pond.

I stood listening without changing my expression. My experience as a young New York reporter decades ago prepared me to be astonished by virtually nothing. This woman before me was articulate and convincing. In her manner and appearance there was no hint of drug or alcohol abuse (she said she used neither); nor did her healthy, smooth complexion, bronzed from the months outdoors, suggest that she was a battered wife. "We argued in the last few years" was all that she would concede about her husband, and when I asked why she had left him, her response was, "I left because I didn't want to live that life anymore."

"Is what you have any better?" I interrupted. She did not reply.

"Look," I said, "I can give you money, but that's not going to help. How about a job? Did you ever hold a job?"

"Yes," she said. "I worked as a hairdresser. In Queens, until the second child was born, I even had my own salon."

"I know people in that business," I said. "If I get appointments, will you show up?"

"Yes."

I guided her toward a nearby telephone booth, but both phones were out of order. It was after five P.M. I was eager to reach my acquaintances before they left for the day. Taking a piece of paper out of my pocket and also some change, I jotted down my home number and told her to contact me from another booth within the hour, by which time I hoped to have arranged for the interviews. Before I left her on Lexington Avenue, I also asked for, and received without delay, the phone number of the home in Queens where she had lived as a wife and mother.

The managers of both Manhattan salons I called agreed to see her the following morning, and both were disposed to hiring her on trial. As I waited at home for the woman's call, I typed letters of introduction for her to give to them, together with their business locations. These

I intended to place in her hands after she called to tell me where to meet her. But she did not call that night. Nor the next day.

Two days later, a Sunday afternoon, I telephoned the number in Queens. After a male voice identified himself as her husband, I told him how I had met her, and of the appointments awaiting her.

"She'll never keep those appointments," the husband assured me. "She doesn't want to work. She doesn't want to stay home with the children. All she wants is to be free and wander around."

"I'm dropping these letters off at your place today," I said, not seeking his permission. His wife had given me the address of the house.

What she had not given me was any insight into why she had left it.

. . .

It was a two-story building on a quiet tree-lined street in a residential neighborhood of tidy but fading lawns, and of new-model automobiles parked along curbs or driveways. The door was opened by a polite man in his late forties, who, after extending his hand, led me into a spacious living room and introduced me to his three children and the mother of his missing wife. The mother occupies the lower level of the house, which has a private entrance, kitchen, living room, bedroom, and bath; the children—two of whom wore braces that their father seemed proud to say he could afford—share the upper portion of the residence, which has three bedrooms, a large kitchen, and a living room and dining area in the rear. On the condition that the family name would not be published— the children claim their schoolmates do not know that their mother has left home—the husband and mother agreed to talk with candor.

"She called us from a phone booth," volunteered the eleven-year-old, "and we all cried and told her we wanted her to come home. She said she could come someday, but . . ."

"She disappeared a few times last year," the husband said, "but just for a few days at a time then. I asked her if she wanted a divorce, and she said no. We took her to psychiatrists, but they said there's nothing really wrong with her. They gave her some pills, which she took for a while, then stopped."

"Did you force her to stop working as a hairdresser?" I asked.

"At first, after the second baby, I said I wanted her home. But later I said for her to go back to work. We have enough money for someone to come in and help out. But the kids are almost old enough now and don't even need it."

The husband doubted that another man was a factor in her absence, adding that her choosing to live in the streets seemed to confirm this.

He would take her back, he said, but since he has little faith in her capacity to reconcile herself with him permanently, he has recently begun proceeding toward a divorce.

Her mother, whose blue eyes and features the missing woman carries with her, spoke sadly about the situation, but she seemed reluctant to unburden herself in the presence of the children and their father. A day later, however, at a table in the cafeteria of the building where she works, she was both forthcoming and tearful as she related her own biographical background and the formative years of her only child.

The mother is now sixty-two. She was born in 1926 in the German town of Delmenhorst, on the Weser River near Bremen. Her father, a factory worker, returned home injured from the Battle of Verdun of 1916, and the harsh penalties imposed upon the German nation for its part in the war seemed to linger in the grimness and penury of her girlhood surroundings from the thirties through the aftermath of the second German defeat, in World War II. Allied bombers hit the Bremen area, and although her home was not hit, she associates that period of her life with rubble, grief, and bitterness. In the final year of the war, 1945, she was sent with other young women to work in the countryside as a farm laborer, replacing the men at the front. During this time, she met a young German soldier and fell in love. Neither ever believed that they would have the funds or opportunity to settle down in marriage, and by 1946, he had drifted out of her life. And she was pregnant.

Her infant girl, born in the spring of 1946, was raised in the home of the child's grandparents, whose scornful attitude toward their unmarried daughter's having a child out of wedlock improved to, at most, resignation in the years to come. They were even relieved when, in 1953, their husbandless daughter met and married a heavy-drinking American merchant seaman, who subsequently provided the money that brought his bride and her seven-year-old daughter to the United States.

Except for the funds, he provided little else. He was in and out of seaports, and drunk when he returned home to their apartment in the Bronx. His wife finally divorced him after nearly seven years of marriage.

By holding two jobs—as a cleaning lady at night, a bookkeeper during the day—she supported herself and her daughter, and she eventually left the Bronx for a garden apartment in Astoria. Her daughter attended school there, and at seventeen she registered at a Manhattan training school for beauticians. A year later she was working in a salon in Woodside, and four years later, when the owner retired, she became the proprietor, with a down payment of three thousand dollars.

Still living with her mother, the daughter bought a new car, hired extra help for the thriving salon, and on two occasions confided to her mother that she was in love. But both relationships ended unhappily. One of her lovers borrowed her car one night, left it parked outside a tavern in Yorkville, and was not heard from again. Her mother seemed to be even more distressed by this than she was, and, in 1977, thinking that she was doing her daughter a good turn, the mother answered an ad placed in the *Staats Zeitung* (a German-language daily) by a man who wished to meet a respectable young woman.

"My daughter has a broken heart," the mother told him on the telephone.

"I also have a broken heart," he replied.

Without telling her daughter, she invited the man to dinner, but much to her relief and delight, the couple appeared to like each other at once. Though a mechanic, the man had clean fingernails, and in addition to earning between one thousand dollars and fifteen hundred dollars a week with overtime, he owned a sizable apartment house in Bensonhurst that was filled with Italian tenants who paid their rent on time.

The daughter's marriage in 1978 was followed by the purchase of the eighty-five-thousand-dollar two-family home (for which the daughter contributed fifty thousand dollars from her savings from the salon). With the birth of the second child, she sold the salon, but until two years ago, when she first began to disappear for days at a time, she did not seem to be disenchanted by her duties as a homemaker and mother.

. . .

During my one and only talk with her, a fortnight ago, the homeless woman indicated that she spends much of her time in the area of the South Street Seaport. It later occurred to me that this might remind her of the river that ran close to her girlhood home in Germany, and that the rubble that she doubtless passes during her excursions through the deteriorating sections of New York might evoke memories of postwar Bremen. It might even be inferred that her wayward course, if that is what it is, is following the path of the wandering soldier who sired her. But such are merely musings.

The reality is that her children, her mother, and her husband—those most intimately connected with her life—appear to be unable to help her. If they cannot, what can we expect of our government? And what is expected of us?

Being a homeless woman with two homes certainly marks her as unique in New York; but how truly unique is she among New Yorkers impelled to withdraw from their inherited place, or wishing to escape institutionalism—be it the institution of marriage or the institutions that we look to for detecting symptoms and providing solutions?

These mysterious people live among us each day, sleep at our doors, walk shoulder-to-shoulder with us in the streets. Yet, regrettably, we do not know them, and too many New Yorkers, with the donation of a few quarters daily, are able to buy their way out of whatever momentary concern or discomfort is caused by the presence of the homeless.

The Kingdoms, the Powers, and the Glories of the *New York Times*

Most journalists are restless voyeurs who see the warts on the world, the imperfections in people and places. The sane scene that is much of life, the great portion of the planet unmarked by madness, does not lure them like riots and raids, crumbling countries and sinking ships, bankers banished to Rio and burning Buddhist nuns—gloom is their game, the spectacle their passion, normality their nemesis.

Journalists travel in packs with transferable tension and they can only guess to what extent their presence in large numbers ignites an incident, turns people on. For press conferences and cameras and microphones have become such an integral part of the happenings of the sixties that nobody today knows whether people make news or news makes people—Premier Ky in Vietnam, feeling no doubt more potent after his sixth magazine-cover story, challenges Red China; after police in New York raided the headquarters of young hoodlums, it was discovered that some gang leaders keep scrapbooks; in Baltimore, a day after the *Huntley-Brinkley Report* mentioned that the city had survived the summer without a race riot, there was a race riot.

When the press is absent, politicians have been known to cancel their speeches, civil-rights marchers to postpone their parades, alarmists to withhold their dire predictions. The troops at the Berlin Wall, largely ignored since Vietnam stole the headlines, coexist casually watching the girls go by. News, if unreported, has no impact; it might as well have not happened at all. Thus the journalist is the important ally of the ambitious, a lamplighter for stars. He is invited to parties, is courted and complimented, has easy access to unlisted telephone numbers and to many levels of life. He may send to America a provocative story of poverty in Africa, of tribal threats and turmoil—and then he may go for a swim in the Ambassador's pool.

A journalist will sometimes mistakenly assume that it is his charm, not his usefulness, that gains such privilege; but most journalists are realistic men not fooled by the game. They use as well as they are used. Still they are restless. Their work, instantly published, is almost instantly forgotten, and they must endlessly search for something new, must stay alive with bylines and not be scooped, must nurture the insatiable appetites of newspapers and networks, the commercial cravings for new faces, fashions, fads, feuds; they must not worry when news seems to be happening because they are there, nor must they ponder the possibility that everything they have witnessed and written in their lifetime may someday occupy only a few lines in the plastic textbooks of the twenty-first century.

And so each day, unhaunted by history, plugged into the *instant*, journalists of every creed, quality, and quirk, report the news of the world as they see it, hear it, believe it, understand it. Then much of it is relayed through America, millions of words a minute, some thousands of which penetrate a large fourteen-floor fact factory on Forty-third Street off Broadway, the New York Times Building, where each weekday afternoon at four o'clock—before it is fit to print, before it can influence the State Department and perplex the president and irritate David Merrick and get the ball rolling on Wall Street and heads rolling in the Congo—it is presented by *Times* editors seated around a conference table to one man, the managing editor, Clifton Daniel.

He is a most interesting-looking man but difficult to describe because the words that quickly catch him best, initially, seem entirely inappropriate for any man who is a man. But the impression persists. Clifton Daniel is almost lovely. It is his face, which is long and pale and soft and dominated by large dark eyes and very long lashes, and his exquisitely groomed, wavy gray hair that makes him seem almost lovely. His suits are very Savile Row, his hands and nails immaculate, his voice a soft, smooth blend of North Carolina, where he was born in a tiny tobacco town, and England, where he came of age as a journalist and squire of fashionable women and was sometimes referred to as the Sheik of Fleet Street.

London in those days, during and just after World War II, was a great city for young American journalists. There was the dramatic story of the blackout and the bombing raids, of the Allied counterattack and triumph. The Americans and British in London shared a warmth and common purpose; British society was democratic at every level, and the image of American correspondents, influenced to a degree by the presence of such eminent ones as Edward R. Murrow, was highly glamorous. If an American, particularly a well-tailored bachelor, also possessed, as did Clifton Daniel, a certain formality and reserve and understated charm—Tory manners that in Daniel's case were partly cultivated out of a small-town Southern boy's shyness—then London could be an even more responsive city; and for Daniel it was.

He was sought out by London hostesses, was often seen escorting distinguished women to the theatre and ballet, and he generally avoided the men's clubs for the drawing-room scene where, sometimes in the company of Bea Lillie and Noel Coward, Margot Fonteyn and Clarissa Spencer-Churchill, who later married Anthony Eden, he could listen to the latest gossip about politics and people as he had many years before when he worked behind the fountain of his father's drugstore in Zebulon.

Zebulon is a quiet little town built up along the sides of a road to Raleigh in the bright leaf-tobacco region of North Carolina, a town with three traffic lights, five policemen, three Protestant churches, and about eighteen hundred people who live mostly in white frame houses and know just about everything there is to know about one another. They are friendly people who do their shopping along the one main street, and many of them stop in at Daniel's drugstore on the corner to catch up on the latest, have a Coke, and say hello to Elbert Clifton Daniel, Sr., a pharmacist in his eighties whose facial features, particularly his eyes, strongly resemble his son's, although his gray wavy hair is shorter and his clothes far less conservative.

Mr. Daniel will sometimes appear at his drugstore wearing a pair of formal gray-striped morning trousers and over them a brown double-breasted jacket, and under it a blue striped shirt and pale polka-dot bow tie, and also a brown hat, black shoes, a brown cane; all of which, on him, looks fine. He is thought of as the town's most distinguished living landmark, being the first man in Zebulon to have a telephone, and nearly everyone is very fond of him, although there are a few, very few, who find him a bit patronizing at times. Twice he served as Mayor, first getting the city to put in running water, then to replace the kerosene streetlamps with electric lights. He had a brief fling at owning the Vakoo movie theatre, and he once merchandised his own brand of liver pills and a diarrhea cure. In the back of his drugstore he usually keeps a bottle of bourbon for the nourishment of his friends and himself.

The marriage of his son to Margaret Truman in 1956 permitted him to become acquainted with Harry Truman, and the two men have gotten along splendidly ever since, Mr. Truman once telling Mr. Daniel: "Hell, you did just as well as I did—you just stayed down in your little town helping the poor people, and I went up and mixed with those rich bastards."

Had it not been for an attack of appendicitis in 1902, when Mr. Daniel was about eighteen years old, he might have never escaped the rugged farm life of his father, his grandfather, and nearly all the other Daniel kin; but the illness enabled him to meet a young doctor from Raleigh who later encouraged him to go into the drug business. And in 1905, after borrowing some money from his grandfather, Zachariah G. Daniel, an illiterate but industrious tobacco farmer who had migrated from England, and after acquiring a drug "permit" from the doctor friend, Clifton Daniel, Sr. bought an interest in his first drugstore.

He practiced pharmacy on his permit until 1911 when he supplemented his training with schooling at Greensboro. In the same year, in his drugstore one day, he saw seated at the counter with other girls, sipping a soda, Miss Elvah Jones. She was the daughter of a tobacco warehouseman, had attended college at Raleigh, having once been the May Queen, and she was very pretty. He quickly courted her and in December of that year, at her grandmother's house in the next county, they were married, and during the following September was born their only child, the future managing editor of the *New York Times*, Elbert Clifton Daniel Jr.

The boy got all the attention and affection that an only child normally gets, and he did most of the right things. He had his first tooth at nine months, was walking within a year, but carefully, revealing a caution that would always be with him, and he displayed a premature aversion to dirt. There was nothing of the farmer in him. He was like his mother in his quiet manner, neat about his clothing, clean and precise. His father later worried a bit when he preferred to stay indoors much of the time, sprawled on the rug reading books, but the boy was very bright in school and obedient at home, and after school he helped out in the drugstore and also sold *Grit* magazine around town, saving his pennies, and there was really nothing the father could justifiably complain about the boy.

The drugstore in those days, much more than now, was a center of social life. The deputy sheriff and the police chief hung out there, as did the farmers talking about the price of tobacco and cotton, and the visiting politicians would drop in to shake hands. There was a piano in the front of the place and, when he was not grinding ice for drinks or delivering things on his bicycle, Tad Chavis, the Negro man, was usually playing ragtime on it, although he was sometimes competing with a loud and scratchy rendition of "In a Little Spanish Town" blaring from the Edison phonograph that stood not far from the piano. There was no radio in the drugstore then, and so young Clifton Daniel, Jr. would occasionally slip across the street to the rear of a feedstore to hear the radio news and baseball scores, and it was there, too, that he remembers hearing about Lindbergh's flight. He never stayed away too long, however, for the drugstore was busy, and one of his jobs was to help with the curb service, thereby getting to know many of the pretty girls who sat out at the tables, and then he would be back inside taking telephone calls for the doctors, or listening to the deputy sheriff's account of some local brawl, and one night Daniel saw walking into the drugstore a man whose throat was cut from ear to ear. Daniel called a doctor. He also called the *Zebulon Record*.

He had been sending news items into the paper all summer, earning five dollars a week; the drugstore, the great clearinghouse for local gossip and news, was a perfect post for a young reporter. When he returned to high school in the fall he continued to write news stories for the *Zebulon Record*, covering student activities and sports. He was never an athlete himself. Young Clifton Daniel had absolutely no ambitions to fulfill on the ball field, and he was becoming a little deaf in his left ear, and he also was on the frail side, although for a while he did some calisthenics in his bathroom at home. One morning, however, he leaned over too far and slipped and broke a front tooth against the bathtub. This ended his physical-culture program for a while, and he sought to satisfy his ego by describing the actions of others, by getting his stories published, seeing his name in the paper. Sometimes, when writing a story that was a collection of local news items, he would separate each item with a small design bearing his initials—ECD—and a few people in town thought this was a bit much.

There was something a little cute and fancy about young Daniel, they said, those few who perhaps were put off by his formality in this so informal town. They saw him developing, too early, a sense of self and a manner that seemed mildly patronizing. But the girls whom he dated liked him very much, liked not only his fine clothes and politeness but also his respect for older people, especially his parents, and they liked the fact that he was the brightest boy in the class and voted the "best looking" in the Wakelon High School yearbook of 1929.

But the girls sensed that they did not have a chance with him, not from anything he said or did but from what he did not say or do. He did not get involved. He had plans, places to visit, things to do. And his first step away from Zebulon was Chapel Hill, home of the University of North Carolina, although now the Depression had begun and nobody had much money. The *Zebulon Record* was offering a year's subscription for a fat hen or a bushel of potatoes. The bank cashier with whom E. C. Daniel Sr. had always dealt advised against sending the boy to college, urging instead that he be trained to someday take over the drug business. But Mr. Daniel, ignoring the advice, began trading drug supplies for corn and chickens, and Mrs. Daniel dressed the chickens and made chicken-salad sandwiches which were sold in the drugstore for ten cents apiece, money to put toward her son's room and board at college. He himself had saved sixty-five dollars from his summer earnings, and so in the fall of 1929 Elbert Clifton Daniel Jr. began his career as a college freshman.

In 1929 the *New York Times* was in the process of becoming, if it had not already become, the most important newspaper in the world. Its great publisher, Adolph Ochs, who in 1896 had purchased the *Times* and begun to revitalize it, was now ill, but his credo—"To give the news impartially, without fear or favor, regardless of any party, sect or interest involved"—was firmly rooted in his staff, and the news department was still under the direction of Ochs's brilliant managing editor, Carr Vattel Van Anda.

Van Anda was an austere and impersonal man, possessing a look that one of his reporters, Alva Johnston, described as a "death ray," and when a group of *Times*men petitioned Van Anda to put bylines on their stories he snapped, "The *Times* is not running a reporters' directory!"

Bylines were the exception on the *Times* then, going mainly to the few star journalists like Edwin L. James, a flamboyant Virginian who would himself become the *Times*' managing editor in the thirties (and be succeeded in turn by two other Southerners: Turner Catledge in 1951, Clifton Daniel in 1964).

But if Carr Van Anda was not a popular folk hero with his staff, as Edwin L. James would become, he was nonetheless respected as few editors would be; for he was not only a superb newsman but also a scholar, a mathematical genius and a student of science and logic. It was he who pushed the *Times* toward its expanded coverage of the great feats in polar exploration and aviation, forming the foundation for the paper's portrait of the space age. He was the first editor to publicize Einstein—and once, in checking over a story about one of Einstein's lectures, discovered that the scientist had made an error in an equation. Van Anda, who read hieroglyphics, printed many stories of significant excavations, and one night, after examining under a magnifying glass the inscription of a four-thousand-year-old Egyptian tomb, he discovered a forgery, and this fact, later confirmed by Egyptologists, led to the conclusion that a young Pharoah, Tut-ankh-Amen, had been assassinated by a military chief named Horemheb. It was Van Anda who disputed the new *Titanic*'s claim to being unsinkable and when the ship's radio went silent, after an emergency call for help, he deduced what had happened and drove his staff to get the story of the disaster that would be a world scoop. During World War I, Carr Van Anda, equipping himself with every available military map, charted the course of battle and he anticipated many future campaigns, getting his reporters there in advance, and the *Times*' coverage during that time was unparalleled.

By 1929, too, while Clifton Daniel attended classes on the North Carolina campus, rarely reading the *Times* and having no particular ambition to work for it, there were rising on the paper many young and talented and ambitious men with their own singular styles and ideas— some of which would find favor for years, and some of which, when Daniel would emerge thirty years later, would be in conflict with the *Times*, would in fact be the foundation for a quiet revolution within the paper, a revolution distinguished for its tactics and intrigue, and one of the few that the *Times* has failed to cover fully.

It is still going on today, though the dust now seems to be settling in the *Times*' third-floor newsroom, and two figures stand very tall and clear, both of them small-town Southern boys. Both are very different. Both are very smooth.

One is Turner Catledge, a smiling, charming, six-footer, born sixty-five years ago in Ackerman, Mississippi. His younger ally, Daniel, is now fifty-four. Catledge spent his best years getting the power; Daniel may spend his using it.

Catledge is a whisky-drinking, joke-telling, onetime political reporter in Washington who could have become a very successful politician. He rarely makes enemies, never makes deals he cannot get out of, never hits things head-on. He moves at oblique angles and shifts, but always with gentility and always guided by what he truly believes to be in the best interest of the *Times*. During Catledge's years as managing editor, from 1951 to 1964—he has since moved up to the newly created position of executive editor, where he is directly answerable only to the forty-year-old Publisher Arthur Ochs Sulzberger—the *New York Times* enjoyed its greatest glory and power; but at that time Catledge was engaged in an almost constant power struggle within the paper, a battle with many distinguished editors and reporters who, during those almost slipshod years after Van Anda left and Edwin James was managing editor, were able to take some power themselves.

It was not that Edwin L. (Jimmy) James, the dashing correspondent of World War I, the boulevardier and horseplayer, the favorite son of Adolph Ochs and Carr Van Anda, was a weak or naive man; it was rather that he was of journalism's old school, a freewheeling reporter who, as an administrator, became easily bored with much of the necessary trivia of the job. While James was managing editor, from 1932 until his death in 1951, the newspaper was becoming bigger, less manageable, expanding its coverage all over the nation and the world; and it was understandable, given James's nature, that other men of talent and ambition, men with their *own* ideas of what was best for the *Times*, would move in and stake claims. Thus the *Times*, in a sense, became splintered into little dukedoms, each duke having his loyal followers and his special territory to protect.

This was contrary to Catledge's concept; he was a believer in the political organization, a self-perpetuating and coordinated institution with unchallenged hard power at the top. The challenge facing Turner Catledge when he became managing editor then was what to do about the dukes.

Had he been on another publication the solution would have been simpler, but on the *Times* it is not easy to remove people, particularly people with some power, or people who might have secret alliances with the publisher or members of his family. *Times*men in key positions like to stay there, they fight to stay there, for employment on the *Times* is very prestigious—doors open elsewhere, favors are for the asking, important people are available, the world seems easier. Also, from the early days of Adolph Ochs, there had been a traditional delicacy toward faithful employees, and people with prestige on the staff were rarely humiliated. Many of the dukes, too, were valuable men who had made, and were still making, important contributions to the paper which, in addition, was a very successful enterprise, and many people saw no reason for change.

If Turner Catledge wished to carve his concept upon the paper, if he wished to stage a revolution and demote the dukes and attempt to bring the power back under the managing editor's office, he had better do it subtly. And he had better be lucky.

In 1929, however, Catledge was just starting out as a *Times* reporter, and Daniel was a college freshman, and many of those who would be affected by the future revolution—Arthur Krock and Lester Markel, James Reston and Drew Middleton, Theodore Bernstein and Harrison Salisbury and Thomas J. Hamilton and A. M. Rosenthal, and dozens more—were either not yet on the scene, or not yet making their move, or many years away from the challenge.

Most of what Clifton Daniel wanted out of college life, he got; and that which he did not get, he did not miss. He joined Phi Delta Theta fraternity, did well in class, wrote for *The Daily Tarheel*. He would have liked to become editor of the *Tarheel*, but not long after joining it he was fired for being, or for seeming to be, a bit cocky with a senior editor. And by the time he was reinstated to the *Tarheel* staff he was out of line for the editor's job.

He did become editor of the campus literary magazine, the *Carolina*, and was elected vice-president of the student body. He could have run for the presidency later but he declined because he had the notion—"somewhat presumptuous," he later conceded—that he was a newspaperman, and he believed that newsmen, in the interest of objectivity, should stay out of party politics and never become irretrievably committed to any one cause or person, a policy shared by nearly all journalists, although at a price. For this detachment from the world they observe robs them of a deeper experience that springs from involvement, and they sometimes become merely voyeurs who see much, feel little. They take death and disaster as casually as a dock strike, and they take for granted their right to publicize the weakness in others, to second-guess the Senate, to criticize other men's plays, but they rarely have to lay it on the line themselves. Of course if journalists become committed to a cause or a great figure they might become apologists or propagandists, flunkies for the famous. Clifton Daniel would know some journalists to whom this would happen, but it would never happen to him. He was always too sure of what he was, what he wanted, and was possibly assisted by a natural aloofness, perhaps even a lack of passion. If he ever made a compromise in his professional or private life, few people would know it, there would be no scandal, he would cover his tracks well.

After graduating from the University of North Carolina in 1933, and after a year on a small newspaper downstate, Clifton Daniel joined the Raleigh *News and Observer*. There between 1934 and 1937 he covered politics and crime, all sorts of assignments, and he met many interesting people, among them Katharine Cornell, the first famous actress he ever interviewed, and Thomas Wolfe, whose novel, *Look Homeward, Angel*, had been published only a few years before. Daniel also met Turner Catledge one day in Raleigh, but it was only a quick, casual meeting—remembered by Daniel, forgotten by Catledge—and the two would not meet again for a couple of years.

Catledge was then the bright young man on the *New York Times*. He was a member of the Washington bureau headed by Arthur Krock, the latter being a powerful duke with more autonomy on the *Times* staff than anyone except Lester Markel, the Sunday editor whose style would one day be likened to that of Louis XIV, The Sun King. Arthur Krock became the chief of the *Times*' Washington bureau in 1932, a propitious move at the time because Krock's predecessor, Richard V. Oulahan, had run a rather disorganized bureau in which reporters did as they pleased, and if three of them wished to cover the same assignment on a particular day, they did, and sometimes all three versions would be sent to New York and be printed.

Krock quickly converted the bureau into a coordinated team, *his* team, and the most ambitious member of the team was Turner Catledge. Catledge sometimes wrote four or six major stories a day, became an expert on tax law, developed new sources throughout Washington; and all this tremendous energy and ambition could have worked against him if he did not also possess a quality that would redeem him.

He had a wonderful way with men. Particularly older men. Particularly older men with power. This is a quality that perhaps cannot be learned but is inherent in certain rare young men who, partly because they are very bright and do not flaunt it, and partly because they are respectful and not privileged, confident but not *too* confident, attract the attention of older men, self-made men, and receive from these men much advice and help. The older men probably see something of themselves in these bright young men, something of what they were, or *think* they were at a similar age. And so they help the younger men up the ladder, feeling no threat because these younger men are also endowed with a fine sense of timing.

Turner Catledge had all this as no other young *Times*men would have it until the arrival in 1939 of James Reston, and it is not surprising that these two would become, in their mannered ways, rivals throughout the forties and fifties, and especially during the *Times'* showdown of the sixties.

One of the first important men to help Catledge was Herbert Hoover who, as Secretary of Commerce in 1927, was on a survey of the Mississippi River flood area; Catledge was there for the Memphis *Commercial Appeal*. Catledge had left his home state of Mississippi for Memphis in 1923, riding the rails with $2.07 in his pocket, and now four years later he had come into prominence as a newsman principally for his vivid reporting on the Mississippi flood. Hoover, an orphan who always admired initiative in young men, was so charmed by Catledge that he wrote a letter in his behalf to Adolph Ochs, publisher of the *New York Times*. It was not until 1929, however, after Hoover had been elected President, that the *Times* hired Catledge.

Arthur Krock also was much impressed with Catledge and by 1936, when Krock was fifty and Catledge thirty-five, Krock hinted that he did not intend to spend his whole life in Washington and that Catledge had the makings of an ideal successor as bureau chief. Catledge was very pleased but he still continued to call him "Mr. Krock," and was not encouraged to do otherwise, and this formality later stiffened a bit when Krock heard that President Roosevelt was also becoming enchanted with Turner Catledge. Krock disliked Roosevelt, and vice versa, due in part to

Krock's turning against the New Deal after 1936, and due also to an episode prior to Roosevelt's inauguration in March of 1933. Roosevelt suspected Krock of attempting to act as an intermediary between someone else and Roosevelt on some action Roosevelt was being pressed to take on becoming President. Roosevelt felt that the other person did not have to go through Krock but could have come directly to the President-elect, and Roosevelt blamed Krock for offering to act as a go-between in an effort to establish himself in an important role.

So after the Democratic National Convention of 1936, possibly as a way of embarrassing Arthur Krock, President Roosevelt told Catledge to feel free to check out stories or acquire information directly from the President; in short, Roosevelt was offering a line of communication that Catledge should use on his own without going through Krock.

Catledge immediately felt uncomfortable and he went to Krock and told him about it, and he also told a very close friend on the United Press, Lyle Wilson. Catledge wanted first to let Krock know that he was not available for such double-dealing and he wanted some intimate friend to know the story, too, and he was lucky that he did. For Krock got the episode mixed up, or at least Catledge felt that he did, and Krock let the word get around that Catledge had been intrigued by Roosevelt's proposition. Catledge, backed by Lyle Wilson, was able to counter Krock's suspicion and to reiterate that, far from being intrigued, he was actually offended by Roosevelt's move, even frightened.

Roosevelt's antipathy toward Krock was actually aimed at others on the *Times* as well, including Arthur Hays Sulzberger who, following the death in 1935 of his father-in-law, Adolph Ochs, assumed the position as publisher. Roosevelt thought he had an opportunity to benefit by a less independent *Times* at the time of the settlement of Mr. Ochs's estate tax. Roosevelt expected that the Ochs family would be forced to go into the money market or sell some of its stock in the *Times* in order to raise the necessary funds.

But when the family got the money by the sale of some of its preferred stock, not its common stock, Roosevelt became very distressed, and he admitted as much to some of his confidants in the Senate. Some editors on the newspaper felt then, and feel now, that Roosevelt's resentment of the *Times* was based on nothing more complicated than the fact that he could not control it. Few active Presidents actually believe in a free press—Truman did not, nor did Eisenhower nor Kennedy nor

Johnson; nor do most newspaper publishers, including those at the *Times*, whenever their own personal stakes are involved, a fact discovered by any writer who has ever attempted to do a publisher's biography.

Turner Catledge, at any rate, never became the Washington bureau chief of the *New York Times*. Krock, who in 1936 was saying that he did not intend to spend his whole life in Washington, was still there thirty years later. In 1938, in fact, a year in which he had condemned the Roosevelt administration for "official favors surreptitiously extended to syndicated columnists who are sympathetic," Krock strangely got an exclusive interview with Roosevelt, for which he received the Pulitzer Prize. Catledge at the same time felt his career had stalled—he was hitting his head "against the bottom of Arthur Krock's chair," he once described it to a friend—and in the winter of 1941, at the age of forty, Catledge quit the *New York Times*. He left for Chicago to become chief correspondent and later editor-in-chief of the *Chicago Sun*. But even before he left, Krock telephoned Sulzberger in New York and told the publisher to keep the door open—Catledge would probably be back.

By 1941, Clifton Daniel had left Raleigh and was working for the Associated Press. He had come up to New York in the Spring of 1937 but had been turned down by nearly all the dailies in New York except the *World-Telegram*, and he turned it down when the offer was only thirty-five dollars a week, ten dollars less than he had been making in Raleigh. His interview at the *Times* was short and he was not very disappointed about being rejected, later explaining: "I was conscious of the *New York Times*, although I did not read it religiously, and I recognized the dignity and importance of working for the *New York Times*, but I did not regard it as a place where I would particularly want to work."

The newsmen whose work he knew best in those days were either working on the afternoon papers or the *Herald-Tribune*—such writers as H. Allen Smith and Joseph Mitchell, the latter a 1929 graduate of the University of North Carolina who would become the great reporter on the *New Yorker* magazine. The *Times* had, as always, many fine reporters and almost no fine writers, one notable exception being Meyer Berger. But some on the *Times* were even not impressed with Berger, one being a night City editor who, shaking his head, once said to Berger, "Mike, you'll never make a newspaperman."

So when the Associated Press offered Clifton Daniel fifty dollars a week he quickly accepted, and for the next three years, from 1937 through 1940, he worked for the AP bureaus in New York and Washington; in November of 1940, at the age of twenty-eight, his dark wavy hair already turning gray, he sailed to Switzerland for the AP on a ship whose passengers included Lady Jersey, a stunning blue-eyed blonde who had been married to the Earl of Jersey, and before that to a Chicago lawyer and to Cary Grant. She would later, after the war, marry a Polish RAF pilot, but in London during the war—a year or so after meeting Daniel on the ship—she and Daniel would become sufficiently well acquainted to cause their friends to speculate the two would some day marry. But Daniel then, and for many years afterward, was not deeply serious about anything except his work, and he knew, too, that if he wished to distinguish himself on the Associated Press it would require a total commitment on his part because the AP had working for it many talented and ambitious young men. There was Drew Middleton and Gladwin Hill and William White, to name a few who would be hired away by the *New York Times*, and there was also James Reston, who by 1939 had already left the AP's London bureau for the *Times*, and had begun to rocket up through the *Times'* hierarchy more quickly, more smoothly than had any young man before him or since.

In addition to his energy and his very lucid style of writing, Reston had the rare quality that Catledge had, a wonderful way with older men. One of the first men to take an interest in him was the former Governor of Ohio, James M. Cox, who owned a string of newspapers and who, in 1920, had run as the Democratic candidate for President. Reston as a young teenager had caddied for Cox at the Dayton Country Club. Reston's family, very poor and pious (his mother wanted him to become a preacher, which as a columnist he later became), had immigrated from Scotland when he was eleven years old. Undistinguished as a student, he neglected books for the golf course, and soon he was shooting in the seventies and winning tournaments and he could have become a professional. But his mother was opposed—"Make something of yourself"— and James Cox advanced him money to help him through the University of Illinois; upon graduating in 1932, Reston went to work on one of Cox's newspapers.

He was hired away in 1933 by Larry MacPhail for a job as traveling secretary for the Cincinnati Reds baseball team, and in 1934 he was writing sports for the Associated Press. By 1937 he was in London with the AP bureau covering sports in summer and the Foreign Office in winter. He was then twenty-eight, was married to a very bright and lively girl who had already had their first son, and soon Reston had caught the eye of Ferdinand Kuhn, the *New York Times'* bureau chief in London. By 1939 Reston was with the *Times*.

His colleagues in the London bureau remember Scotty Reston as a man who seemed to be fast at everything except at a typewriter. There, surrounded by his notes and several open books out of which he picked tidbits of sagacity, he slowly composed his thoughts and arranged his words as few newsmen ever take the time to do. Outside the office he was neither the life of the party nor a playboy: it was work and then home to his wife, Sally, of whom he was both proud and impressed. She was a Fulton from Sycamore, Illinois, a member of Phi Beta Kappa, the daughter of a lawyer, of whom Reston said, smiling, "I married above me."

In 1941, with Sally expecting their second child, and with the big political story shifting to Washington as the United States prepared to move into the war, Reston arranged a transfer to Mr. Krock's bureau. A year later Reston's book, *Prelude to Victory*, was published to rave reviews, and the next thing that his colleagues in London heard was that Scotty Reston had become assistant to the *Times'* publisher, Arthur Hays Sulzberger, and would accompany Mr. Sulzberger on a trip to the Soviet Union. That it was a very valuable trip, one that broadened the understanding of both men, there is no doubt; that the trip was a social success that brought the *Times'* publisher and his young star closer as men—this is debatable. For the interoffice word after the trip was that Reston, with his early-to-bed habits and his rigidly moral character, palled on Sulzberger, an extremely sophisticated man who drank well and had an eye for an ankle, and who, away from his work, knew the art of relaxation. Sulzberger never ceased being an admirer of Reston the journalist; but Reston the epicurean, the man to take long trips with: this was something else. For this there was only one man. Catledge.

Turner Catledge had returned to the *Times* in the spring of 1943. He had been unhappy in Chicago, despite the $26,500 salary, and returned to the *Times* for $12,000. In the fall of 1944, while scouting the political campaign in Fargo, North Dakota, Catledge received a telegram from Arthur Hays Sulzberger asking him if he would be interested in taking a trip with the publisher to inspect the Pacific front. Catledge wired back his acceptance, and in November they began their 27,000-mile flight with a stop at San Francisco. They checked into the Mark Hopkins Hotel, went almost immediately to the Top of the Mark for a few drinks before dinner. They were seated at a comfortable divan, and through the big windows that surrounded them they could see the panorama of the north side of the city, the neck of San Francisco Bay with the ships coming and going, and to the left, the Golden Gate Bridge.

They ordered a Scotch, then a second round. On the third round Sulzberger proposed that they be "doubles." Then they ordered two more "doubles" and continued to talk about everything—the *Times*, the San Francisco landscape, the *Times*, women, the *Times*, the strange workings of the Oriental mind. They ordered still another round of "doubles." When the waiter brought them, Sulzberger asked, "Are you sure these are doubles?" The waiter said, "Am I sure? You've drunk practically a bottle already."

They had a few more rounds and then they stood up to go to dinner. But before they left, Arthur Hays Sulzberger looked at Catledge, then extended his hand, saying, "Well, you pass."

In January, 1945, Turner Catledge was named assistant managing editor, second in command to Edwin L. James. The other editors were neither surprised nor disappointed; none had regarded themselves as likely successors to James, except possibly Bruce Rae, a fine reporter who had become an assistant managing editor. But Rae made the mistake one day of sitting in James's chair when the managing editor was out ill. When James heard about it, he was furious.

Where one sits in the *Times'* newsroom is not a casual matter. Young reporters of no special status are generally assigned to sit near the back of the room, close to the Sports Department; and as the years go by and people die and the young reporter becomes more seasoned and not so young, he is moved up closer to the front. But he must never move on his own initiative. There was one bright reporter who, after being told that he would help cover the labor beat, cleaned out his desk near the back of the room and moved up five rows into an empty desk vacated by one of the labor reporters who had quit. The recognition of the new occupant a few days later by an assistant City editor resulted in a reappraisal of the younger reporter's assets, and within a day he was back at his old desk, within a year or so he was out of the newspaper business.

Clifton Daniel, in February of 1944, resigned from the Associated Press in London and was hired by the *New York Times* on the recommendation of the *Times'* London bureau chief, Raymond Daniell, who is no relation. Raymond Daniell had been a first-rate *Times* reporter since 1928, reporting on the Scottsboro case and Huey Long's rise to power, the sharecropper disputes in Arkansas and coal-miner troubles in Kentucky. He had been in Mexico City in 1939 but, as the European war spread, he was quickly reassigned to London where, in 1940, his quarters at Lincoln's Inn were shattered by bombs and he and his colleagues moved the *Times* bureau into the Savoy Hotel, where they also lived. Since London time is five hours ahead of New York, the staff usually wrote until dawn while bombs shook the city; they slept through the afternoons, raids or no raids, and then after their customary round of Martinis they were back at work on what were called "inraids" and "outraids"—the "inraids" being the German attacks on Great Britain, the "outraids" being the retaliation by the RAF.

When Raymond Daniell first became aware of the AP reporter with the similar name, he did not particularly like him, especially his looks. A little too smooth and suave. And this first impression was fortified by other reporters' observations about Clifton Daniel: he seemed haughty, he never removed his jacket in the office, he was the only newspaperman they had ever known who had lapels on his vests—and they made many other points about his clothes and his hair, as reporters would continue to do for years, even speculating in 1956 that Clifton Daniel owned more suits than Harry Truman ever sold.

But Raymond Daniell dug more deeply into the character of the man. And he learned that Clifton Daniel was not only a very fast and facile writer, but had often been put in charge of running the AP's London bureau during its most hectic hours and had always functioned calmly and efficiently; furthermore Daniel was known for his loyalty to the AP bureau chief and was not the sort who would ever overstep his boundaries or attempt to take over.

So Ray Daniell offered him a job and Daniel accepted. But first, taking some time off, he visited New York where a rather unusual thing happened that nearly cost him his job on the *New York Times*. Daniel had been invited to deliver a short speech about wartime London to a luncheon gathering of The Dutch Treat Club and, noticing the servicemen in the audience, he proceeded with anecdotes that he thought the G.I.'s might enjoy. He gave one vivid description of an American colonel falling into a fountain during the blackout, and he also told the servicemen that if they got to London they need not worry about women; there were plenty of girls on the streets, Daniel said, and they were easy to pick up.

Seated in the audience, becoming very indignant and barely suppressing his rage, was General Julius Ochs Adler, a high executive on the *Times* and a member of the ruling family. This profane and irreverent newspaperman was not *Times* material, General Adler declared later at the *Times* office. And it took a great deal of persuasion on the part of more tolerant *Times*men to get General Adler to withdraw his objection and give Daniel a chance. Daniel did well for the *Times* in London. Night after night he sat among his colleagues in the Savoy or in the field, writing stories that would carry his byline the next day on Page One.

On a single day in November, riding in a jeep behind the advancing First Army, Clifton Daniel visited three countries and filed news stories from each—Eupen, Belgium; Aachen, Germany; and Vaals, the Netherlands. Then, in March of 1945, he was in Paris watching as "the big, dirty, green trucks speed along the Rue La Fayette, their heavy tires singing on the cobblestones and their canvas tops snapping in the winter wind. The men in the back," Daniel wrote, "are tired and cramped after eleven hours on the road. The last wisecrack was made a hundred miles back. But one of them peers out, sees the name of the street and says, 'La Fayette, we're here.' The truck growls to a halt . . . The men dismount, a little stiff at first, light up cigarettes and start looking. They inspect the cornices of the Opera House, watch the crowds swirling past the Galeries Lafayette and eye the passing girls—always the girls . . ."

By spring, Daniel was back in London describing the city as the blackout restrictions were lifted, but before he could become adjusted to the light and tranquility he was sent to North Africa and back to the sound of gunfire and rioting; then from Egypt he went to Iran, arriving in Tabriz with two other journalists hours ahead of the Iranian Army that was to take over the city from a collapsing Soviet-backed Azerbaijanian rebel regime. As Daniel and the two others rode into town they were greeted by thousands of villagers lined along the road, and several sheep were sacrificed in their honor. The ceremony, the highest honor that a Persian can pay, consisted of beheading a sheep on one side of the road as the traveler approaches and carrying the head to the other side of the road; the traveler then passes between the body and the head.

The exotic sights and sounds, the headline makers and headhunters from the Middle East to Great Britain—this was Daniel's world for the next seven years, although now, in 1966, all those events and faces are, if not forgotten, rarely remembered by anyone except those who were there, like Daniel, watching twenty years ago in Dhahran as a fat roasted hump of young camel was set before King Ibn Saud; listening at midnight from his hotel in Jerusalem as the troops below with rifles shuffled through the sloping street near Zion Square; dancing and dining in Cairo at Shepheard's with a pretty English girl when King Farouk arrived and asked Daniel and the girl to join him for a drink and a discussion about things that now mean little. Then Daniel was back in London observing "an elderly cherub with a cigar almost as big as the butt end of a billiard cue"—Winston Churchill, one of the few names that survives the momentary madness that makes headlines; the others quickly die or fade—Naguib, Mossadegh, Klaus Fuchs. Men like Daniel go off to new names, new places, never getting *involved*, although sometimes they worry about the impermanence of their work and wonder where it will lead them.

Daniel would have liked to have become chief of the *Times'* London bureau, but Drew Middleton, suspected by a few New York editors of having a private line of communication with the publisher, Arthur Hays Sulzberger, got the job. Daniel was assigned to replace Middleton in Germany and, as an Anglophile, he could barely abide the Germans. His reporting was uninspired, sometimes noticeably disdainful: "BERLIN— In the cold, dirty slush of last night's snow a few thousand of Berlin's millions stood along Potsdamer Strasse today watching the custodians of Germany's destiny roll by in a fleet of limousines. They were typical Berliners, seedy, cynical and slangy . . ."

In New York, Catledge was having his troubles too. He had been separated from his wife in 1948 and was spending a good deal of time in Sardi's bar, so much in fact that his picture was soon hanging on the wall and his name was on the menu ("Veal Cutlet Catledge"); and his dream of bringing the power back to the managing editor's office in New York, of demoting the dukes, was very slow in materializing. Though Catledge had been Sulzberger's appointee, the publisher never did give him carte blanche—no editor gets that on the *Times*—and there were also rising up around Mr. Sulzberger many new young men who had a good deal to say about anything Catledge did, or tried to do.

One was Orvil Dryfoos, a friend of Reston's, a onetime Wall Street broker who, after marrying a Sulzberger daughter, became an assistant to the publisher and eventually, in 1961, would become the publisher himself. Another was Amory Howe Bradford, a tall, blond Yaleman who had married Carol Warburg Rothschild, whose family knew the Sulzbergers. Bradford would also become very influential on the *Times*, and remain so until the early sixties.

James Reston was also a power, particularly after taking over in 1953 as chief of Krock's twenty-four-man Washington bureau, a concession quickly made when Reston contemplated quitting the *New York Times* for a better job on the *Washington Post*; and the most autonomous duke in the New York office, of course, was the Sunday editor, Lester Markel, who started at the paper in 1923 with a staff of only three editors, a secretary, and an office boy. By 1951 he had a staff of eighty-four, including fifty-eight editors, layout and picture crews, and special correspondents in Paris, London, and Washington.

And Turner Catledge, though he had become the No. 2 man under Edwin L. James in 1945, was no further along in 1951; James was ill much of the time, but he was still the managing editor and Catledge never crossed him, even though the veteran gossips around the office generally agreed that James was hardly Sulzberger's favorite person. James had been *Ochs*'s managing editor, they pointed out, and Adolph Ochs—whose only daughter had married Arthur Hays Sulzberger in 1917—used to make remarks about Sulzberger's night life to James, observations that must have quietly amused James who, years before, had been privy to some of Adolph Ochs's nocturnal excursions through Paris and elsewhere.

When Ochs died in 1935 and Sulzberger became publisher, he was never entirely comfortable around James, it was said, although this might have been due to their difference in style—Sulzberger preferred the more sedate, subtle manners of his favorite city, London, while James responded to the frisky freedom of Paris and remained the boulevardier long after he ceased being the *Times*' chief correspondent there. In the New York office he dressed with a flair, kicked his polished shoes or rapped his cane against the elevator when it moved too slowly, placed bets with his bookmaker who worked as a news clerk in the rear of the city room (the bookie remained there until, years after James's death, he was quietly transferred into the *Times'* financial-news department).

Through these years Catledge, waiting patiently and trying to keep his balance, never was entirely certain that he would succeed James; there was always the possibility that Reston might want the job; or perhaps Cyrus L. Sulzberger, the publisher's nephew who now had James's old Paris assignment as the *Times'* chief foreign correspondent. During the six years that Catledge was James's understudy he was exceedingly careful, provoking James's anger only once, and that was over James's son, Michel.

Michel James, born in France but educated at Princeton, was up for employment as a *Times* reporter at the suggestion of Cyrus Sulzberger, and Catledge later suspected a plot. Michel James, Catledge believed, would become a foreign correspondent under Cyrus Sulzberger (who then was virtually in charge of all *Times* foreign correspondents) and would serve as Sulzberger's hostage.

Catledge strongly opposed the hiring of Michel James. Edwin James became very angry. Michel James was hired and soon became a most interesting addition to the staff. He was a very thin, zany young man who dressed himself in very narrow, rather bizarre clothes, lived in Greenwich Village, and frequented the more far-out parties. He was also an excellent photographer, often of subjects that the *Times* never would have found fit to print.

As a writer he had talent, but as a foreign correspondent he ran up enormous expense accounts, would be incommunicado sometimes for days, weeks, and then might suddenly appear in Cambodia or Bonn or in Paris with a pet monkey on his back, a lively little animal that absolutely terrified the *Times* bureau chief in Paris, Harold Callender.

On a staff saturated with men who take themselves seriously at all times, too seriously sometimes, Michel James was a refreshing figure, but Catledge saw little humor in his presence on the *Times* for those years he remained. As to whether Michel James was of any use as a hostage, it was never possible to tell. For in December of 1951, Edwin L. James died. And Arthur Hays Sulzberger's memo on the bulletin board of the newsroom read:

To the Staff: When death takes a valued member of an organization, it is always a sad occasion. Such it was with the passing of

Mr. Edwin L. James. But the institution must go on, and I have today appointed Turner Catledge to the post of managing editor of the *Times* . . ."

Now Catledge, while causing as little commotion as possible, began his campaign to centralize the paper, to bring friendly forces into his camp. In 1952 he promoted two men to the rank of assistant managing editor, Robert E. Garst and Theodore M. Bernstein. At the same time he tried to make it clear to both men, as clearly as he could without being offensive, that they would go no further, would never succeed him as the managing editor.

No objections were raised at the time, but in the years that followed, as Turner Catledge focused his attention elsewhere, Theodore Bernstein became increasingly powerful. Responding perhaps to Catledge's call for good writing, Theodore Bernstein established himself as the final arbiter of what was good. He had been an outstanding professor of journalism at Columbia University, then a dedicated *Times* deskman who in 1939 took charge of all war copy, and later he edited the Churchill memoirs for the *Times*, as well as those of Cordell Hull and General Walter Bedell Smith. As a person, Bernstein was warm and friendly, very approachable; with a pencil in his hand, however, he was cold and dogmatic, a strict believer in rules, especially *his* rules. From his office in the southeast corner of the city room, a section called the "bullpen" and populated by subordinate editors who shared most of his opinions on news and grammar, Bernstein, in addition to his many other duties, published a little paper called *Winners & Sinners* that was distributed to *Times*men in New York and throughout the world; it listed examples of their work, good and bad, that had appeared recently in the *Times*, and it also included a recitation of Mr. Bernstein's rules and comments. These were memorized by deskmen throughout the vast city room, and these men were held accountable by Bernstein for the maintenance of his principles; thus the deskmen, in the interest of a more readable and grammatical newspaper, gained new power with Bernstein as their mentor—he had become the *Times*' grammarian or, as *Encounter* magazine later suggested, its "governess."

Such a position, of course, made Bernstein a villain with those reporters who had their own ideas about writing. They charged that the deskmen, overreacting to Bernstein's rules, were merely hatchet men who deleted from stories the choicest phrases and gems of originality. Catledge did not become involved in the feud at this time. If Bernstein's men went too far they could always be checked, and the quicker pace of postwar life, the coming of television, the increased cost of news production, among other factors, required that the *Times* become a more tightly edited paper for faster reading. Also, *somebody* had to worry about the proper uses of "that" or "which," "whom" or "who," and so Catledge now concerned himself with other more pressing problems, and there were many.

Ever since the beginning of World War II, when the workday in the city room was expanded so that the *Times* could publish the maximum amount of late-breaking news, there had been a lack of coordination between various editors of the "day side" and "night side"—neither knew what the other was up to, there was competition, intrigue. There was also throughout the *Times'* many departments—City, Science, Sports, Financial, a dozen more—a dangerous commitment to the traditional way of doing things. Editors in some of these departments would sometimes peek back at the *Times'* edition of exactly one year ago, would see how certain stories had been approached, laid out, written; then they would try to duplicate that day one year later.

The morale was low on the New York local staff. It had long been running a poor third in performance behind the prestigious Foreign staff, which often attracted away the best New York men, and the National staff, which was led by Reston's elite corps in Washington. (Reston, incidentally, at that time hired his own men—usually tall, tweedy men who were deceptively bright and were born and reared, preferably, some hundreds of miles from New York City.)

The Sports staff was sluggish, and Catledge decided that he would retire the Sports editor as soon as possible. The staff was sectioned off into little cliques and there was tension. There had even been a fight between the makeup man, Frank Blunk, and the slot man, Harry Heeren. Blunk had told Heeren to stop sending up copy for the first edition, there was no more room, and Heeren replied, "Don't you tell me when to cut off copy!"

"Com'on, Harry," Blunk had said, "the first edition's in, forget it."

"I will not forget it!"

"Well if you don't keep your mouth shut, I'll hit you in the nose."

Heeren opened his mouth, Blunk hit him in the nose.

Heeren ran through the city room into the bullpen to make an official complaint to Bernstein. The next day Frank Blunk, standing in Catledge's office, explained that he had been trying for years to get a transfer to the writing staff, being weary of working indoors near Harry Heeren. So Catledge quickly acted; he made Blunk a reporter specializing in auto races, a plush job that would take him to Florida and Nassau much of the winter; and it confirmed for Blunk the notion that small men in big institutions frequently get what they want only after raising some hell.

The death of Anne O'Hare McCormick, the foreign-affairs columnist, opened up that busy job for Cyrus Sulzberger, and he no longer sought to influence the running of the *Times*' overseas bureaus. Catledge himself took trips abroad and spent time with correspondents, and he frequently was amazed at how well they lived, the number of servants they had, the size of their homes.

In Mexico he visited the young bureau chief, Sydney Gruson, who explained at the outset: "Okay, Turner, while you're here we can go off each morning and see people, and I'll make phone calls, and I'll pretend that this is the way I really work here. Or," Gruson said, eyes lighting up, "we can do what I really do here. I own five racehorses, I see them run two or three times a week, and I play golf three or four times a week. And, well, how do you want to do it, Turner?"

"Don't be silly," Catledge said, "we'll do it the way you always do it."

So during the next week they had a magnificent time. They went to several parties, they bet on Gruson's horses, losing every time, and went to the bullfights, where Gruson had arranged for a bull to be dedicated in honor of Catledge.

Ten days later, after Catledge had returned to New York, Gruson received word that his Mexican assignment was over. He was to report back to the New York office. Some months later he was assigned to Prague. Catledge maintained that his Mexico trip had nothing to do with it. (Gruson did extremely well during his assignment in Eastern Europe, and also in Bonn and London; and he became, in 1965, the *Times*' foreign-news editor.)

One of the major personnel problems facing Catledge in 1954 was finding a replacement in Russia for Harrison E. Salisbury. Salisbury, a tall and remote individualist—he was once fired as editor of the University of Minnesota daily newspaper for smoking in the library—had been the *Times*man in Moscow since 1949. He had worked long and hard under the most adverse conditions—the Stalin era, censorship—and yet Catledge had no other qualified *Times*man who wished to go to Moscow. Then Clifton Daniel volunteered.

Catledge was delighted. It confirmed for him many of the things he had come to accept about Daniel: in fact, Catledge had for the last two years been thinking of Clifton Daniel as a future executive, a possible successor, being impressed with Daniel's performance in the London bureau, both as an administrator and newsman, and Catledge also had been pleased with Daniel's attitude in accepting the Bonn assignment. Daniel was eleven years younger than Catledge, was an organization man who could operate within the corporate ego of the *Times*. And—he was a Southerner. Take away all that fancy English tailoring, that long wavy hair and courtly manner, and Daniel was what Catledge was—a country boy who said "sir" to his superiors, and had reverence for the Southern past and big-city dreams for the future.

So Clifton Daniel returned to New York to study Russian at Columbia University. One day after class he had lunch at Sardi's, checking his Russian first reader with the blonde in the cloakroom. He also took a trip down to Zebulon to see his parents and friends, and while in the Zebulon post office he was approached by the clerk, Whitley Chamblee, who leaned forward and whispered, "Did I hear you're going to *Russia*?"

After Daniel confirmed it, Whitley Chamblee asked, "I wonder, when you're there, if you would buy me one of those cuckoo clocks."

"Whitley, I don't believe they make cuckoo clocks in Russia," Daniel said. "They make them in Germany and Switzerland. But, well, if I find one, I'll send it to you."

A year later Clifton Daniel was in Geneva for the Big Four Conference. He had flown there from Moscow to join a team of *Times*men reporting the big story. While there he also bought a cuckoo clock and mailed it to the postman in Zebulon.

Daniel arrived in Moscow in the late summer of 1954, a vintage period in Russian news—Stalin only eighteen months dead, Krushchev emerging with a new party line that would include vodka toasts and receptions in the Great Kremlin Palace; at one reception, Daniel reported to the readers of the *Times*, "I was as close to Mr. Malenkov as this paper is to your nose."

His reporting in the *New York Times* was remarkable in that it captured not only the political rumblings but also the mood of the people: the audience at the Bolshoi and the barber in Kharkov; the athletes preparing for the Olympics, and the fashion models wearing designs of "socialist realism" in this land where "bosoms are still bosoms, a waist is a waist, hips are hips, and there is no doubt about what they are and where they are situated." He reported, too, how tipping—a "relic of the dark bourgeoisie past"—was a necessary reality despite Government disapproval, and he also described the arrival of winter:

"This was Christmas morning in Russia, and a cruel snow-laden wind blowing straight out of the pages of Russian history and literature whipped across roofs and through the frozen streets of Moscow. At midnight the bells in the tower of Yelokhovskaya Cathedral in the northern quarter of the city set up an insistent clangor. The faithful of the Russian Orthodox Church—women tightly wrapped in shawls and men in fur-collared coats and caps—hastened through the churchyard to escape the icy bite of the wind."

Since Daniel was then the only permanent correspondent of a Western non-Communist newspaper in the Russian capital, he was able to pick his subjects at will and write them well and not have to contend with editorial second-guessing that would have come from New York had there been rival papers' men in Moscow focusing on government spokesmen with their endless pronouncements. And not being part of a pack, Daniel had to work harder than he ever had. He developed an ulcer and lost between thirty and forty pounds. In November of 1955, Turner Catledge, acting on orders from Arthur Hays Sulzberger—who had by this time received letters from *Times*men commenting on how bad Daniel had looked at the Big Four Conference in Geneva—ordered Daniel home immediately.

He returned, emaciated, but was not long in recovering, and soon was working in the New York office. He had been named *an* assistant to the foreign news editor, although nobody in the city room knew precisely what this meant, including possibly *the* foreign news editor. But it seemed obvious from the way Daniel moved around the room, and from the way the room moved around him, that he was not going to remain an assistant to the foreign news editor for very long.

Daniel's desk, which normally would have given a clue, was in a nondescript spot. It was on the south side of the room, where all the senior editors sit, but it was partially obscured by a post. It was also up a bit between two lady secretaries, equidistant from the Foreign editor and the "bullpen." He also rarely remained seated. Usually he walked slowly around the big room, his glasses sometimes tucked like a tiara into the top of his silver hair. Sometimes he would stop, sit down, and chat with reporters or deskmen in the Science department, or in Sports, or Education, or Financial, or Society. Occasionally he would return to one of these departments for a whole week or two, sitting in various places, and conversing in a very casual, disarming way about the *New York Times*, and asking occasionally what they liked about working there, or did not like.

He was living at the Algonquin Hotel then, and was spotted at night also in Sardi's after the theatre, and was once seen at the opera with a tall, striking brunette.

After they had gone twice more to the opera they became a "twosome" in Walter Winchell's column. The lady was mildly upset, partly because she felt that Daniel, a *Times* editor in a gossip column, might be very embarrassed, especially when their relationship had been so innocent: a drink, dinner, the opera, another drink perhaps, then home. Directly. A pleasant good night in front of the doorman. That was it.

She had met Clifton Daniel at a New York party prior to his leaving for Moscow, had received one postcard from him, and was now pleased to be seeing him again. And, hoping that he would not be angered by the Winchell item, she telephoned Daniel at the *Times*.

He could not have been nicer. He only laughed when the Winchell subject was brought up, and hardly seemed sorry about the item appearing—which, she later told a friend, "kind of surprised me."

Shortly after that, in March of 1956, she read in the newspapers the engagement announcement of Margaret Truman to Clifton Daniel. She wrote a note of congratulations to Daniel, and received in turn a note thanking *her* "for being such a fine cover-up for myself and Margaret."

The brunette was "devastated" by the note, and she neither spoke to nor saw Clifton Daniel again for two years. Now, looking back, she concedes that perhaps she was wrong to have reacted as she did: perhaps he was being "light" or "humorous."

Clifton Daniel met Margaret Truman in November, 1955, at the New York home of Mrs. George Backer, a friend of Daniel's from the forties in London. Mrs. Backer's husband, the politically active New York, who was once publisher of the *New York Post*, was out of town, and so there were only Turner Catledge and Daniel for dinner, in addition to Madeleine Sherwood, widow of Robert Sherwood. After dinner, others came. Among them were Alan Campbell, who had been married to Dorothy Parker, and Mr. Campbell's date, Margaret Truman.

Margaret and Campbell had been to Edna Ferber's for dinner, and were merely stopping in, at Campbell's insistence, for a quick nightcap at the Backers'. Mrs. Backer introduced Daniel to Margaret Truman.

To this day Daniel remembers very sharply the smallest details about her that night—her wonderful complexion, never suggested in her photographs, and the way she wore her hair, her shoes, the dark blue Fontana dress with the plunging neckline: Daniel recalling to a friend years later, "I looked down the neck of that dress and I haven't looked back since."

Soon, at the Backers', Daniel and Miss Truman were conversing in a corner, he telling her that if she, the daughter of a prominent political figure, had been reared in Russia she would be "practically unknown," because the politicians there shun publicity for their families. This interested her, and he continued to talk in his worldly way, and before she left he had made a date for lunch.

They were married in Independence, Missouri, on April 21, 1956. She was thirty-two, he was forty-three. The wedding, in Trinity Protestant Episcopal Church where she once sang in the choir, was witnessed by about fifty relatives and close friends and the maid and housekeeper from the Truman home. Most of those present were from the two small towns in which the bride and bridegroom grew up. The best man was Daniel's boyhood friend from Zebulon, John K. Barrow Jr., a college roommate and fraternity brother who operated a big lumber business in Ahoskie, North Carolina. The ushers were George Backer and Turner Catledge.

Within the next five years Clifton Daniel moved steadily upward, becoming assistant to the managing editor in 1957, and *the* assistant managing editor in 1959. In this capacity he became a Catledge troubleshooter and the author of many long, highly critical memos to the staff, which in turn became highly critical of him. One day in the city room Margaret Daniel, making an infrequent visit, was introduced to a reporter who said, "Oh, it's a pleasure meeting you, Mrs. Daniel, I *love* your father."

"What about my husband?" she asked.

"That," he said, forcing a smile, "I'll have to think about."

While the Catledge-Daniel influence was undoubtedly increasing during these years, it did not go unchallenged. Reston was still a singular power in Washington. During the steel strike in 1959 when the *Times'* top labor reporter, A. H. Raskin, who worked out of the New York office, appeared at the Washington bureau to continue his coverage of the developments—a presidential panel was about to hold hearings on a possible emergency injunction—Reston blocked him. The steel story had moved into the Washington area and Reston wanted one of his men, namely his own labor specialist, Joseph Loftus, to take over the story; and Loftus did. A. H. Raskin returned to New York. Turner Catledge, out of the office at the time, was angry when he learned of it and he made a loud interoffice speech about how the *Times* was now being run from Forty-third Street; but no one really wanted to have a showdown with Reston at this time.

Reston's close friend, Orvil Dryfoos, was then president of the New York Times Company and heir-apparent to his father-in-law; and the expected happened in 1961 when Arthur Hays Sulzberger, seventy years old and not in good health, made Orvil Dryfoos the publisher. While Dryfoos and Catledge shared a convincing cordiality and mutual respect, it was not to be compared with the warm affection that existed between Dryfoos and Reston. Reston, too, was the poet laureate of the paper, a man whose writing had a lyrical quality even when dealing with the more ponderous issues of the day; and his staff, fashioned in his own image, had unquestionably enhanced the prestige of the *Times*. Reston did not covet Catledge's job, such as it was, for he would probably lose more than he would gain; he would have to leave Washington for New York, a city he never liked, and he would have to give up his column, a thing he could probably never do.

For the column in the *New York Times* was the podium from which Reston could spread his Calvinist view of life throughout the land, thrilling thousands with his sound logic and wit, influencing scholars, students, and politicians, sometimes infuriating such presidents as Eisenhower, who once asked, "Who the hell does he think he is, telling me how to run the country?"

And so as long as Reston had his column and could run his bureau as he wished—a prerogative he thought reasonable since he was held responsible for its performance—he would remain in Washington, a reasonably happy man. And that is what he was for as long as Dryfoos lived. In the spring of 1963, at the age of fifty, Orvil Dryfoos died.

He died of a heart ailment shortly after the settlement of a 114-day New York newspaper strike, a tedious and strenuous period that, some of his friends insist, impaired his health. It was he who, at a crucial moment when negotiations seemed about to break up in angry recriminations, persuaded the chief negotiators to resume talks and submerge their hostility. Much of this hostility had been directed at Dryfoos' own colleague and adviser, Amory Bradford, the *Times'* general manager who was then chief spokesman for the New York publishers' committee with the union. In a remarkable example of independent journalism, the *New York Times*, in a long analysis published after the strike but before Dryfoos died, reported that Amory Bradford had brought "an attitude of such icy disdain into the conference rooms that the mediator often felt he ought to ask the hotel to send up more heat." This story by A. H. Raskin also characterized Bradford as an "aloof" man who operated on a "short fuse" and had called the Mayor's strike methods "foolish" and had become "sick and tired of the whole proceedings."

When Catledge read A. H. Raskin's story, he immediately called Dryfoos and asked him to look at it. Dryfoos said he would when it appeared in the *Times*. Catledge urged him to read it prior to publication. So Dryfoos took the story with him to Central Park, where he could read it alone near the lake, and Catledge remained in the office uncertain of Dryfoos' reaction and whether the story would ever be published. Later Dryfoos returned the story, telling Catledge to let it run.

When Amory Bradford saw a copy of Raskin's story, he became enraged and urged Dryfoos to have the story killed. Dryfoos replied that he did not feel it was his responsibility to censor the news. He knew that Catledge had absolute faith in Raskin's accuracy and the story would be published as planned.

At Orvil Dryfoos' funeral, attended by two thousand persons at Temple Emanu-El on Fifth Avenue in New York, Amory Bradford did not sit among the many *Times* editors near the front. He sat several rows back, and Harrison Salisbury, who has an eye for such things, immediately foresaw Bradford's resignation.

James Reston delivered the eulogy of Orvil Dryfoos. It was a beautifully composed portrait of the publisher, revealing touching insights into the man's mind and ideals. Reston recalled that in the city room on election night, 1960, Dryfoos was the first man to "sense that we had gone out on a limb for Kennedy too early and insisted that we reconsider. And again in 1961," Reston continued, "when we were on the point of reporting a premature invasion of Cuba, his courteous questions and wise judgment held us back."

This last point seemed to carry just the slightest sting for the New York editors. *They* had planned to play up the Bay of Pigs invasion plan, but Dryfoos, agreeing with Reston that it was not in the national interest, had the story toned down and had eliminated from it any phraseology stating that the invasion of Cuba was imminent. (Three years later, in June of 1966, after the power had shifted within the *Times*, Clifton Daniel would make a speech at the World Press Institute in Minneapolis that would get back a bit at Reston: Daniel would say that the Bay of Pigs operation "might well have been canceled and the country would have been saved enormous embarrassment if the *New York Times* and other newspapers had been more diligent in the performance of their duty," and he would also report President Kennedy's later concession to Turner Catledge: "If you had printed more about the operation you would have saved us from a colossal mistake.")

After the Dryfoos funeral there were weeks of intense guessing in the city room as to whom the next publisher would be. Various names were mentioned: John Oakes, the editorial writer whose late father, Ochs's brother, had changed the family name during World War I because of the Germanic flavor of "Ochs"; there was Ruth Sulzberger Golden, Arthur Hays Sulzberger's daughter who was then publisher of the *Chattanooga Times*, first published in 1878 by Adolph Ochs; there were individuals who were not part of the family, including James Reston; and there was Arthur Hays Sulzberger's thirty-seven-year-old son, Arthur Ochs Sulzberger, known by his nickname, "Punch," given him at home because his youngest sister was called Judy.

Punch Sulzberger was a charming and completely unostentatious young man, but many people around the newspaper seriously doubted that he was yet old enough or mature enough to take over the *New York Times*. As a young boy he had many problems in school, and his older sister Ruth, making light of it once in the *Times'* house organ, wrote: "Nearly every school in the vicinity of New York was graced with

Punch's presence at one time or another. They were all delighted to have him, but wanted him as something other than a spectator."

He, too, was always amusing when recalling his days at Browning or Lawrence Smith or Loomis, or while he was tutoring at Morningside. But on rare occasions, though he tried to conceal it with his laughter and his casual manner, there was a hint of deep hurt, the dark memory of displeasure from his father. "They sent me to St. Bernard's, then based on the English school system, and I rebelled," he once said. "I was a natural left-hander, but I was made to write with my right. And the result even now is that I do a lot of flipping—instead of writing '197' I'll reverse it to '179.' Anyway, I was at St. Bernard's for maybe five or six years, and I still get those letters addressed 'Old Boy.'" Then, lips hardening, he added quietly, "I never gave them a penny."

He joined the Marines in 1943. He served in the Philippines and Japan, remembering fondly a certain tough Marine Corporal Rossides "who helped me grow up." After his release from the Marines in 1946 he entered Columbia ("my old man was on the board") and made the dean's list; and then during the Korean war he was recalled and made a lieutenant. By 1954, after a year on the *Milwaukee Journal* as a reporter, Punch Sulzberger came to the *New York Times* where, until the death of Orville Dryfoos, almost nobody in the city room thought, or knew, very much about him. He was just Punch, the smiling son of Arthur Hays Sulzberger, a dark curly-haired boy smoking a pipe, wearing a Paul Stuart suit, saying hello to everyone in the elevator, sometimes wandering through the newsroom and looking up at the walls inspecting the paint, or scrutinizing the air-conditioning ducts. Later in the afternoon, once the four-o'clock news conference was over, Punch would usually slip into a little room behind the managing editor's office and sit down and chat and have a few drinks with his very close friend, Turner Catledge.

Catledge and he had been friends for years, although there was nothing unusual about this; Catledge seemed to be friends with everybody for years—copyboys and Senators, bellhops and bootleggers. And it seemed natural that Punch Sulzberger—who, like Catledge, had marital difficulties and was in no rush to get home—would wind up in Catledge's smoky little room at five o'clock drinking with Catledge and the other members of the "club": Joe Alduino, the comptroller, and Irvin Taubkin from Promotion, both of whom had marriage problems; and also Nat Goldstein, the circulation manager, whose wife accepted his "marriage" to the *Times* and never counted on his appearances at home.

Turner Catledge had a very paternal way with young Sulzberger without ever being condescending; he gave advice willingly, but Punch made his own decisions. Through the years their friendship deepened, and this at a time when many top *Times*men were merely polite to Punch. Even James Reston, when he would come flying into New York from Washington, would, after a quick handshake and hello, breeze past Punch into the office of the *Times*' publisher, Orvil Dryfoos. Everyone on the *Times*, seeing Dryfoos in apparent good health, expected that he would remain the chief executive through the 1980s, and hardly anyone expected that Punch, until then, would be anything but Punch.

Almost one month after Dryfoos' death, Punch Sulzberger became publisher of the *New York Times*. At thirty-seven, he was the youngest publisher the *Times* had ever had. His appointment was made known through a statement from his seventy-two-year-old father, the *Times*' chairman of the board. This statement also accepted, with regret, the resignation of Amory Bradford. "Amory Bradford has been a valuable source of strength and leadership in our organization," the statement read. "We are sorry he has decided to resign. He will be greatly missed."

Within Punch Sulzberger's first year as publisher, he devised the plans for the *Times*' most dramatic shakeup in history. His intent was to appoint Turner Catledge to the newly established office of executive editor, meaning that Catledge would have unquestioned authority over Lester Markel's Sunday department, over Reston's bureau in Washington, and over all *Times*men and *Times* bureaus at home and overseas. Markel would become "associate editor" and get his name on the *Times*' masthead, as would James Reston, still writing the column; both Markel and Reston would be consulted and respected on the paper, but neither of them would again have the power to challenge Catledge.

Markel's protests were vigorous, but he was then seventy, the Sunday editor for forty-one years. Sulzberger, while recognizing Markel's enormous contributions, insisted on replacing him with a judicious man named Daniel Schwarz, who had been an assistant to Markel since 1939. Most of Markel's staff welcomed the change. His autocratic rule had cracked the spirit of many writers and editors through the years; on occasions some had actually broken down and cried, others had gone off and written bad novels about him. "For all those years," one editor said, "Lester Markel was our great Jewish father-figure, and we were his sons—and he had a way of convincing us that we were always failing him."

Reston in Washington was different. His staff admired him and tried to identify with him; he was self-assured, very informal—even the office boys called him "Scotty"—and, when he spoke, there was something in the timbre of his wonderful distant voice, the words he slowly chose, the way he paused, that gave to almost everything he said the ring of instant history.

When some of his intimates on the bureau heard of Sulzberger's plan, they were shocked, but not surprised. Nothing from New York, no matter how preposterous, would surprise them, they said. Two years before, in 1962, Harrison Salisbury had been appointed the National editor. Since all stories written by *Times*men in bureaus around the nation, including the Washington bureau, had to go through the National editor's desk, Harrison Salisbury had the prerogative of pressuring Washington a bit; and he did. He had an obsession about suspecting plots and sinister deals in the American government, they said, and when these stories did not materialize they felt he thought they were vulnerable—soft on their sources, protecting their friends on Capitol Hill. Reston's men countercharged that Salisbury possessed a conspiratorial mind, the result of too much time spent covering the Communists in Russia—or, as one *Times*man in Washington put it: "Salisbury spent so many years watching who was standing next to Stalin that now *he's* standing next to Stalin!"

Yet Salisbury had continued to pepper the Washington bureau with memos, ideas, questions: Was there any Murchison money behind that Johnson deal? What was Abe Fortas *really* up to? Is it true, as rumored, that the State Department would recognize Mongolia? (The Washington men said that Salisbury had asked that last question so many times that the State Department probably will recognize Mongolia.)

It was Salisbury, they said, and probably Clifton Daniel, too, who made the decision to publish President Kennedy's S.O.B. remark in the *Times* during the Administration's confrontation with the steel industry in April of 1962. Wallace Carroll of the Washington bureau had written in his story that President Kennedy had been enraged at the steel men's decision to raise prices across the board, had spoken unflatteringly of them, but Carroll did not attribute to Kennedy the direct quotation that would later appear in his story ("My father always told me that all business men were sons of bitches but I never believed it till now!"); it was the New York editors, tipped off by a news source they trusted, who identified these words as the president's. So Salisbury called up Carroll and told him to write an insertion that would include this quotation. Carroll said that *he* had not heard the president use such language. When Salisbury persisted, Carroll snapped back, "The hell with it—you write it in yourself!"

If James Reston had not been so busy at this time writing his column and running the bureau, trying also to keep in touch with his Washington contacts, including his family, he could have made a full-time career of fighting the editors in New York. But Reston was now approaching his middle fifties and was resigned to an attitude of give-and-take (with the ageless Arthur Krock muttering in the background that when *he* was bureau chief he took nothing from New York), and Reston might have continued along these lines had he not been informed of Punch Sulzberger's plan to centralize the *Times'* news operation with Catledge in charge of everything.

Reston reacted, and his friends in Washington and elsewhere rallied behind him, urging him to go to New York and make a pitch for the big job—not for himself, but in the interest of saving the *New York Times* from the destructive elements they saw encircling it. And if the executive editorship had been offered Reston, they later said, he would have taken it, even though it would have undoubtedly meant his leaving Washington to live in New York, and giving up his column. But the job was not offered. Other alternatives were made for Reston's coming to New York in a higher executive capacity, but these would not have checked the central order of things with Catledge at the top.

Reston, in his discussions with Sulzberger, tried other approaches, suggesting that the youthful publisher might be wise to surround himself not with older men but rather with the bright young men of his own generation—such men as Tom Wicker, Max Frankel, and Anthony Lewis (all of the Washington bureau). But Sulzberger by that time was already committed to his plan for combining all the news elements under one senior editor, a plan that Catledge had been envisioning for twenty years.

With the cards so stacked, James Reston contemplated his resignation. His bureau manager in Washington, Wallace Carroll—whom Dryfoos had viewed as Markel's successor in the Sunday department—did resign in the summer of 1963, becoming editor and publisher of the *Winston-Salem Journal and Sentinel*. Carroll had been on the *New York Times* since 1955, and his resignation did not carry with it the same emotional torment that Reston's would have, because Reston, who had joined the paper in 1939, had grown with it, earning and receiving from it national fame and more literary freedom than any *Times*man before him or since.

Still Reston had immense pride, and he could not be submissive to New York. Also he now had an offer from his close friend, Katharine Graham, president of the Washington Post Company, whereby he would not only continue as a syndicated columnist but would also have a hand at guiding this paper up to perhaps a challenging position, as well as helping to run the company's other publication, *Newsweek* magazine. He would receive enough money and stock benefits to guarantee that he and his family would be quite rich. He thought it over, discussing it also with such friends as Walter Lippmann. In the end, Reston turned it down. He could not leave the *Times*.

So he continued with his column which, appearing on the editorial page, did not make him answerable to the news department. Reston's choice as successor, Tom Wicker, did get the job, although receiving beforehand a short briefing from Catledge on the new organizational chain of command. Tom Wicker was then thirty-seven, a superb journalist whose description from Dallas of the Kennedy assassination took up more than a page of the *Times*' November 23, 1963, issue. A native of North Carolina, a graduate of the University of North Carolina, Wicker had once been interviewed, while wearing a beard, by Clifton Daniel; he was not hired. In 1960, without the beard, and having written six novels (three under a pseudonym), Wicker went to see Reston; he was hired. Reston's two other bright young men in Washington, Max Frankel and Anthony Lewis, were not entirely joyful over Wicker's appointment as bureau chief. Frankel, the diplomatic correspondent, remained on the bureau, however, resisting a later temptation from *The Reporter* magazine. Anthony Lewis left Washington to take over the *Times*' London bureau, replacing Sydney Gruson who returned to New York as the Foreign editor, replacing Emanuel R. Freedman, who became an assistant managing editor. Harrison Salisbury, who vacated his National editor's job to a hustling Atlanta-born reporter named Claude Sitton, moved up to become *the* assistant managing editor, the third man, under Daniel and Catledge.

Before most of these changes had been made, Catledge had gone off to Tokyo to try to convince the *Times'* correspondent there, A. M. Rosenthal, to return home and become editor of the New York staff, which was then being rather rigidly run by a stout, ruddy man who had gone to Princeton, and by his assistant, a former colonel. Rosenthal, just over forty, had been considered by many to be the *Times'* best writer-reporter combination. His stories from Japan, and before that from Poland and India, were incisive and warm, very readable and sensitive to the nuances of politics and people. His story on a visit to Auschwitz is a journalistic classic: "And so there is no news to report from Auschwitz. There is merely the compulsion to write something about it, a compulsion that grows out of a restless feeling that to have visited Auschwitz and then turned away without having said or written anything would be a most grievous act of discourtesy to those who died here."

Rosenthal had been a reporter on the *New York Times* since 1944, while still an undergraduate at City College of New York. Though very anxious to become a foreign correspondent with his own country to cover, Rosenthal was unable to get such an assignment until 1954—not because he was unqualified before that, but rather because of an incident that occurred in 1948 while he was in Paris helping to cover the United Nations' General Assembly session there. Returning to his hotel room one day, he noticed that a twenty-dollar Travelers Check had been removed from his bureau drawer. He angrily reported this to the concierge, hinting that if it were not returned he would deduct that amount from his bill. The concierge, equally angry, telephoned the *Times'* office in Paris and reported young Rosenthal's assertiveness to Cyrus Sulzberger.

Back in New York, Rosenthal continued to work in the United Nations bureau, being unable, though he often tried, to get his assignment changed for the next six years. Several years later, after he had achieved his stature as a correspondent and had won the Pulitzer Prize, Rosenthal was driving to Geneva with Cyrus Sulzberger. As they talked, Sulzberger, suddenly and out of context, brought up the hotel incident of 1948. He admitted, somewhat casually, that Rosenthal had been kept in New York all those years because he, Sulzberger, had wanted it that way. He explained that Rosenthal in those early days had seemed the sort who would cause problems. Rosenthal felt the tension building within himself now, in the car; he thought of all the frustrating years at the UN, and thought, too, that if Sulzberger's influence as an overseas duke had been continued into the fifties, he might have never gotten to be a correspondent. The recollection of this silly, little impulsive moment in a hotel, and the realization of the harsh consequences, caused Rosenthal now to feel such a whirling sensation of both nausea and fury that he could barely, just barely, control himself until they reached Geneva.

Turner Catledge, long before approaching Rosenthal in Tokyo about the New York editor's job, debated the logic of removing from the *Times* one of the bylines that readers looked for, and sticking that man behind a desk. The idea of doing this had originally been Theodore Bernstein's; Catledge became intrigued with it because it was, for the *Times*, a rather drastic move, somewhat insane. Rosenthal had no experience as an editor, had been away from New York for nearly a decade, and might be intimidated by the enormity of the job itself—yet the New York staff, Catledge felt, was lethargic, needed a real shot to get it going again, and maybe this drastic move would bring results.

Rosenthal was responsive to the idea, but he really wanted to do a column, "Asia," for the editorial page. Catledge hates columns. He calls them a "malignancy" and prefers a paper with just news, well-written news, no columns that allow reporters to sound off on days when they often have nothing to say. If Rosenthal would take this editor's job, Catledge said, selling it hard now, Rosenthal each day would have not just *one* byline—he'd have *forty* bylines, *fifty* bylines: each story by one of Rosenthal's men would represent part of him, *Rosenthal*, and the gratification each night, the challenge each morning, would be something Rosenthal could never imagine until he tried it.

While Catledge remained briefly in the Orient, Rosenthal spent a good deal of time with him, and revealed finally that he would give the job a try. Catledge was delighted. He looked forward to Rosenthal's finishing the Tokyo assignment and coming home. Later, before Catledge left for New York, he discussed other things with Rosenthal—among them the fact that there would be a new column in the paper after all—one by Russell Baker. Catledge tried not to look too deeply into Rosenthal's face—but he knew that, had he hurled a bucket of cow dung into it, Rosenthal's expression would have been about the same.

A casual visitor to the *New York Times* city room during these years, between 1962 through 1964, would never have guessed that there was then in progress an institutional power shift and struggle of more magnitude than any in the *Times'* history. The city room would seem as quiet as ever: rows and rows of gray-metal desks occupied by reporters speaking calmly into telephones; in other parts of the room, seated behind long curved tables, would be deskmen, heads down, heads up, gazing softly into space for a headline. The headline might concern murder, riots, rapes, war— but the deskman's contact with these problems would be with a pencil. Over his head, racing across the ceiling, but quietly, would be a mechanical snake curving and hooking its way forward, clutching between its tiny metal tentacles single pieces of paper; it would transport each piece from the glass-enclosed telegraph room, in the distance, through the city room, down a hall, then into a remote room behind the morgue and into the hand of a deaf-mute seated behind the keyboard of a sturdy black machine. The only overpowering voice in this big newsroom would come from the silver microphone that rests on the desk of the Metropolitan editor—and is occasionally picked up by a clerk when asked to page a reporter: "Mr. Arnold, Metropolitan Desk"; and Mr. Arnold, with a soft sigh, would get up from his desk and begin the walk up the aisle toward the big desk centered near the front of the room.

A casual reader of the *New York Times*, too, would have no idea that there would be going on then a quiet revolution. There would be small announcement stories inside the paper (reading as if *everybody* was being promoted)—and even big front-page stories announcing the appointment of Punch Sulzberger, or mourning the death of Orvil Dryfoos—but none would offer any insight into the ramifications.

During these same years, and continuing through 1966, the *New York Times* would publish several stories of other institutional revolutions within such places as the *Saturday Evening Post*, as well as print interpretive pieces on the events leading up to the demise of the *New York Mirror* in 1963 and the *Herald Tribune* in August of 1966; and the *Times* would spark its news columns, too, with in-depth stories about the CIA and the "black-power" battle, about Franklin D. Roosevelt's mistress and the New Left, and oral contraceptives.

Yet the more than seven hundred thousand daily readers of the *New York Times* would get only dull reporting couched in institutional phrases when it would come to the story of Turner Catledge's triumph— and the rise of Daniel—a story that headed the second section of the *Times* on September 2, 1964. The headline read: CATLEDGE NAMED EXECUTIVE EDITOR OF TIMES, and the small second lines banked underneath: *Market, Reston Raised to Associate Editors—Schwarz Sunday Chief; Daniel Managing Editor—Wicker Will Direct Washington Bureau.*

The *Times* story began: "Six major changes in editorial assignments for *The New York Times* were announced yesterday by Arthur Ochs Sulzberger, publisher."

The big office and the little back room that Catledge occupied as managing editor was taken over by Daniel; and Catledge moved into a big new office—with a *new* little back room. Instead of being entered from the city room, as was his old office, Catledge's present office is now reachable only through an outside hall: meaning that if Catledge might wish to step out the door thirty times a day and ascend to the fourteenth floor to see Punch Sulzberger, or if Sulzberger might wish to come down to the third floor thirty times a day to see Catledge, both men might do so without being watched by the city-room gossips.

When Clifton Daniel moved into Catledge's old office, which is thirty-five feet long and eighteen feet wide, he made dramatic changes in the decor. One of the first things he did was to convert Catledge's little room, which smacked of turn-of-the-century Tammany, into a tastefully appointed sitting room. On the walls are now hung photographs showing the Clifton Daniels at the White House with the Lyndon Johnsons, the Harry Trumans, the John F. Kennedys—these being but a sample of many such photographs that the Daniels have, a few of which, blurred, were taken by Jacqueline Kennedy.

Behind Clifton Daniel's sitting room there is a cozy bar and bathroom; only Daniel and Catledge, among the third-floor news editors, and Theodore Bernstein, have private offices with bathrooms. Bernstein, who is as conspicuously informal as Daniel is formal, likes, in his subtle way, to mock the much larger and grander office that Daniel occupies directly across the newsroom. When Daniel ordered for his floor a brand-new blue-black tweed rug, Bernstein requested (and received) for *his* floor a chunk of the old tattered Catledge rug that was being pulled up, possibly to be junked. While Daniel sits in his traditional English office that contains, in addition to his desk, a new oval conference table surrounded by eighteen Bank of England chairs, Theodore Bernstein sits, with his shirt sleeves rolled up to the elbow, on an old wooden chair behind a scratchy desk, upon which he writes with flawless grammar on the cheapest memo paper he can find.

In the two years that Clifton Daniel has been managing editor he admits to having raised his voice in anger only once, refusing further clarification. Others in the city room, however, believe his estimate to be on the conservative side, claiming to have heard Daniel locked in a quarrel with Theodore Bernstein on at least a half-dozen occasions— usually the result of Bernstein's having passed off an irreverent remark about one of Daniel's pet projects, most likely the women's page.

While Daniel has been instrumental in several of the *Times*' big changes for the better—the expanded coverage of cultural news, the more literate obituaries, the encouragement of flavor and mood in "hard news" stories that formerly would have been done in a purely routine way—he is more quickly credited with (or blamed for) the women's page.

Its critics say that the women's page gets too much space, and they particularly oppose the publication of lengthy stories by Charlotte Curtis, a five-foot fast-stepping blonde, describing the activities of wealthy wastrels from Palm Beach to New York at a time when most of America is moving toward the goals of a more egalitarian society. Miss Curtis, however, is rarely flattering to her subjects, though many may lack the wit to realize this—but, what is more important about Miss Curtis' work, is that Clifton Daniel likes to read it. The deskmen, therefore, rarely trim her stories, and she is extremely careful with her facts, knowing that should she make an error Daniel will surely catch her.

Some years ago, in a story on Princess Radziwill, she mentioned the Prince's nickname, "Stash," only to receive the next day a memo from Daniel noting that while it was pronounced "Stash," it was spelled "Stas." Having previously checked the spelling with Pamela Turnure, then secretary to Prince Radziwill's sister-in-law, Jacqueline Kennedy, Miss Curtis telephoned Mr. Daniel to inform him that he was wrong—it was spelled "Stash."

"On what authority?" he asked.

"The White House," she quickly answered.

"Well, when I knew him," Daniel said, "it was spelled S-t-a-s."

He hung up. She thought that was the end of it. But Daniel tracked the Prince down in Europe, and some months later Miss Curtis got another memo from Daniel—it was "Stas."

Another change on the *Times* during Daniel's early days as managing editor, one that nearly caused paroxysms of panic among the Old Guard in the city room, began with the arrival from Japan of A. M. Rosenthal, the new Metropolitan editor. A quick and vibrant man, dark-haired and wearing horn-rimmed glasses, rather short and seeming ten years younger than his forty years, Rosenthal's primary commitment was to the livelier coverage of New York, and he was not at all interested in the way the city room used to be run.

Previously, at least in the opinion of one reporter who had lived for years in Europe, the city room had been run somewhat along the lines of a Paris café. In the late afternoon, he noted, the reporters at their desks would lean back in their chairs, sip coffee, read the newspapers and observe other people walking back and forth in front of them. There was always a card game at one of the desks, always a conventional gathering at another, and there was also a late-afternoon tranquility about the place that induced sleep. Some of the men and women who were having love affairs would, after the senior editors had disappeared into the four P.M. news conference, slip away to one of the hotels in the Times Square area, having only to remember to place an occasional precautionary call to a friend in the city room and to return before 6:20, for that was when the editor would stroll through the city room giving his traditional "good-night" to individuals on the early shift.

There had been a reporter named Albert J. Gordon who had once left for home at the end of the day without a "good-night"; later reached by phone he was told that the editor wished to discuss with him a most important matter—*now*, and in person. Gordon lived at an inconvenient distance from the office, and it was also then raining heavily, but he reappeared in the city room as soon as he could. There, wet and sullen, he stood for a few seconds in front of the City desk until the editor looked up and said, almost with a smile, "Good-night, Mr. Gordon."

In those days, too, there was a traditional method in assigning stories; the best local stories each morning were given to the front-row veterans, and the younger reporters near the back usually ended up with such stories as a water-main break in Yorkville or a small fire in Flushing, or were sent up to Watertown, New York, to cover the training activities of the Seventy-seventh Division, General Julius Ochs Adler's old outfit, a traditional "must" on the assignment sheet.

Younger New York reporters who wrote with a certain flair in those days were never completely trusted by their superiors in the city room, the assumption being that "writers" would compromise the facts in the interest of better literature; such staff men therefore usually were assigned to cover the weather or parades or the Bronx Zoo and the circus—where, if the quotes were brightened a bit, there was a reasonably good chance that the clowns and animals would not complain to the Letters department.

The arrival of A. M. Rosenthal, of course, changed all this. Now, suddenly, stories were not only supposed to be accurate and complete— but also "written." As a result some of the senior *Times*men, losing out to younger men who were superior writers, became embittered and helped spread the rumor that the new policy was to "fake" stories. And when Rosenthal would assign "project" stories that would perhaps require three or four days' research and would make greater demands on the reporter's ability to organize his facts and weave them with transition, there was the angry reaction from some that the newspaper was now a "magazine."

Even more unpopular than Rosenthal at this time was Rosenthal's hand-picked assistant, a lanky creative tower of tension named Arthur Gelb. The staff's main objection to Gelb was that he had too many "wild" ideas. Each morning, fresh off the train from Westchester, Gelb's tall, thin figure would come breezing into the city room with pockets packed with ideas—twenty ideas, thirty ideas: people to interview, tips to check, angles to investigate, grand "projects" that might take weeks to complete. Some of these ideas were brilliant, most had merit, a few *were* wild, all meant work, lots of work. So the less-ambitious *Times*men, whenever they saw Gelb getting up from his desk and about to look around, would head for the men's room, or to the dictionaries located behind posts.

Inevitably, most of Gelb's ideas went to the eager young men, and he employed an almost hypnotic manner in communicating his ideas to them. He would whisper. First he would put an arm around a young man, would walk him down the aisle, and then would whisper, very confidentially, hand over mouth, into the young man's ear—the inference being that this particular idea was so great that Gelb did not want to risk its being overheard by other reporters who would surely become envious. Finally, before the young reporter would leave the city room to embark on the assignment, Gelb would whisper again, "And remember, *there's a great deal of interest in this story.*" There was the barest hint that this idea might be Rosenthal's, or maybe even Daniel's or Catledge's, and the young reporter had better do his best. Then, after the reporter had gone, Gelb would have his arm around another young man, and again there would be the parting whisper: "And remember, *there's a great deal of interest in this story.*"

Rosenthal and Gelb—behind their backs they were occasionally called Rosencrantz and Guildenstern—would later read the stories as they came in, page by page, and would check to see that the touches and angles that they had requested were in the story. Then they would try to assure that the story was not overedited by one of Bernstein's deskmen; on occasion, in order to prevent the cutting of a certain paragraph or phrase, Rosenthal would carry the fight to Bernstein himself.

When Rosenthal was particularly pleased with the way a story had been done, the reporter would receive a congratulatory memo, and Rosenthal also pressured Daniel and Catledge into quickly producing big raises for certain of his favorites. One of his young stars was R. W. Apple, Jr., whose popularity with older *Times*men was hardly enhanced by the rumor that, after a few months on Rosenthal's staff, he was making $350 a week.

If so, he was earning it. An indefatigable young man with a round smiling face and a crew cut, the look of a slightly overweight West Point cadet, Apple was very gung-ho; he never stopped running, the perspiration showing through his shirt by two P.M., and he never dismissed one of Gelb's ideas without giving it a try. The result was that Apple got more good stories into the paper than anybody on Rosenthal's staff. This is not what bothered his older colleagues so much, for they soon recognized his ability to get a story and write it; what really unsettled them was Apple's incredible enthusiasm for *everything* he had been assigned to cover—a boring Board of Estimate hearing, a talk with the tax commissioner, a repetition of campaign speeches by Bobby Kennedy— and Apple's insistence, once he'd returned, on telling everybody in the city room about what he had seen or heard, or what had happened to him while on the story. Once, returning from the Democratic National Convention, Apple burst into the city room to report that Ethel Kennedy had sneaked up and pinched his behind on the boardwalk in Atlantic City.

Many other staff members, too, soon caught some of this enthusiasm, and the *Times'* coverage of the city was expanded to include lengthy investigative reports on New York's hospitals and its homosexuals, its interracial marriages and its bookmakers. One exclusive story about a screaming girl being murdered one night in Queens, while thirty-eight people heard her and did nothing, provoked many editorials and follow-up stories about New York's "inertia." (None considered the possibility that if New Yorkers did not have this built-in resistance to screams in the night, to screaming headlines and the loud forecasters of alarm and hate, there might only be mayhem in New York and political assassination: so perhaps human inertia, which permits some to die, allows others to live.)

Nevertheless the spark that Catledge had wanted in the city room was supplied by Rosenthal and Gelb, and one victim of all the chasing, writing, and rewriting was the late-afternoon card game. Another was the traditional "good-night," inasmuch as Rosenthal did not care when his reporters came and went, so long as they got the story. A third result was that the national and foreign staffs, once so superior to New York's, were now beginning to feel the pressure and competition for space on Page One.

Claude Sitton, the National editor, drove his staff harder, especially such reporters as Roy Reed, who was assigned to cover racial demonstrations in the South, Sitton's beat during his reporting days. After James Meredith had been shot in Mississippi, and a wire-service photograph of his prone body on the road was received in New York, Sitton grabbed the photo and scanned its edges closely, asking, "Where's Roy Reed?"

Tom Wicker in Washington became the target of Daniel's troubleshooter, Harrison Salisbury, and was chided for not producing enough front-page exclusives. Later there were discussions in New York about replacing Wicker as the bureau chief in Washington. This increased the animosity in Washington toward Salisbury and, to a lesser degree, Daniel—Salisbury being referred to as "Rasputin."

James Reston staunchly defended Wicker. But New York kept up its attack. There was not only the recurring theme that the Washington bureau was overly protective of its friends in government, but Wicker himself was blamed both for his running of the bureau and his performance as a reporter. He was just not coming up with big exclusive stories, they said, although failing to explain what specific big stories he was missing, nor how he was supposed to get exclusives that his own specialists were obviously not getting. The New York editors pointed out that Reston had come up with numerous exclusives during his younger days in Washington, but Reston quickly came back with the argument that Washington in those days was different—the war had just ended, it was a world of emerging nations, news was more easily gotten. Today, he said, Washington is pretty much a one-man town, Johnsonville, and if Wicker were the sort who was merely interested in protecting his own flank from New York's attack he could have focused each day on the President's movements and moods.

This volleying went back and forth between New York and Washington for more than a year, with some in the bureau contending that it was no more than New York's taking further vengeance on Washington, making Wicker pay for all the years of autonomy enjoyed by Reston and Krock.

But New York seemed committed to its decision to replace Tom Wicker as late as July of 1966. With the possible retirement of Arthur Krock, who would be eighty in November—though he seemed as nimble as when he joined the *Times* in 1927—there would be room on the editorial page for a column by Wicker.

Then, inexplicably, New York changed its plan. Perhaps cognizant of the low morale in Washington, perhaps unable to replace Wicker with an individual who could run the bureau better, the New York editors reversed themselves. Wicker now was told that he would remain as bureau chief *and* write a column. Wicker was pleased, but also weary of office politics. He did not want to remain the bureau chief if he had to be continuously bombarded by New York, and he communicated this to Catledge. If Wicker were to succeed as the bureau chief, he knew, he could not afford to be regarded in New York as just Reston's boy, or anybody else's boy. He had to be the actual choice of the New York editors, including Turner Catledge. When he put this notion up to New York, he was assured that he was New York's choice.

Suddenly there were new rumors in the New York city room. Salisbury was out. Rosenthal was sitting at Salisbury's desk. Gelb was at Rosenthal's desk. Rosenthal was Daniel's heir apparent. Where was Daniel? Where was Catledge? Who was running the store?

These rumors—prompted perhaps by Salisbury's going on a round-the-world reporting trip, and by his recently expressed desire to get back to writing after four years in the city room—continued throughout the summer.

It had been a wonderful summer for Clifton Daniel. His wife had delivered their fourth son; the *Times* was stronger than ever, unshaken by all the internal movement; and he, as its managing editor, was being recognized as something of a celebrity. He was included in the 1966 edition of *Current Biography*, and magazine writers made appointments to see him—no longer because he was married to a President's daughter, but because of his position at the helm of one of the few newspapers that seemed certain of survival.

As one being interviewed, however, he is not nearly so smooth as when he is conducting an interview. Once he kept a man from the *Saturday Evening Post* waiting for forty-five minutes. Then instead of merely apologizing for the delay, Daniel perhaps tried to make light of it—as he had years ago, possibly, in that note to the brunette lady he called a "fine cover-up" for his courtship with Margaret. Daniel's greeting to the magazine writer was, "If someone had kept *me* waiting for forty-five minutes when I was a reporter, I'd have gotten up and left." The man from the *Post* said nothing. But interviewers always get in the last word, and his article about the *Times* was hardly flattering to Daniel.

Mrs. Daniel, who has had so much more experience than her husband in such matters, will sometimes sit in when he is being interviewed at home; and one evening, after he had tossed off a remark that might have seemed conceited in print, she quickly edged forward on the sofa and warned, "Watch out, he'll print that."

"No, he won't print that," Daniel said, casually dismissing her fears.

"He *will*," she said, nodding.

"No, I won't," the magazine writer said. "Someday I may come to you for a job."

"Yes, and you'll not get one if you print that," Daniel said.

"He couldn't be less concerned," Margaret said.

"That's not true," the writer said.

"He couldn't be *less* concerned," Margaret repeated, more firmly, still shaking her head at what Daniel had said.

The most endearing thing about Daniel at home is his obvious delight in his four children. With them he is entirely relaxed, delightfully informal—a manner that seems beyond him in the office. On weekends he is seen often in Central Park with his older boys—Clifton Truman Daniel, nine, and William Wallace Daniel, seven—and whenever he makes airplane trips he usually checks the terminal's toy counters to see what he may buy to take home. In summertime the Daniels vacate their

Park Avenue duplex for a house in Bedford, New York, and Daniel commutes to the *Times*. When he returns in the evening Margaret is waiting at the station, always parked in the same spot. When she sees him, she honks her horn. He comes over, perfectly pressed, not a hair out of place, and gets into the driver's seat as she slides over. He kisses her on the cheek. She begins to talk as he starts up the engine of a Chevrolet station wagon. Then he spins the car around, and they begin the drive home—a typical American couple.

He is, she says, somewhat like her father. Mr. Truman, though not known for it, was also something of a "dude"; while he is known for his Giv'em-Hell-Harry manner, Mr. Truman at home was reserved and he never swore. "The only cussing done at home was by my mother," Margaret said. Both men, she continues, are "very tough characters, in a nice way," adding, "I couldn't get along with a man that wasn't definite, tough." The two men are also very compatible, and when a writer visited Mr. Truman in Independence, Missouri, earlier this year about Clifton Daniel, Harry Truman's last words were the gentle warning: "You'd better write something nice about my son-in-law. He's a good boy, an ideal son-in-law. He's never done anything to embarrass me." Mr. Truman paused for a second, then said, "And I don't *think* I've done anything to embarrass him."

The Daniels occasionally take the children to visit the Trumans in Missouri, and Daniel himself often takes one or two of his boys to revisit Zebulon. Margaret is "terrified" of airplanes and avoids any trip that she can, but Daniel likes to fly, enjoying the comfort of first-class travel. He is in tune with the tidiness of terminals, the well-dressed people; he relishes the two drinks before dinner served by winsome stewardesses who appeal to him not only because of their good grooming and precise tailoring, their pleasant smiles and desire to please—but also because of their almost ritualistic movements as they bend to serve, so graceful and controlled. "They are America's geisha girls," he once observed, flying back to New York after a speech in the Midwest. Then he said, almost wistfully, "I never knew an airline stewardess. A few of them used to live in the building I was in years ago in London. I used to hear them at night. But I never knew one." Then he said, "Premier Ky's wife was once an airline stewardess." He thought for a second. "Very pretty."

The speeches that Daniel makes around the country, usually

concerning the role of a free press, are delivered in his style of cool elegance, and are followed by questions from the audience. People are very curious about the *Times*, and many of them get from hearing and seeing Daniel a confirmation of their own ideas about the paper, its calm posture and pride in appearance, the respect for its tradition and the certainty of its virtue. They get from Daniel the image the institution has of itself, which is not necessarily all the reality beneath the surface. For there are other sides to the *Times*, other speeches made by *Times*men gathered at a Forty-third Street bar, or *Times*men talking to themselves in bed at four A.M., that reveal the frustration in working for a place so large, so solvent and sure—a fact factory where the workers realize the too-apparent truth: they are replaceable. The paper can get along without any of them. The executives like to deny it, and nobody likes to talk about it, but it is true.

And this truth evokes both sadness and bitterness in many who deeply love the paper, who have romanticized and personalized it, thought of it as some great gray goddess with whom they were having an affair—forgetting that no matter who they are, nor how well they have performed, they will soon be too old for her. She is ageless and they must yield to newer, younger men, and sometimes they are replaced as casually as light bulbs in a great movie marquee—changed automatically, though luminous as ever, once they reach a certain age; and this act does not go unnoticed by *Times*men still on the scene. They deplore the departure of older men such as Brooks Atkinson, who has not revisited the paper since; and William L. ("Atomic Bill") Laurence, the science writer; and the baseball writer, John Drebinger, who at his retirement party announced, after a few drinks, "Well, if I'd known retirement was so great, I'd have done it long ago," to which a *Times* executive responded, coolly, "Well, then, why did you give us so much trouble, John?"

Automation is everywhere, the complex problem shared by big business throughout the world, and yet at the *New York Times* there is the lingering notion that journalism is not a business, but a calling, and there is resentment in the city room on election night when a half-dozen machines are rolled in to do what the late Leo Egan used to do so well, predict the outcome; and there is vengeance among the ink-stained workers in the composing room for the increasing number of machines that can do everything better than men—except strike. There is irreverence in the city room for those items that promote communication without contact—the memos, the silver microphone on the City desk; and there is perhaps a realization among the high executives, too, that though the *Times* has long thrived on keeping "in touch," it has now grown to such enormity that it does not really know what is going on under its own roof. In the spring of 1966 there was the announcement in the *Times*' house organ that a team of trained psychologists, working under the auspices of an independent research organization, Daniel Yankelovich, Inc., would interview a "scientifically selected random sample" of *Times* employees in an effort "to determine how, in this large and varied organization, it can establish greater rapport with the men and women who work for it."

None of these intrafamilial matters are hinted at in any of the public speeches by Clifton Daniel or other executives; and the audiences who listen, and the subscribers who each day read the *Times*—and indeed, many who work for it, including the *Times*' editorial board—are not aware that there is any difference in what the *Times* seems to be, and what it is. The editorial writers, for example, continue to publish their lofty principles—they condemn congestion on city streets (ignoring the traffic jams caused at night by *Times* delivery trucks parked below); they lament the passing of landmarks, the demolition of historic buildings (not explaining why the newspaper sold its famous Times Tower building to Allied Chemical, nor why the celebrated electric-light sign that once rotated *Times* headlines around the building is now run by *Life* magazine). The *Times* is quick to denounce the suppression of news and ideas, even when such may be contrary to its own editorial policy, and yet in recent years its news department has refused to print anything by Herbert L. Matthews, who now sits rather quietly in room 1048 along a corridor of editorial writers. In 1963 Matthews revisited Cuba and Fidel Castro—who profited so greatly from Matthews' interviews prior to the revolution—and, upon his return, offered to write articles; but the news department refused. He had embarrassed the paper, he knows, and yet even now Matthews believes that Castro was not a Communist when the revolution began.

In the spring of 1966, Herbert Matthews returned to Cuba, again representing the *Times*' editorial board, not its news department; while there he reacquainted himself with Fidel Castro and Cuba, amassing twenty-five thousand words of notes. The news department again, upon his return to New York, declined his offer to write for it. So now

Matthews writes anonymously for the *Times'* editorial page on Latin American affairs, including those in Cuba—about which he has often been critical; other than that, he devotes himself to his books and to his belief that history will finally absolve him. But at the age of sixty-six, he is not counting on a clearance during his own lifetime.

Clifton Daniel appears at the *New York Times* each morning around ten, having read all the newspapers including the *Wall Street Journal* and, until recently, *Women's Wear Daily*. His secretary, Pat, who greets him outside his office, is an extremely pretty young woman who dresses impeccably—he chose her himself, and one is not surprised. "I am interested," he admits, "in appearances," and this extends to not only individuals' grooming or clothes, but also to the manner in which they conduct their private lives. He objects to being described as "puritanical," indicating that it matters little to him if the whole staff of the *New York Times* is involved in a vast assortment of pleasurable pursuits, sexual or otherwise; he is concerned, however, with "appearances."

Daniel's day is a smoothly run schedule of exits and entrances by subordinate editors seeking his advice or affirmation, and by strangers seeking his confirmation prior to employment on the *Times*. He also reserves time, prior to the four-o'clock news conference in his office, to reread those portions of the *Times* that bothered him slightly, perhaps because of the vagueness of the wording; or the sense that the reporter was becoming *involved*, the unpardonable sin; or maybe there had been an error that would require a "Correction," always an upsetting item on his agenda.

As he read the paper on one balmy summer day in 1966 he did not notice the item at first; it was on Page 30, and it was printed in agate type deep within a list announcing the names of City College students who had received awards: and yet there it was: "BRETT AWARD to the student who has worked hardest under a great handicap—Jake Barnes."

To anyone who has read Hemingway's *The Sun Also Rises*, the references are clear: Lady Brett and the impotent hero who loves her, Jake Barnes. In the *Times*!

A. M. Rosenthal, whose deskmen had edited and checked the story, had not noticed it, either, until the next day, after it had run through all editions; and he learned of it through a phone call from *Newsweek* magazine, which thought it was very funny.

Rosenthal saw nothing funny about the item. He was immediately infuriated. If the young *Times* correspondent who had been assigned to the City College story had been guilty of deliberately inserting false information into the *Times'* news columns, there was no recourse but to fire him. Many years ago, A. J. Liebling, then employed as a deskman in the Sports department, had done something like this; instead of listing the correct name of the basketball referee in the agate box score, as was required, Liebling—who always experienced difficulty in getting the correspondents to remember to get the referee's name—would merely write, in place of the name, the Italian word *Ignoto*—"unknown." Mr. Ignoto's name would appear on sometimes two, three, or even four basketball games a night—far too energetic and omnipresent a man to be believed for very long. When the prank became known, Liebling was fired, and he went on to use his imagination more wisely on the *New Yorker*.

The difficulty in the City College incident was that the correspondent who *might* have been guilty—Rosenthal had not yet called him—was Clyde Haberman, one of Rosenthal's favorites, a young man of twenty-one who reminded Rosenthal very much of himself: Haberman was skinny and driving, as Rosenthal had been twenty years ago when *he* was the City College correspondent, and Haberman had quickly demonstrated an ability to sense a story, then to write it well. In the eight months he had been the City College correspondent, Clyde Haberman had produced more than sixty pieces, a remarkable achievement for an individual whose beat was limited to one campus. Rosenthal also knew how dedicated Haberman was to journalism, how determined he seemed to be in making the grade on the *Times*, in no time at all, Rosenthal believed, Clyde Haberman would be recognized as one of the bright young men of the *New York Times*.

But if Haberman had inserted the Brett Award, Rosenthal knew, he would have to go. There was no chance of supporting a young man in this situation as Rosenthal had supported another man, a Negro named Junius Griffin, who had written for the *Times* about the existence of a "Blood Brother" gang in Harlem, militant men trained in karate who would soon move on Manhattan if things did not get better. Immediately, in Harlem and throughout New York, there were angry denials about the veracity of the Blood Brothers—some people challenging the story as an exaggeration, others calling it an outright hoax. Rosenthal checked it, and even today claims that Junius Griffin was not writing fiction; but the

Times was loudly criticized then by other newspapers and periodicals—an opportunity never missed when they think the *Times* is wrong—and Rosenthal himself was mocked by some of the Old Guard in the city room. The Blood Brother story, they said, was "Rosenthal's Bay of Pigs."

Clyde Haberman was in bed when Rosenthal called his home in the Bronx. Haberman had been awakened fifteen minutes before by a call from the City College publicity department saying it had been receiving inquiries about the "Brett Award." It was then, and only then, that Haberman remembered that he had forgotten to remove the humorous award, as he had intended, from the long list before turning it into the desk. The Brett Award had come into his head after an hour of boredom and drowsiness in having to type the long, unending list of prizes and awards that, Haberman was sure, nobody read. He gave an award to "Jake Barnes," then laughed and continued to type; later he became busy with something else, forgetting about Barnes and Lady Brett as he turned the story in—and it took the morning phone calls to remind him, first from the college press agent, then from Rosenthal himself.

"Clyde," Rosenthal began, softly, "did you see the City College prize list this morning?"

"Yes."

"Did you see a Brett Award?"

"Yes."

"How did that get there?"

"I, uh, guess I put it in," Clyde Haberman said, timidly, "in a moment of silliness."

"You did," Rosenthal said, slowly, the voice getting hard. "Well, that moment finished you in newspapers."

Haberman could not believe the words. His first reaction, as he later related it to a friend, was to be stunned by Rosenthal: "Finished with newspapers! He must be kidding! It isn't possible over an inane thing like this!"

Haberman got dressed, having been told by Rosenthal to appear in the city room immediately, but even as he rode the subway to Times Square, Haberman could not believe that he was finished at the *Times*. Rosenthal, who had learned from personal experience the importance of a second chance on the *Times*, Rosenthal, the author of that classic on the Warsaw ghetto—"so sentimental," Haberman had said, upon rereading it, "that you'd think he would be ashamed to expose such raw emotion"—Rosenthal was merely upset by the incident. Haberman knew him well enough to sense that Rosenthal regarded a joke on the *Times* to be a joke on him; yet he was confident, once the lack of malicious intent had been explained, that the mistake would pass and be forgotten.

It was noon when Haberman entered the city room. Nearly everybody was out to lunch. He walked up to the City desk and addressed a broad-shouldered gray-haired clerk named Charley Bevilacqua who had been there for years.

"Is Mr. Rosenthal in?" Haberman asked.

"Out to lunch," Bevilacqua said.

Haberman walked away, but Bevilacqua called after him, harshly, "You'd better stick around. He wants to talk to you."

Haberman wanted to whirl around and say, "No kidding, you idiot, why didn't someone tell me?", but being in no position to act offensively, he retreated meekly into the city room's rows and rows of empty desks, occupied only by the obituary writer, Alden Whitman, a reporter, Bernard Weinraub, and a young man on tryout, Steve Conn, a friend of Haberman's.

"Hey, Clyde," Conn said, laughing, "did you see that Brett Award in the paper today."

Haberman admitted writing it, and Conn smacked a hand gently against his forehead and groaned, "Oh, *God.*"

Haberman took a seat in the middle of the city room to await Rosenthal's return from lunch. He focused on the silver microphone up ahead—a most intimidating gadget, he always thought, for most young men on the paper: they feared, after having turned in their story, the sight of the editor picking up the microphone and booming out their names, paging them to the City desk to explain their ambiguities or errors. Just from the sound from the microphone, Haberman knew, a young reporter could usually tell the mood of the editor: if the editor paged the reporter in a snappy, peremptory tone—*"Mr. Haberman!"* very quick—it meant that there was only a small question, one that the editor wished to hastily discuss so he could get on to other matters elsewhere; but if the editor languished on the sound of a young man's name—*"Mr. H a b e r m a n"*—then the editor's patience was thin, and the matter was very serious indeed.

Twenty-five minutes later Haberman saw Rosenthal walk into the city room, then stride toward his desk. Haberman lowered his head as he heard the microphone being picked up; it was the voice of Charley Bevilacqua, a low sad note of finality, "*Mr. H a b e r m a n.*"

Haberman got up and began the long walk up the aisle, passing the rows of empty desks, thinking suddenly of a course he had taken under Paddy Chayefsky in screenplay-writing, and wishing he had a camera panning the room to capture permanently the starkness of the scene.

"Sit down," Rosenthal said. Then, as he sat, Haberman heard Rosenthal begin, "You will never be able to write for this newspaper again."

Haberman now accepted the reality of it all, and yet made one final attempt at reminding Rosenthal of the work he had done from City College, the many exclusives and features, and Rosenthal cut him off: "Yes, and that's why you acted like a fool—I had backed you, and written memos about you, and you could have been on staff in a year or two . . . You made me look like a jackass. You made the *Times* look like a jackass."

Then, his voice softening and becoming sad, Rosenthal explained that the most inviolate thing the *Times* had was its news columns: people should be able to believe *every* word, and there would never be tolerance for tampering. Further, Rosenthal said, if Haberman were pardoned, the discipline of the whole staff would suffer—any one of them could err and then say, "Well, Haberman got away with it."

There was a pause, and in this time Rosenthal's voice shifted to yet another mood—hope for Haberman, not on the *Times* but somewhere else. Haberman had talent, Rosenthal said, and now it was a question of accepting the fact that it was all over with the Gray Lady and moving on determinedly to make the grade somewhere else.

Rosenthal talked with him for another five minutes, warmly and enthusiastically; then the two men stood up, and shook hands. Haberman walked back, shaken, to a desk to type out his resignation. Clifton Daniel knew what was going on; Rosenthal had conferred with him, and also with other editors in Daniel's office, and they all agreed to accept the resignation as soon as Haberman could type it out.

Having done so, and handed it in, Haberman was aware that other people in the city room were now watching him. He did not linger. He quickly left the city room and waited in the hall for an elevator, and was surprised to see the tall figure of Arthur Gelb running after him calling, "Clyde, wait."

Haberman had never particularly liked Gelb, having been influenced by the Old Guard's view; but now Gelb was deeply concerned only about Haberman, and he reassured the younger man that the world was not over, there were brighter days ahead. Haberman thanked him and was very moved by Gelb's concern.

Then Haberman rode the elevator down to the first floor, not pausing as he passed the stern statue of Adolph Ochs in the lobby, nor stopping to talk with the few friends he met coming through the revolving door. He would return to City College for his final session in the fall, and then after graduation worry about what would happen next. The next day there was a "Correction" in the *Times*, only a single paragraph, yet it reaffirmed that despite all the shifting and shuffling of people and ideas, there are some things that never change at the *Times*. The paragraph, written by Clifton Daniel, read:

> In Wednesday's issue, *The New York Times* published a list of prizes and awards presented at the City College commencement. Included was a "Brett Award." There is no such award. It was put in as a reporter's prank. *The Times* regrets the publication of this fictitious item.

Gino's Long Run

There is a restaurant on Lexington Avenue near Sixty-first Street called Gino, which has not changed its policies much in a half century—no reservations, no credit cards, no earringed waiters. And yet, as a long-time customer, I have found Gino to be enduringly contemporary, rejuvenating itself constantly with the arrival of young men and women who first came to the restaurant as children and now, in this city of liberal and radical tolerances, become reactionary at dinnertime, preferring old-fashioned Italian family dinners where the management is conservative, the prices are moderate, and some of the veteran waiters still wear clip-on bow ties. Gino's food prices will actually be rolled back to their 1945 level on Friday and Saturday of this week, as the restaurant celebrates its fiftieth anniversary. This means that the $7.25 antipasto will be 60¢; lamb chops at $23.95 will drop to $2.50; and coffee will be served free with the compliments of Gino himself, whose full name is Gino Circiello, and who, at eighty-three, will step out of retirement for a two-day event.

In 1944, while working as an assistant manager of Caruso's restaurant on East Fifty-ninth Street, Gino saw a rental sign on the ground floor of a brownstone on Lexington Avenue near Bloomingdale's. He did not see an Italian restaurant nearby, and thought that this street of shoppers was an ideal place for one. The brownstone's upper-floor tenants were thriving as hairdressers and dressmakers, and on the fourth floor was a music teacher who spent her summers in the Catskills, always accompanied by her mini-size piano, which was lowered and raised by ropes outside her window. Gino liked the neighborhood and the neighbors, and, together with two partners, he signed a five-year lease at a monthly cost in rent and taxes for four hundred dollars—a cost that the present proprietors (two of Gino's former waiters and his chef) have seen rise to a current monthly rate of about twenty thousand dollars.

Fittingly, the restaurant's décor and furnishings have changed little through the years. Near its front door is the mahogany bar that Gino bought on the Bowery during the winter of 1945; in the dining area behind the bar are Gino's twenty-seven original tables. Covering most of the sidewalls and the vestibule of the rectangular restaurant is tomato-red wallpaper across which four rows of zebras are shown leaping unharmed through fusillades of flying arrows. One night recently, after a couple of Sambucas, I counted three hundred and fourteen zebras, and I saw for the first time that a single stripe was missing from the rumps of half the animals.

When I mentioned this to Gino, he admitted in a roundabout way that the wallpaper possessed an artistic touch of negligence. He explained that after the restaurant was forced to close briefly in the 1970s, owing to a kitchen fire, he had the wallpaper remade by a young designer, and the designer somehow failed to copy a stripe near the tail of the smaller of a pair of zebras that were the prototypes for all the zebras in the pattern. This oversight was repeated throughout, marring the regularity of one zebra in every pair. Before Gino noticed the mistake, however, the rolls of paper had been glued to his restaurant's walls. And, in true Gino tradition, he decided against changing anything. Several years later, when the wallpaper again was replaced, because its colors were faded and its texture was deteriorating, the pattern was repeated in conformity with the past—with a tomato-red background and with half the zebras missing a stripe.

The Kingdom and the Tower

When Arthur Gelb joined the *New York Times* as a copyboy in 1944, the uniformed elevator men wore white gloves, the desk editors donned green eye shades, and reporters making phone calls from the third-floor newsroom had to be connected by one of the dozen female operators seated at the eleventh-floor switchboard (perhaps the most vibrant center of gossip in all of New York); and up on the fourteenth floor, adjoining the publisher's office, was a private apartment visited on occasion by the publisher's mistress—and there was also nearby a bedroom for the publisher's valet, a gentleman of high moral character and undaunted discretion.

The *Times'* citadel of communication, whose neo-Gothic finials, scallops and fleurs-de-lis at 229 West Forty-third Street were in accord with young Arthur Gelb's vision of himself as an aspiring vassal in the House of Ochs, is now operational within the *Times'* recently occupied skyscraper on Eighth Avenue between Fortieth and Forty-first streets, thus terminating Mr. Gelb's ties to where he had invested sixty-three years of his working life and left him at his current age of eighty-three as the most enduring employee in the history of the paper.

Having risen from copyboy to reporter in 1947, and from Metro editor in 1967 to managing editor (1986 to 1990), and thereafter a fixture in the corporate hierarchy overseeing the paper's scholarship programs and other forms of munificence, Mr. Gelb now continues his relationship with the *Times* as a consultant and, for whatever it is worth in an age when the journalism he knew and practiced may be on the cutting edge of oblivion, he exists as the institution's éminence grise and one of its ceremonial hosts for such events as last Thursday evening's farewell party to the chateau of the Good Gray Lady on West Forty-third Street.

Hundreds of the paper's employees and their guests were invited to dance in the aisles and drink beer in the vacated third-floor area where Mr. Gelb had once overseen the metro staff and where his present-day successor, Joe Sexton, a physically fit and bespectacled man of forty-seven who had a salt-and-pepper goatee and was wearing a light blue cotton shirt darkened with his perspiration, danced with such tireless vigor around the room that he got the attention of someone with a digital camera and, promptly, his picture was available around the globe via *Gawker* along with a written account of the event:

> It was like Dorkfest 2007. The newsroom, filled with empty desks which were lousy with dustballs, contained about a hundred pizzas, 500 bottles of beer, and hundreds of journalists, editors and photogs sweating it out to the sounds . . . It was so crowded that it was nearly impossible to make the rounds, so some hopped up on the desks and filing cabinets and shimmied to the beat.
>
> But the best was Joe Sexton, Metro Editor, who is always a relaxed, jovial presence in the newsroom, always encouraging social outings, and he's a huge hip-hop fan, so nobody could hold a candle to his moves. He was on that dance floor for at least a couple of hours, drenched in sweat.

Watching from the sidelines, with his facial expression suggesting benign noninvolvement, was Mr. Gelb in a suit and tie chatting with some of the *Times* veterans, myself included, with whom he had dined an hour earlier at Sardi's on West Forty-fourth Street, next to the rear entrance of the Times Building. At the dinner, Mr. Gelb had begun by expressing condolences over the deaths of such *Times*men as David Halberstam, R. W. Apple, Jr., Sammy Solovitz (a pint-sized lifetime copyboy), and Abe Rosenthal, who had preceded Mr. Gelb as the Metro editor and whose leadership in the newsroom was often defined by the staff as a reign of terror.

Bernard Weinraub remembered being in the men's room one day when Abe Rosenthal walked in and asked, "Hey, Bernie, you think I'm losing weight?"

Mr. Weinraub regarded him momentarily, then replied, "No, Abe, I don't think you are."

"You son of a bitch!" Abe shouted, abruptly leaving the room.

The stunned young Bernard Weinraub soon hurried over to where Mr. Gelb was sitting and, after relating the incident, asked, "Arthur, is this the end of my career?"

"I'm not sure," responded Mr. Gelb.

Another reporter told a bathroom story regarding Michiko Kakutani, who, shortly after being hired as a cultural reporter, collapsed in tears and refused to leave the ladies' room for a half hour after being told that Rosenthal was critical of the clichés he found in her writing.

For no particular reason, certainly none having to do with Rosenthal, Joseph Lelyveld (former reporter and executive editor) made reference to the suicidal death of a venerable and zealously reliable staff member named Russell Porter, who one day left the Times Building and jumped out of his apartment window.

Many other recollections of shared experiences good and bad were exchanged by Mr. Gelb's twenty guests, and the digressions might have continued at length had he not interrupted everyone by saying: "C'mon, it's getting late—let's go to the party."

After leading the way out of Sardi's, he paused on the sidewalk to remove from his pocket a key that he said held special meaning. "This key was given to me many years ago by [then publisher] Punch Sulzberger and it provides a shortcut from Sardi's into the *Times*, meaning you don't have to walk all the way around the block to get in. Oh, I've used this key thousands of times, and now, on this night, I'll be using it for the last time."

He then inserted the key into the lock of a metal door that was a few steps above what had once been a loading dock for *Times* delivery trucks, and soon we were following Mr. Gelb through the mail room which was directly over where the huge printing presses used to function until this operation was transferred in 1997 to plants out of town. Still, as we passed one row of tanks, there was evidence of ink oozing out.

Following our ride on one of the back elevators up to the third floor, we immediately heard the loud music blaring from two self-powered Mackie speakers affixed to ten-foot-high tripods that overlooked the Metro desk, and the LP records spinning around on two turntables sequentially introduced us to the voices of James Brown ("Sex Machine"),

Aretha Franklin ("Respect"), Michael Jackson ("Don't Stop 'Til You Get Enough"), Diana Ross ("I'm Coming Out"), Justin Timberlake ("SexyBack"), and the Temptations ("Ain't Too Proud to Beg"). In rhythm with all of this music was the redoubtable Joe Sexton, and within the crowds of other dancers and onlookers—it was not easy to distinguish between them—were such newsroom notables as the executive editor, Bill Keller; a managing editor, John Geddes; and an assistant managing editor, William E. Schmidt.

It had been Mr. Schmidt's secretary, along with Mr. Sexton, who had arranged for the services of the disc jockey known professionally as "DJ Herbert Holler"—but as "Kenny" to his friends—and who rents himself out (along with his hundreds of vinyl records and his two-channel Rane mixer) for $1,000 an hour. While he refused to reveal his rate of pay from the *Times*, he did say that Mr. Keller did not want him to leave at their prearranged ten P.M. exit.

"Can we get you to spin another hour?" Mr. Keller asked, but Kenny said, "I can't," explaining that he had another private party to go to downtown in the meatpacking district. "But," he added, "I'll put on one more long dance." He selected "Love Thang" by First Choice.

The evening was very successful, in the opinion of Charles Kaiser, a writer who had worked as a metro reporter for the *Times* until 1980, having first gained Mr. Gelb's attention in the early 1970s when Mr. Kaiser was a Columbia student serving as a stringer. "What we saw in this place tonight was what you'd never have seen when I started as a reporter here in 1974," he said, adding, "You saw all these young people of color, and people of all kinds dancing with one another—men dancing with men, men dancing with women, women dancing with women—and it really reflects the fundamental change in the *Times* since Arthur Ochs Sulzberger Jr. became the publisher [in 1992]. When he started out here in the early 1980s as an assistant Metro editor, he figured out who all the gay reporters were, and then he took each of them to lunch, and one by one he said: 'I know you're gay—don't worry about it. When Abe Rosenthal leaves I'll make sure that the fact that you're gay will make no difference in your career.'"

After the music stopped, most people left the building; but others were free to roam around, and even wander up to the executive suite on the fourteenth floor, as I did, to get a final look at the exalted domestic quarters occupied many years ago by the publisher, the publisher's mistress, and the publisher's valet. Although the beds are gone, I assumed that what I saw was pretty much as things looked a half-century ago, notwithstanding the fact that there are draperies sprawled along the floor, and the ornate chandeliers were dislodged from the ceiling, and a few plush chairs, tables, and other furniture were scattered here and there and sometimes turned upside down. One object that remains in place, however, is an elegantly carved oak-wood grandfather's clock that stands about ten feet high and displays a medallion that marks it as a gift to Adolph S. Ochs from the citizens of Chattanooga, dated December 8, 1892. This was when Ochs was publisher of the *Chattanooga Times*, and the clock was presented to him four years before he left the South to take over the failing *New York Times*, whose founding editor, Henry J. Raymond, had introduced the *Times* in 1851 with offices downtown at 113 Nassau Street. The clock is still ticking perfectly. It will not be available to the auctioneers, having been claimed by Ochs' fifty-five-year-old great-grandson and present publisher, Arthur Ochs Sulzberger Jr.

While the interior of this building at 229 West Forty-third Street that the staff first inhabited in 1913 will soon be gutted by its new owner—an Israeli diamond billionaire named Lev Leviev who paid $525 million for the property, and might well convert the interior to profitable usage beyond anything imagined by the heirs of Ochs—the façade of the building will remain as it now is in accord with the building's landmark status.

The *Times'* new headquarters building on Eighth Avenue, a fifty-two-story "shimmering tower of transparent glass" (words by Paul Goldberger), has already received much welcoming attention from architectural critics and has elicited few negative comments from members of the staff, even though the top editors were more prestigiously endowed when they were at 229 West Forty-third—which is to say that in the old place anyone holding the rank of managing editor or above (be it Mr. Gelb, Rosenthal, or Mr. Sulzberger) had offices with private bathrooms. But not in the new place. Not even Mr. Sulzberger will have one, as he apparently wishes to convey his egalitarian sensibilities, whether they truly exist within him or not, and at the same time he emphasizes his paper's devotion to transparency by making it virtually impossible for any reporter or editor in this glass-walled emporium to enjoy a single moment of privacy—be it a furtive gesture of flirtatiousness expressed across the aisle toward a co-worker, or an upraised index finger in the face of an irascible colleague. But it behooves me not to enlarge upon my meanderings, for I have only briefly visited the new premises, having done so during the past weekend while accompanied by Mr. Gelb and two amiable *Times* escorts who deal harmoniously with Mr. Sulzberger.

Among the things that Mr. Gelb and I learned during our visit are the following:

- Of the building's 52 floors, only the lower 20 are being used by the newspaper, the rest being rentals.
- While there were less than 40 conference rooms in the old building, there are 113 conference rooms in this new one, giving me the impression that Mr. Sulzberger is inclined toward a talkier *Times* management.
- In the old building, especially when Mr. Gelb and I were employed there together during the 1960s, we routinely mingled and associated with multitudes of fellow employees who were members of the working class: We sat among ink-stained printers in the cafeteria, and we knew the first names of many of the *Times*' elevator men, the carpenters, the electricians, floor sweepers, and so on—nearly all of whom, I believe, took satisfaction in being affiliated with the *Times*, and in their neighborhoods this affiliation no doubt bestowed upon them a prideful identity. But now in the twenty-first-century *Times*, the employment is largely monocultural, and while blue-collar workers abound on the premises they lack the old-time sense of kinship because they are sent in by outside contractors.

In the lobby of the new building, as Mr. Gelb and I headed home and thanked our escorts for showing us around, I noticed a bronze statue of Adolph S. Ochs that had held the preeminent position in the lobby of Forty-third Street, but now in the new building it was positioned at an oblique angle behind the reception desk, with the statue's foundation wrapped in packing cloth, and the imperial gaze seemingly adrift.

"Where's that going to go?" I asked one of the escorts.

"We don't know yet," he replied.

Travels with a Diva

On an August night this past summer, the opera singer Marina Poplavskaya lay motionless for nearly three hours on the floor of her mother's apartment in Moscow, having collapsed shortly after four A.M. from inhaling noxious smoke from the forest fires that were burning out of control in the countryside; she was feverish and had no clothes on, after a sleepless night in hundred-degree heat with no air conditioning. Since Russia began keeping weather records, a hundred and thirty years ago, there had never been a heat wave comparable to this one. And never before in Poplavskaya's career as a soprano, in which she had frequently performed from a prone position and was often dead or dying by the final curtain—smothered by her husband in "Otello," stabbed by her own hand in "Turandot," drowned in boiling water in "La Juive," wasted with tuberculosis in "La Traviata"—had she imagined that the melodramatic scenes she had regularly given voice to would bear any relation to her life offstage.

Even after she was revived by two emergency medical technicians, who had come to the apartment at around eight A.M. in response to a call from her mother, Poplavskaya, who is thirty-three, lacked the strength to get to her feet. Her mother placed cool wet towels on her forehead and supported the back of her neck with a chilled bottle of Friuli wine that Poplavskaya had bought at the duty-free shop in the Frankfurt airport the week before.

She had just enough strength to telephone a friend.

"Darling, I'm about to die," she whispered into the receiver. "And so I ask that you help take care of my mother!"

A few days earlier, Poplavskaya had returned to Moscow for a visit with her mother and her grandmother before going on the road again: first to Buenos Aires, as a soloist in two concerts under the direction of Daniel Barenboim; next to Barcelona, to sing the part of Micaela in "Carmen"; and then to the Metropolitan Opera House, in New York, where, in November, she would appear as the mismated Queen Elisabeth of Valois in "Don Carlo." On New Year's Eve, she is scheduled to open in "La Traviata," singing the role of the self-sacrificing courtesan Violetta Valéry.

Poplavskaya made her début at the Met in December of 2007, as Natasha Rostova, the hopeful but abandoned maiden-in-waiting in "War and Peace," and she returned in 2009, with "Turandot." Of "Turandot," Anthony Tommasini wrote in the *Times* that "the most complete performance came from the elegant Russian soprano, Marina Poplavskaya, as Liù, the slave girl . . . She sang with warmth, beautifully earthy colorings and captivating pianissimo high notes."

Since then, she has kept a busy performing schedule, being increasingly in demand and shuttling between opera houses around the world. I had been introduced to her in New York, when she was rehearsing for "War and Peace." One night, she came out to dinner with me and my wife and a few friends, at Elaine's. During dessert, she suddenly got up from the table, raised her arms, and began to sing a Russian folk song. The noisy diners stopped talking. After serenading the restaurant with a few more, she bowed deeply and undoubtedly became the first opera singer at Elaine's to get a standing ovation.

Marina Poplavskaya was still a relative unknown in New York. During rehearsals, she had been relegated to the second cast, with the soprano Irina Mataeva singing the role of Natasha in the first cast. The Met's general manager, Peter Gelb, however, had become much taken by Poplavskaya's singing and stage manner, and, shortly before the opening, the two sopranos switched places. "Her presence is extraordinary," Gelb told me. "Some singers have it, others do not. It's something beyond practice—it's a natural phenomenon. She has it."

Aside from her powerful voice, which emanates from a body that retains its robustness through her devotion to such physical exercises as swimming and salsa dancing, her most distinctive features are her expressive blue-gray eyes, pearl-white complexion, and blonde hair, which falls to her waist.

On the occasions when I saw Poplavskaya during the run of "War and Peace," and two years later, during "Turandot," we discussed the possibility of my visiting her in Moscow. I was curious to see what it was like for an independent young singer on the rise to travel back and forth between the world's leading stages, with no fixed home, coping with the challenge of singing well while enduring the fatigues and frustrations of travel—the canceled flights, the visa problems, the lost luggage, the tedium of checking in and out of hotels. I had never been to Russia, and when she suggested that late summer would be a good time to come I made the arrangements. As it turned out, my travel dates coincided with the forest fires and the heat wave that were smothering Moscow. Despite Poplavskaya's warnings—she called to tell me about the night she spent unconscious on her mother's floor—I stuck to my plan and told her that I would be happy to wait out the weather in my air-conditioned hotel near Red Square. She relented, asking only that I bring from New York as many surgical masks as I could find. They were in short supply, she said, since people were wearing them not only in the streets but also in their workplaces and homes.

As my plane made its descent into Moscow, I could smell smoke from the fires thousands of feet below. An hour later, my cab pulled up to the Hotel National, and I could only vaguely make out the clock tower of the Kremlin and St. Basil's Cathedral, a few hundred yards away. While I was unpacking, Poplavskaya called to confirm our lunch date for the following day, but she told me that my promised tour of the city would have to be cut short. She could barely speak, much less sing, and with her hectic schedule in the weeks ahead—requiring that she perform in Buenos Aires, Barcelona, and New York—it was essential that she recover her health as quickly as possible. The cool air in Argentina, where it was winter, was a good place to start.

And so, during the following days, I saw a bit of Moscow, traveling in an air-conditioned 2002 Toyota silver hatchback that was driven by Poplavskaya's mother, Elena, who serves as her daughter's chauffeur, not only in Moscow but in foreign cities as well. Elena has always appreciated classical music; Poplavskaya told me that while her mother was in labor with her, she was singing Schubert's "Ave Maria." Elena's goal as a young woman had been to become a competitive bicyclist, but she was forced to abandon the idea after she was struck by a truck in a drunk-driving accident. As part of her rehabilitation regimen, she exercised at a local swimming pool, and that was where she met her future husband and Marina's father, Vladimir. He had bumped into her in the water, and he apologized. Elena told me that this was the first and last time that Vladimir apologized for anything. In 1976, after a quick courtship, during which she found him at times to be obstinate and evasive (she never really knew what he did for a living), she married him. Marina was born the following year, and by the time her brother, Stanislav, arrived, in 1982, her parents' marriage was so contentious that she lived most of the time with her grandmother.

I was taken to visit the grandmother, Tamara, on my second day in Moscow. She is a plain but vital woman with alert brown eyes, a rosy complexion, and silver hair that she wears secured in a short ponytail. She lives as a widow in a tidy two-room apartment on the twelfth floor of a much patched and repainted gray cement building.

The first thing I saw when I entered the living room with Poplavskaya and her mother was a large poster of the singer, advertising a performance at Covent Garden. It bore the caption "Turbocharged. Marina can do 0–60 in one second. Decibels that is. One voice. Complete control. Total power. Va va voom." A bookcase contained works by such writers as Georges Simenon, Mark Twain, Leo Tolstoy, and Alexandre Dumas père and fils.

"At the age of eight, I would sit here reading Dostoyevsky, Tolstoy, and all the Russian greats, because they were right here on the wall in front of me," Poplavskaya said, seated between her grandmother and her mother on a sofa. She described her childhood self as a blend of precocity and immaturity—a third-grade misfit whom many of her teachers and fellow-students resented, because she was in the habit of using big words. When she was bored in class, she recalled, she would interrupt the proceedings with a song. After she had done that a few times, some of her teachers pronounced her mentally disturbed and recommended that she be sent to a facility where such children received special treatment.

At this, Poplavskaya's mother and grandmother exchanged some soft words in Russian. What they were saying, as Poplavskaya translated, was that her so-called mental problems in school had nothing to do with her but were the result of the backwardness of the Soviet education system.

Poplavskaya got up to show me around the apartment. She pointed out the sofa in the living room where she had slept as a child, and the spot where she once kept cages containing a hamster, turtles, and a parrot. She said that she had not been allowed to have pets at her parents' apartment. After they separated, she said, everyone in the family except her father moved in with her grandmother. She never understood or cared for the remote man her mother had married, but even so, she said, "I always missed having a father." Elena now lives alone in the apartment in central Moscow. When Poplavskaya is in town, she stays with her mother and sleeps on the couch.

On my last night in Moscow, I arranged with the concierge to be awakened the following morning at 4:30. I was to meet Poplavskaya at the airport for a 7:25 flight to Madrid, where we would change planes and travel for another sixteen hours to Buenos Aires. Poplavskaya's mother would be taking her to the airport but would not be joining us on the trip.

I was a bit concerned about seeing Poplavskaya that morning, because the previous evening a slight rift had developed between us. The ill-feeling had begun shortly after we left her grandmother's apartment. Her mother had gone off to do errands, and Poplavskaya wanted to walk me around the old neighborhood. She showed me her school, and the playground where she had fallen and cut her lip as a child. Suddenly, she looked at her watch and said, "Oh, it's getting late! I must get to my rehearsal!" She added, "You're making me talk too much."

She ran and I followed her, watching as she held her right hand in the air in the direction of the oncoming traffic. Several taxi drivers slowed, but she waved them away. "They're thieves," she told me. "They overcharge, and they also might kidnap and kill you. We stay away from them."

A private car pulled up, and she leaned in to speak to the young man behind the wheel. Grabbing the rear door handle, she motioned for me to get in. Within seconds, we were speeding through traffic and soon arrived at our destination. The man, who revealed that he was a professional race-car driver, refused Poplavskaya's offer to pay him.

I followed her into a small recital hall that had a piano in front and a few dozen folding chairs arranged in uneven rows behind it. Except for Poplavskaya and her accompanist, I was the only one present, and for at least an hour I sat in the back enjoying the vibrancy of her voice as she sang, in Latin, lines from Verdi's *Requiem*, which she was to perform in Buenos Aires as a soloist with La Scala's orchestra and chorus.

Every once in a while during the rehearsal, she suddenly stopped singing. She stood and stared at the sheet music she held at eye level and began to shake her head in a way that sent her long loose hair thrashing about in whiplash fashion. She spoke harshly to the pianist, who would draw himself up and sit quietly, looking down at the keyboard. Tense moments of silence followed, punctuated only by a sound coming from Poplavskaya's cell phone, which sat on a nearby table. The phone had been programmed to function as a metronome. No matter what Poplavskaya was doing, it performed its duty: tick-tock, tick-tock, tick-tock.

Then, after nodding at the accompanist, she started again, singing in Latin:

"Quid sum miser tunc dicturus?" ("What shall I say, wretch that I am?") . . . "Lacrimosa dies illa qua resurget ex favilla iudicandus homo reus." ("Tearful will be that day, when shall rise out of the ashes the guilty to be judged.")

The word "lacrimosa" seemed to present a problem regarding pitch or intonation, and she paused to repeat it many times: "Lacrimosa! . . . Lacrimosa! . . . Lacrimosa!" Once, as she sang the word, she slammed her right palm down on the top of the piano.

The pianist sat in silence.

Tick-tock, tick-tock, tick-tock.

After the rehearsal, she and the pianist parted cordially. Then she walked over to me and said she was sorry that I had to sit through such a trying session. She stiffened and went on to suggest that her flawed singing and her fatigue were partly attributable to having me around. With her voice rising, and her tone almost as harsh as when she had been talking to the pianist, she said that answering so many of my questions and serving as my interpreter with her mother and grandmother had taken a toll on her throat. It was my fault that she had sung so poorly.

I expressed my regrets and promised that, from now on, I would be content to attend her performances and restrict our conversations to times of her choosing. The next morning, I was relieved, when I spotted Poplavskaya across the business-class lounge at the airport, to see her smiling at me and waving me in her direction.

After landing in Madrid, we had a beer together while we waited to change planes, and she told me a long story about sleeping on an airport bench in London one night in 2008 because of a visa mix-up. This sort of thing was almost unavoidable, she said, because, with her career moving so quickly and with enticing opportunities being offered on short notice, her travel dates were often switched at the last minute.

A few examples: In early January of 2008, she flew to Moscow from New York, having completed the run of "War and Peace" at the Met. Then she went right back to New York, because she could not resist the opportunity to perform at Avery Fisher Hall on January 25 with the conductor Leon Botstein and his American Symphony Orchestra, in a concert called "The Russian Futurists." During that period, Poplavskaya spent a lot of time in London, where she appeared in four productions under the auspices of the Royal Opera House: "Götterdämmerung," "Don Giovanni," "Eugene Onegin," and "Don Carlo." During her final scene on the last night of "Onegin," as she walked offstage she stumbled and fell, chipping a bone in her foot and tearing a few ligaments. She had to cancel a flight to Spain, where she had planned to visit San Lorenzo Escorial, a royal palace, as a method of preparing emotionally for her role as the queen in "Don Carlo." She walked with crutches for two and a half months, and when she was rehearsing for "Don Carlo" she wore an air boot under her gown to ease the pain. Six weeks later, she was singing the part of Desdemona in the Salzburg Festival's production of "Otello," conducted by Riccardo Muti. Her schedule is booked for the next five years.

With the plane to Buenos Aires ready for boarding, I followed a few steps behind Poplavskaya. Not for the first time did I notice how gracefully she carries herself and how nearly perfect is her posture, her spine straight, her shoulders back, her head held high. Her carry-on bag, slung over her right shoulder, appeared to be very heavy, but she carried it with ease. Inside it, in addition to her laptop, which contains downloaded recordings of hundreds of operas and symphonies, she keeps many books and instructional pamphlets. That day, she had a copy of "Practical Method of Italian Singing," by Nicola Vaccai (1790–1848), and "Esercizi per la Vocalizzazione," by Girolamo Crescentini, an eighteenth-century Italian castrato. She also carried the full operatic score of "Carmen," all six hundred and fifty-three pages of it. She is one of the few opera singers who not only know their own part in each opera and concert but are also familiar with the parts played by every other singer and instrumentalist in the orchestra.

In her bag, she also had the two-hundred-and-seventy-page conductor's score of Verdi's *Requiem*, which she had annotated with penciled notations. She carries a dozen or so colored pencils with her, each representing to her a particular emotional color or key. Her notes on the score are color-coded to signify mood shifts or changes in harmonics. B minor is represented by emerald green, C major by a shade of goldish red.

Shortly after we took off, Poplavskaya removed a headset from her bag and, after placing it over her ears, began listening to Beethoven's Ninth Symphony, one of the pieces she would be performing under Barenboim in Buenos Aires. She briefly lent me the earphones so that I could appreciate the sound quality. Then, after she had readjusted it over her ears, she leaned back in her seat and closed her eyes.

I tried to get some sleep, too, but I kept recalling scenes and sights from my brief visit to Moscow—the Bolshoi Theatre, the Pushkin State Museum of Fine Arts, the food market where I had watched as Poplavskaya skipped down the aisle pushing a cart filled with groceries for her grandmother, humming along with Bach's Brandenburg Concerto No. 2, which was playing over a loudspeaker.

It was evident that she had loved music all her life. Her beloved grandmother Tamara played the guitar and taught her folk songs. (She has mixed feelings about her grandfather Sergei, who had trouble holding his liquor and his job. He once took young Marina to a barber, who, without consulting her, lopped off her long braids. Later, she surmised that he had sold her hair to pay his bar bill.)

When Poplavskaya was nine, she told me, she was home alone after school one day when she heard an announcement on the radio that the Bolshoi Theatre was auditioning youngsters for its children's choir. She immediately headed to the arts center, leaving a note on the kitchen table for her mother and grandmother. After a fifty-minute subway ride and a forty-minute bus ride, she stood in line outside the recital hall for a few hours with more than a hundred other children, all of them escorted by parents or guardians. When it was her turn, she took her place onstage in front of a director, who sat behind a desk. He ignored her and looked around, as if he expected to speak first to the adult who had brought her. Then he turned to her and asked, "Why are you here?"

"That's a strange question," she replied. "I'm here to sing."

"And what will you sing?"

"I can sing many things," Poplavskaya said, "but I'll start with a folk song."

After she had sung two songs, the director asked, "And now would you like to sing the scales?"

"I find that odd," she told him. "Because I've already sung."

"Oh, this little girl has a strong character," the director said.

"May I go now?" she asked.

"Don't you want to wait for the results?" a pianist asked.

"No, I must get home," Poplavskaya said. She wrote down her telephone number for them, and said, "Please call me. If I've passed, fine. If not, I shall sing in another choir."

It was nearly ten P.M. when Poplavskaya returned home. Her mother was angry at her, but she asked, "Well, did you at least pass?"

"They will call," Poplavskaya said. "Or maybe they won't."

A week later, Elena got a call from the director, who told her, "Your extraordinary child has been accepted for a probation period to sing with the Bolshoi Theatre Choir. We will pay her sixty rubles a month."

With her first paycheck, Poplavskaya bought herself a pair of red leather boots. Before long, she was singing with the choir at concerts and operas all over Russia and Europe, requiring at times that she be excused from school. This did little to increase her popularity with her teachers and her fellow students.

At fifteen, having completed the tenth grade, her last year at school, she enrolled at the Ippolitov-Ivanov Music Institute, in Moscow, where she studied with a stern Siberian-born teacher named Peter Tarasov. Three years later, Poplavskaya fell in love with and married a language teacher named Victor Ivanovsky, who was twenty-two years her senior and the son of the venerable Russian tenor Vladimir Ivanovsky. Tarasov became infuriated with Poplavskaya, warning that her marriage would be the end of her career. "He thought I exchanged my talent for the family life and he got so furious that he didn't coach or speak to me for two years," she told me.

As it happened, the career went on and the marriage ended. Poplavskaya would have four husbands over the next eleven years—two legal and two common-law—without any of them altering her routine of living out of a suitcase and traveling all over the world in search of competitive musical events offering prize money and prestige.

In 1997, when she was nineteen, she won first prize for her group in the Bella Voce competition for young Russian singers. In 1999, she took second prize in the Elena Obraztsova International Competition for young opera singers, in St. Petersburg. A year later, in Belgium, she was a finalist in the Queen Elisabeth Competition.

By this time, her marriage to Victor Ivanovsky was over. As she later described it in an e-mail to me, "I left in February 2002 at 4:30 in the morning after I was another time told that I am not a good wife, as I do not manage well with my 'obligations' as a house wife. Meaning: ironing tons of clothing, washing everyday toilet and bathroom, after I am back home from my studies (which was after ten P.M. sometimes) . . . I just left, I ran from not being free, from it, from not being understood and not being loved."

That August, while seeking a divorce, Poplavskaya pledged herself, in her fashion, to a tenor from Kazakhstan whom she referred to as her "social husband." She lived with him for a while in her grandmother's apartment. She was then twenty-five and a soloist at the Bolshoi Theatre, soon to make her operatic début singing the role of Ann Truelove in Stravinsky's "The Rake's Progress." By the following March, she had a new "social husband," a Greek diplomat posted in Moscow. She was on the Bolshoi stage a good deal that year, first in Tchaikovsky's "Mazeppa," and then in Wagner's "Flying Dutchman." In June, during the second act of "Dutchman," her character sings the famous lines about the cursed Dutchman needing a faithful wife, and is crushed in the arms of the bass-baritone who plays him. She found herself enjoying the feeling. "It was," she told me, "love from one sight."

In keeping with Poplavskaya's preference for older men, the bass-baritone who played the Dutchman was an American some thirty years her senior named Robert Hale. (She ultimately married Hale in a Presbyterian church in Arizona, on August 2, 2006. Within a few months, she had filed for a divorce.)

When she met Hale onstage at the Bolshoi, she was less fluent in English than in German, French, and Italian. But after she rented an apartment in London that year, under the auspices of the Covent Garden Young Artists Programme, her mastery of English improved. So did her mastery of public relations. The British press praised her singing but was particularly charmed by her personality and her offstage antics.

One morning in 2005, she had a nine-o'clock audition at the Royal Opera House and was also expected to be in Moscow that evening at the International Performing Arts Center to rehearse for her role in Stravinsky's "Les Noces." After completing her audition, she rushed out the stage door, still wearing her long concert dress, and met, by prearrangement, a motorcycle driver who was employed by a courier service. They sped from the center of London to the airport in twenty-five minutes, Poplavskaya's arms wrapped around the man's waist and her hair streaming from under a helmet. She made her eleven A.M. flight and was in Moscow by early evening, in time for the rehearsal. The London papers covered the motorbike incident, and, later, the Royal Opera House created an ad campaign featuring her that resulted in the "Turbocharged" poster I had seen in her grandmother's apartment.

After sleeping for several hours on the plane, I turned and saw Poplavskaya still wearing her headset and with both eyes closed, except that now she was waving a yellow pencil in front of her face, as if holding a baton, unmindful of the attention she was attracting among a few passengers.

Finally, nearly twenty-four hours after leaving the smoldering city of Moscow, we landed in Buenos Aires. The weather was frigid—winter in the Southern Hemisphere. A driver sent by the concert's promoters met us and took us to a small hotel in the center of town, across the street from the ornate Teatro Colón. Unable to get a room in the hotel where Poplavskaya was staying, I had found accommodations a few doors away, at a larger hotel called the Panamericano, although I was told by the desk clerk there that, owing to a forthcoming convention, I would be able to stay for only five days. Poplavskaya's first concert, conducted by Barenboim, would not occur for nearly two weeks.

But, even before I had completed my registration at the hotel's front desk, I heard my name being called in a loud and strident voice. Turning, I saw Poplavskaya walking swiftly in my direction bearing a large suitcase in each hand, her carry-on bag slung over a shoulder. Making no attempt to conceal her agitation, she announced that the other hotel had assigned her to a smoking room, and she could not accept this. She went on to say that the manager had refused to give her another room, and, furthermore, he expected her to pay for the first room. She had protested so vociferously that the manager finally backed down, being by then relieved just to have her remove her hostile presence from his lobby.

Now she asked the Panamericano's desk clerk for a nonsmoking room. Fortunately, he had one available, but he made it clear, as he had to me, that she could stay for only five days. She was eager to be off the road, though, and so, after we had registered, we headed toward the elevator, porters following with our luggage. As we said good night, we made a plan to meet for breakfast.

The next morning, I did not see her. Nor did I telephone her. This would be my policy throughout our five-day stay at the Panamericano. She called me with enough regularity that I never felt out of touch. I knew that, before big performances, she sometimes sought seclusion for days at a time.

But she was unpredictable. Sometimes she appeared to hate being alone, and she would suddenly call to suggest that we take a walk or dine at one of the waterside steak restaurants on the Puerto Madero. More often than not, after she had taken a bite of what the chef had presented, she would send it back with word that the meat was insufficiently tender or too salty. Once, after the chef had washed the salt off her steak and returned it, she complained that the meat had come back too wet.

On mornings when we had breakfast together in the hotel's dining room, it was rare that she did not find something to complain about: the table linen was unclean, or the glassware was smudged, or there were too many flies buzzing around the buffet table. Once, she carefully trapped two flies in an empty glass; then, after placing her hand over the top of it, she carried it over to the maître d' and said, "Here, this is yours."

I was sometimes less amused than embarrassed by her demanding nature. After she had complained to the chambermaid about stains she found on her mattress, she reminded me that her grandmother Tamara had worked for a while as a chambermaid in a hotel, after she was forced to retire from her job working in an automobile plant. Her grandmother had been meticulous, she said, supervising other chambermaids and holding them to her own high standard. As a young girl, Poplavskaya would sometimes accompany Tamara as she made her rounds. I got the impression that she was holding the people who served her—the Panamericano's chambermaids, chef, and waiters—to the same artistic standards that a conductor demanded of an orchestra. At the hotel, she asked to switch rooms at least twice, and once she demanded that an electrician be sent to her room to check the heating system.

One evening when we were returning from dinner, after Poplavskaya had paid the taxi driver, she looked at the change and announced that he had given her counterfeit bills. She and the driver got into an argument. We had already stepped out of the taxi, but, as the argument escalated, the driver pulled away from the hotel, with the cab's rear door still open, and with Poplavskaya's handbag on the back seat. She ran into the street after the cab and, unable to catch up with it, screamed, "Police! Police!"

The Panamericano's doorman was standing inside the entrance to the hotel, but he did not respond. A female guest witnessed the episode, however, and wrote down the taxi's license plate number. I later accompanied Poplavskaya to the police station as she filed a report, but even though the license plate number was made available to the authorities, nothing was done to retrieve Poplavskaya's lost handbag—which contained her wallet, filled with credit cards and cash—or to apprehend the taxi driver.

After returning from the police station, Poplavskaya told the Panamericano's night manager that she would not pay her bill because there had been no doorman on duty to provide proper security. When we checked out of the Panamericano, Poplavskaya had not only succeeded in getting her bill significantly reduced; she had also seen to it that five hundred dollars was deducted from my bill. We had booked two new rooms in a hotel across the street called the NH Tango, but the Panamericano's porters would not transport our luggage there. Nor would the new hotel's porters come to us. So Poplavskaya took a brass-arched trolley from the Panamericano's lobby, piled our many pieces of luggage onto it, and rolled it outside and onto the avenue 9 de Julio. The avenue 9 de Julio is a fourteen-lane boulevard with four-lane streets on either side, and, as Poplavskaya piloted the trolley across, it bumped over multiple train tracks, dodging buses and cars and crowds of puzzled pedestrians, tourists, and panhandlers. Twenty minutes later, she gave the wheeled conveyance a final shove, and it rolled past a security guard and right into the lobby of the NH Tango. Because we were pre-registered, she pushed the cart, which was the property of the Panamericano, right past the Tango's porters, directly into the elevator, and up to her room on the ninth floor.

During the weeks in Argentina, Poplavskaya had some time to get acquainted with Barenboim, whom she worked with for the first time in Buenos Aires. (He was born in Buenos Aires, and the concerts were part of a series of events commemorating the sixtieth anniversary of his career as a conductor.) She told me that the part she was singing in Verdi's *Requiem* is more demanding than any operatic role she sings, and she was nervous. One afternoon, we sat in the Teatro Colón watching

Barenboim rehearse the orchestra. The theatre's ornate chairs are uphol-stered in red velvet, and their carved-wood backs are topped with gold filigree; Poplavskaya sat fidgeting, poking at one of the gold decorations with a metal hair clip. Later, she said to me, "Oh, I hope I will be good enough for him."

Several days later, on August 25, in front of a capacity audience at the Teatro Colón, whose horseshoe-shaped auditorium has 2,478 seats, with additional standing-room space for 500, Barenboim conducted Beethoven's Ninth Symphony. Poplavskaya was well received. The critic Margarita Pollini, in *Ámbito Financiero*, wrote, "The level of the soloists (wisely placed between the choir and the orchestra) showed its highest peak with the soprano Marina Poplavskaya, with such a voice that the very difficult Beethoven melismas did not sound strident almost for the first time."

Poplavskaya was also in good form five nights later, when Barenboim conducted Verdi's *Requiem*. Sitting in the audience, I could hardly wait for her to sing the word "lacrimosa." This time, she had no trouble with it. As I listened to her, I thought about her voice: making that sound requires such energy and skill, yet it never sounded forced. At one point, she held a note for ten seconds, and it cut like a diamond sabre right through the sounds of a hundred choral singers and a hundred instrumentalists.

Backstage, after the concert, Barenboim told her, "You are blessed with an exceptional voice, and you have trained it very well." (Later that evening, he told me that he had never known a singer who worked with a conductor's score.) He asked her to meet with him soon in Berlin, where he lives, to discuss the possibility of participating in projects under his direction at the Staatsoper, the Berlin State Opera.

The Teatro Colón hosted parties after each of the concerts in Buenos Aires, and Poplavskaya was often at Barenboim's side, although she smoothly stepped away whenever he reached into his pocket for one of his thick, gold-labelled cigars ("Edicion Limitada 2010") and struck a match under it. Far from Moscow, she was still avoiding smoke.

The next day, when she packed for Barcelona, to rehearse for "Carmen," she made sure to include her bathing suit, so that she could take some restorative dips in the Mediterranean. She also packed a stuffed toy dog, which she had bought for a euro in Rome, and which she takes with her everywhere. When she gets cold in bed at night, she places the dog over her throat for comfort. (The careful packing ended up being in vain: the airline lost her luggage en route to Barcelona.)

She had already arranged for the rental of a three-room apartment in Barcelona, within a short walk of the Gran Teatre del Liceu, where the "Carmen" rehearsals would be held. Poplavskaya was to sing the part of Micaela, the demure love match seeking the attention of Don José, played by the tenor Roberto Alagna. Among the challenges confronting her in this opera was having to sing in French, which she had not done, so she arranged to work with a special tutor. She felt quite comfortable with Alagna, having heard him sing before, and was looking forward to joining him at the Met this month, where he is appearing opposite her in "Don Carlo."

Poplavskaya left Barcelona and, after stopping in Berlin and Moscow, arrived in New York in late October to start rehearsals for "Don Carlo." She is singing the part of Elisabeth, a role that is considered particularly challenging in terms of interpretation. Through a Ukrainian-born friend, she found a nice furnished apartment near Lincoln Center for a hundred and fifteen dollars a day. She will live in it for more than two months, through the runs of "Don Carlo" and "La Traviata." Her living room, on the twenty-second floor, overlooks the twelve-story Empire Hotel, and sometimes, when he is standing near his window, she can see her co-star, Alagna.

On the afternoon of the "Don Carlo" opening, after Poplavskaya cooked herself a late lunch (meat ragout with vegetables and a glass of water), she walked over to Lincoln Center, with her cell phone turned off and her mind on the music that she would soon be singing. She passed through security at the Met's stage door and went to her dressing room. For the next half hour, while doing warmup vocalizing exercises, she set about sanitizing her quarters, wiping the top of her vanity table and all the surfaces around it with paper towels doused in Purell. Her dressing room measures about ten feet by twelve; against one wall is an upright Yamaha piano, and against another is a sofa covered in coral brocade. There is a bathroom with a shower, and Poplavskaya brings her own towels from home, having more than once complained to her Ukrainian friend that those provided by the Met did not conform to her standards of cleanliness.

Shortly after seven o'clock, wearing the hunting attire of Elisabeth of Valois, Poplavskaya was onstage wandering through the forest near

Fontainebleau when, by chance, she meets Don Carlo (Alagna), the son of the Spanish king. It is "love from one sight," as Poplavskaya might have phrased it, but it would not survive Act I. By Act V, more than four hours later, Poplavskaya is lying onstage with Don Carlo dying in her arms, bringing to a close their love and Verdi's long opera. When it was over, the audience whooped and applauded for many minutes, and the next day, in the *Times*, Anthony Tommasini wrote, "The lovely Russian soprano Marina Poplavskaya, as Elisabeth, does not have a classic Verdi voice. Still, with her luminous singing, beautiful pianissimo high notes and unforced power, she was a noble, elegant Elisabeth. Somehow, the cool Russian colorings of her voice brought out the apartness of the character, a young woman in a loveless marriage in a foreign land."

It was nearly midnight before Poplavskaya left her dressing room, having changed into a simple long-sleeved black jersey and a skirt that she had purchased the day before. She was on her way to a gala party on the Met's mezzanine. Onstage, the "Don Carlo" set was being noisily dismantled, and the crew was setting up scenery for the next day's rehearsals of Puccini's "La Fanciulla del West." On her way to the party, Poplavskaya paused in the hallway to put some personal items into her locker. Hanging there, in a cloth bag, were a pair of red patent-leather pumps with five-inch heels. She will wear them onstage on New Year's Eve, when she sings the role of Violetta in "La Traviata."

Four Hundred Dresses

Elaine Kaufman, the renowned and rotund proprietress of Elaine's restaurant, on the Upper East Side, who died, at eighty-one, on December 3, left behind, among her worldly possessions, four hundred custom-made dresses. Last month, she purchased several lengths of fabric, in anticipation of wanting something new to wear in the holiday season.

"Elaine was not thinking of dying," Linda Clare Meisner, Kaufman's dressmaker, said the other day at her studio, on Central Park West. "A few weeks before she went into the hospital, we took a car down to Mendel Goldberg Fabrics, on Hester Street, where they get the most luxurious fabrics direct from Europe. This is not the kind of place for buying leftovers on Seventh Avenue! Elaine was saying, 'Oh, look at that beautiful embroidered brocade over there! It would work well in a coat-dress!' And soon out comes her AmEx Gold card and she's spending six thousand dollars for several pieces of fabric. Coming uptown, she was very happy. Oh, dear Elaine—she was such a fabric junkie."

Meisner, an energetic Texan of sixty-nine, with brown eyes and ash-blonde hair pulled into a tight bun, was a dancer (she once appeared at the Metropolitan Opera) before devoting herself to creating couture apparel. She made the first of her four hundred dresses for Kaufman in 1990. Meisner called it a "triangle dress," composed of five yards of colorful Italian silk and costing about $2,000. Over the years, Kaufman spent about $800,000 on dresses by Meisner, either triangle style or coat-dress style.

Often the fittings were conducted at midday in Elaine's restaurant, which, since the insufficiently profitable luncheon trade was ended in 1988, was relatively private, especially in the smaller side dining room known as Siberia. Here Meisner would lay out the fabric on a table and, with an extra-long tape measure of a type primarily used for upholstery, she would lasso Kaufman's waist. Meisner said, "Measuring and creating clothing for Elaine was like painting a mural in motion."

Now that Kaufman has departed, Meisner worries about the fate of her client's wardrobe. She assumes that the dresses are hanging in the gigantic closets of Kaufman's apartment, around the corner from the restaurant. Four of them are in Meisner's studio, awaiting repair. (A few years ago, Kaufman sent one back that had never been worn; Meisner believes that she must have associated it somehow with George Plimpton, a beloved customer who had died the day it was delivered.) Not knowing what else to do with the dresses and the six thousand dollars' worth of unused fabric, Meisner is holding on to them. She may contact Kaufman's business partner, Diane Becker, but wishes to wait a decent interval before intruding.

Becker, who often sat in Siberia watching while Meisner took Kaufman's measurements, is now serving as the restaurant's manager and supervising its day-to-day operation. A slender, hazel-eyed woman, she started working at the restaurant in 1984 as a daytime waitress and manager. In 1988, she became Kaufman's chief assistant and, most people believe, is her chosen successor.

"Am I the next Elaine?" Becker asked one day last week, at the restaurant. She shook her head. "How could anyone replace Elaine? But she left the restaurant in loving hands, and I and the rest of the staff will care for it and for her customers the way she would have wanted." She went on, "But don't think that Elaine is not still running the show. She had a longtime habit—something she picked up as a kid born at the start of the Depression to Russian Jewish parents who emigrated to the Bronx. Whenever she passed a public phone, she'd stick her fingers into the coin return, fishing around for change. At the restaurant in the afternoon, she'd often sit near the two phones and absent-mindedly check for change. I'd say to her, 'Elaine, since people started using cell phones, you haven't gotten change out of those phones in years.' She'd check anyway. And she never got any change.

"A few days after she died, I was at the restaurant, telling Richie, our awning cleaner, that story," Becker continued. "For effect, I stuck my hand into one of the coin returns and, to my surprise, I pulled out a quarter. When I put my hand into the other phone, I pulled out another quarter. Only this one was accompanied by a penny. That was Elaine getting the last laugh and wishing me luck."

High Notes

On a bright Sunday afternoon shortly after one o'clock in Manhattan, a few days before his eighty-fifth birthday, which he would modestly acknowledge on August 3 by dining at a neighborhood restaurant on the East Side with his wife, Susan—who, within a few weeks, would be celebrating her own, forty-fifth birthday—Tony Bennett was standing behind a microphone at the Avatar Studios, on West Fifty-third Street, rehearsing a few lines from "The Lady Is a Tramp" while awaiting the presence of Lady Gaga.

Lady Gaga was expected to arrive at two o'clock, with her hairdresser, her makeup artist, her creative director, her vocal coach, her producer, her security guards, and others who know her by her pre-fame name, Stefani Germanotta; and then, after she had warmed up, she would join Bennett in singing "The Lady Is a Tramp," the final recording for his latest album of duets, "Duets II," which will be released by RPM Records/Columbia on September 20. It is a sequel to his 2006 Grammy Award–winning album, and sixteen other singers had already collaborated with him. They included John Mayer ("One for My Baby"), Carrie Underwood ("It Had to Be You"), Queen Latifah ("Who Can I Turn To?"), Mariah Carey ("When Do the Bells Ring for Me?"), Aretha Franklin ("How Do You Keep the Music Playing?"), Willie Nelson ("On the Sunny Side of the Street"), Andrea Bocelli ("Stranger in Paradise"), and Amy Winehouse ("Body and Soul"). Bennett and Winehouse had sung together in London in March, four months before her death, in July, at twenty-seven, following years of familiarity with drugs and alcohol.

Over dinner a couple of weeks before the session with Lady Gaga, Bennett told me that he had been concerned about Winehouse's well-being when he spent time with her in London. He said, "I wanted to tell her that she needed to shape up or she could end up destroying herself." In August, he appeared on the MTV Video Music Awards in a special tribute to Winehouse, saying, "She was a true jazz artist in the tradition of Ella Fitzgerald and Billie Holiday." After the broadcast, he told a reporter, "What I wanted to do, I wanted to stop her. I wanted to tell her that many years ago I was naughty also with some drugs." He went on, "Woody Allen's manager at the time"—Jack Rollins—"said he knew Lenny Bruce, and he said one sentence that changed my life. He said, 'He sinned against his talent.' I wanted to tell her that."

As a few dozen people gathered within the glass-enclosed control room anticipating Lady Gaga's appearance, Bennett was standing alone on a white platform, in the center of the studio. He had on a hand-tailored Brioni tux with a red pocket square, a white shirt, and a black tie that had been a gift from his drummer, and he was singing the introductory verse to "The Lady Is a Tramp," the Rodgers and Hart show tune from their 1937 musical, "Babes in Arms":

> I've wined and dined on Mulligan stew and never wished for
>   turkey
> as I hitched and hiked and grifted, too, from Maine to
>   Albuquerque.

He then turned toward his musical director, Lee Musiker, a sharp-featured, energetic, dark-haired man of fifty-five, who sat behind a grand piano, a few yards away. "Let me ask you something," Bennett began, in his characteristically soft and deferential manner. "Can you go up another key?"

"You want me to raise it up more?" Musiker asked.

Bennett nodded. And, as Musiker's fingers moved with accelerated energy along the keyboard, Bennett appeared to be more contented as he again sang the opening lines of the intro:

> I've wined and dined on Mulligan stew
> and never wished for turkey.

After he had satisfactorily rehearsed the next eight lines of the intro, which he planned to sing alone on the record before participating with Lady Gaga in the duet, he decided to rest his voice for a while. She was due in about half an hour.

"I did my scales today," he said, as he stepped down from the platform. Bennett practices scales for fifteen to twenty minutes every day, singing along to a small tape recorder that plays a cassette of exercises created by his longtime teacher, the late Pietro D'Andrea. Once, I heard Bennett say, "The first day you don't do the scales, you know. The second day, the musicians know. The third day, the audience knows."

At Avatar, he popped a dime-size yellow lozenge into his mouth and headed over to the control room to spend some time with his guests and family members, including Susan, who is often with him when he sings.

A week earlier, she had flown with him and his quartet to concerts in Reno, Las Vegas, and Denver, three of nearly a hundred appearances he makes every year around the nation and overseas; and she intends to be in the audience on Sunday evening, September 18, when he and his quartet are scheduled to present a few dozen of his favorite songs from the stage of the Metropolitan Opera House. But, no matter where Tony Bennett is featured, what he sings and how he sings have pretty much remained the same for most of his more than sixty years as an entertainer. As his friend Count Basie once reminded him, "Why change an apple?"

Susan began dating Bennett in 1985, on the eve of his fifty-ninth birthday, when she was eighteen. Her mother, Marion Crow, a fourth-generation native of the San Francisco Bay Area—and a devotee of Bennett's music since her student days at the Convent of the Sacred Heart, in the early fifties—had introduced Susan to the singer five years earlier. Marion and her husband, Dayl Crow—a broker with Merrill Lynch who had been a fighter pilot in Korea—were vacationing in Las Vegas, accompanied by their daughter. After they had seen Bennett's show, they bumped into each other outside the venue, and Marion initiated the introduction. Susan shyly shook hands with the singer but was quickly put at ease by his graciousness.

Marion and Dayl had first met Bennett in New York many years before, in 1966. Dayl Crow was in the city on business and was staying with Marion at the Plaza. After she read that Bennett was booked at the Copacabana, she asked Dayl to get tickets. While they were having a drink at their table before the show, a young woman photographer stopped by and offered to take their picture.

"Yes," Marion replied, "but only if Tony Bennett is in it."

Soon the photographer returned to say that Bennett would see them in his dressing room before the performance, and it was there that he posed with them. Marion was two months pregnant with Susan. Forty-one years later, after she married Tony Bennett, in 2007, Susan explained to a reporter, "It was a prenatal influence that led me to him."

Their marriage, in a civil ceremony in New York, at which Mario and Matilda Cuomo were the principal witnesses, had been preceded by a twenty-four-year courtship, owing to Bennett's prolonged and contentious separation from his second wife, Sandra, with whom he has two daughters—Johanna, born in 1969, and Antonia, in 1974. He retains a warm relationship with both. Antonia, a singer, often travels with him and his musicians, opens his shows, and occasionally does a few numbers with him onstage, including a Sondheim song, "Old Friends."

Bennett's marriage, in 1952, to his first wife, Patricia, ended more amicably; and Patricia and Tony's two sons, Danny, born in 1954, and Daegal, a year later, are both professionally engaged in their father's career and were among those waiting for Lady Gaga. Danny, a well-proportioned six-footer who boxes in a gym about three times a week, is Bennett's manager. He has hazel eyes, a receding hairline, and an engaging demeanor not lacking in self-assurance. His somewhat shorter but equally fit brother, Daegal, who has inherited their father's green eyes and Roman nose, is in charge of sound.

Daegal—commonly called Dae, pronounced "day"—has his own recording studio, in Englewood, New Jersey. Earlier in the week, a seventeen-piece orchestra had met there to prerecord the music that would soon flow through the system at Avatar and blend in with Tony Bennett's and Lady Gaga's voices as they sang into their microphones. Dae believed it was more efficient to have the orchestra complete its work in the New Jersey studio, where the acoustics were ideal and which afforded the Bennett organization some flexibility when coping with the tight schedules imposed by most of the high-profile singers it sought for the duets.

Dae knew that Lady Gaga's time was very limited. As he waited for her to arrive at Avatar, he seemed unable to relax, sitting in the rear of the control room. When his father waved in his direction, Dae failed to notice him, because he was focusing on the console, a black soundboard about five feet wide and lined vertically and horizontally with rows of illuminated knobs (green, red, yellow, amber) that alternately cast slight reflections upon his forehead.

Danny Bennett was standing behind him, looking through the big window at a documentary film crew wheeling a camera along tracks laid on the studio floor near the white platform. Also in the control room, close to the doorway, were two longtime friends of Bennett's—seventy-year-old Leonard Riggio, the chairman of Barnes & Noble, and seventy-one-year-old Joseph Segreto, who owns a restaurant called Eleven 79, in New Orleans, and first met Bennett in Las Vegas in 1961, when Segreto was a roadie for a band from Philadelphia that was playing in the lounge of the Sahara.

Both Segreto and Riggio were smartly attired, and Susan, who has blonde hair and brown eyes, stood talking with them. She was wearing orange linen pants with a yellow-and-white-striped short-sleeved shirt and sandals.

As Bennett joined them, Segreto patted him on the back and complimented him on how well he had sung the intro. Bennett smiled but changed the subject to Lady Gaga, whom he recalled meeting in early May when they had each performed at a charity event for the Robin Hood Foundation at the Javits Convention Center. He also met her mother and father that night, he said, as well as a young man who had told him, "I'm her boyfriend, so you'd better watch out."

The others laughed. Segreto shook his head. "She's big," he said.

"She's going to be bigger than Elvis Presley," Bennett said.

He went on to describe Lady Gaga as being enormously talented not only as a singer but as a dancer and a pianist—and he suggested that, at the same time, under all her makeup and marketing, she was just a normal human being, "a sweet little Italian-American girl who studied at NYU."

Bennett and his friends stood talking near the door for the next fifteen minutes, discussing, among other things, his upcoming show at the Metropolitan Opera. That reminded Riggio of a story about Luciano Pavarotti doing a book signing at Barnes & Noble.

"There were five thousand people lined up outside," Riggio said.

Bennett let out a low whistle.

"So we go inside the store, and Pavarotti, you know, he is signing slow, and talking to people, and the people are giving him pictures, and other books, to sign, and I feel bad for the people outside, so I'm saying, 'Only one book!' and I'm trying to move it. So Pavarotti looks at me, and he smacks me in the face, and he goes, 'Mind-a your own-a business-a!'"

Everybody laughed, and Bennett offered his own Pavarotti story.

He said, "I remember Sinatra once asked Pavarotti, 'How do you sing a soft high note?' and Pavarotti replied, 'You keep-a your mouth closed!'"

Conversation turned to Bennett's forthcoming visit to New Orleans, where he will join Riggio and Riggio's wife, Louise, in celebrating the completion of the 101st house built under the auspices of the couple's nonprofit foundation, Project Home Again in New Orleans, which has provided furnished housing, without cost, to low- and moderate-income families wishing to reestablish themselves in the city following Hurricane Katrina. Bennett said that he and his quartet would entertain the Riggios and the other celebrants there on November 11, and Segreto promised to cook something special at his restaurant. Segreto has developed a warm relationship with the couple ever since they launched their foundation, and Leonard Riggio has acknowledged it by naming one of his many racehorses, a two-year-old thoroughbred, Mr. Segreto.

"How about that, Tony?" Riggio called out, as Segreto took a little bow.

"That's nice," Bennett replied, and gave his signature smile. He then conceded being a frequenter of racetracks back in the seventies, when he lived in Los Angeles, and he remembered one day when he went to the track at the invitation of Cary Grant.

"All the women were just fainting as he's walking," Bennett recalled. "All the women in the boxes fainting. Cary Grant, you know. So I said, 'You come here often?' 'Yes,' he said. 'I own the track.'"

"He owns it?" Segreto exclaimed, in his gravelly voice.

"He owns it," Bennett repeated.

"Probably Fred Astaire paid for it," Segreto said, "because he used to go betting with two hands. Who bet more on horses than two guys, friends of yours, Mickey Rooney and Fred Astaire?"

"I didn't know that," Bennett said.

"Fred Astaire was at the track all the time," Segreto went on. Then Segreto mentioned the name of a woman who was once involved with

Astaire, a woman whom Bennett was also acquainted with, and Bennett thought for a moment and then said, in a lowered voice, "She messed him up."

"Oh sure she messed him up," Segreto declared knowingly. "But he was such a great fan of the races."

Lee Musiker approached Bennett from behind and asked, "You want to do a couple of warmups before she arrives?"

"OK," he said. With a little nod toward Susan and his friends, he turned and headed back into the studio, where he soon resumed his earlier position on the white platform. While Musiker began playing the piano, Bennett, microphone in hand, began to sing, without full voice, the first lines of the duet he would soon record:

She gets too hungry for dinner at eight,
Loves the theater but she never comes late.

On the music stand in front of him, in case he forgot the lyrics to "The Lady Is a Tramp," there were three sheets of paper on which were printed, in large letters, triple-spaced, every word of the song—approximately forty lines that he and Lady Gaga would alternately deliver, with her words printed in red and his in black.

GAGA: I never bother with people I hate . . .
BENNETT: Doesn't dig crap games with barons and earls . . .
GAGA: I won't go to Harlem in ermine and pearls
I won't dish the dirt with the rest of those girls

But before he had completed his second run-through of the tune, his attention was drawn to the sounds of a crowd of newly arrived people—who, having exited the freight elevator, had proceeded down a hall in the direction of the control room, led by Lady Gaga, a slender young woman with aquamarine bobbed hair. She wore dark glasses, a long black lace gown that you could see through, and, over it, a sleeveless black leather motorcycle jacket, unzipped, with studs on the lapels. A silver buckle dangled from a belt that flapped along her right thigh as she ran gleefully toward Bennett.

"Hello, Tony!" she called out, her arms extended.

"Oh, great!" he exclaimed, stepping down from the platform to embrace her as she removed her dark glasses, revealing a small scimitar-shaped stroke of eyeliner beside each of her eyes, extending back toward the temple, resembling a couple of anchovies. As Musiker rose from the piano bench to shake hands with her, Dae and Danny were on their way down from the control room to review the recording procedure. When she removed her leather jacket, and Bennett tried to assist her, she good-naturedly shoved him away, saying, "No, that's OK. Don't you hold a thing." She dangled the jacket in the air until a young man hastened into the studio to take it and carry it to her dressing room.

Lady Gaga stood silently near the piano for a few seconds, looking around the studio and up at the ceiling, which was thirty-five feet at its highest point. She was tugging at the waist of her black lace gown, which she said had been designed by Tom Ford. The gown was so long that several inches of it swept along the floor, and had twisted around her ankles. It was impossible to see the shoes she was wearing, but underneath the lace dress she had on what looked like a black bikini.

"I love the way you wrap that skirt," Bennett said finally. "It's fabulous."

"I thought I'd give a little twist for you, Tony," she said.

Bennett was eager to tell her a story. "I've got to tell you that when my wife and I exercise we look out our window at a synagogue right across the street." He said that some men were working hard erecting a scaffolding there. "And then I noticed that, on the side of their truck, in big letters, the word 'Gaga' was painted!"

"Working so hard!" she said, and laughed.

Danny Bennett came up and introduced himself, and then pointed out his brother.

"Such an honor to meet you, wow, hello," she began, and then she asked some questions, such as "Do we both use the same mic?" (no, there was one for each singer) and "Should I use headphones?" Dae explained that his father did not want headphones, after which she turned to Bennett and said, "I love that you don't want them."

"Beautiful gown" was his reply.

"Thank you," she responded. "I wore it for you. The whole thing, head to toe, as in 'What would Tony want?'"

"Great," he continued, his bronzed face creased with its almost permanent smile.

She then asked Danny Bennett whether or not there was a limit on the rehearsal time before they began the recording.

"As many times as you want to rehearse it, or do it—anything," Danny said. "Everyone's really flexible here."

"Great," she said. "Thank you," and then in a loud voice she said, "Test," and proceeded on her own, without the accompaniment of the prerecorded music, to sing, "That's why this chick is a tramp."

Bennett laughed.

Then she corrected herself. "That's why the lady is a tramp," she sang, pronouncing the last word "tray-amp."

She was having fun, inflecting a slight Southern redneck intonation and a bit of "Guys and Dolls" spirit into the music of Rodgers and Hart: the words "I never bother with people I hate" she sang as "Eye-ha never bother with people I hay-yate."

Bennett joined in: "Doesn't dig crap games, with barons and earls."

When she followed with "I won't go to Harlem in ermine and pearls," she pronounced the words as "oimens" and "poils."

"Oh, I'm so nervous!" she said.

"No, it's terrific," he said.

"If I tap out, you can just tell 'em that it was all planned."

"Sounds great," he responded.

Then, after they had laughed through the rest of the song, she turned to him and asked, "What was it like with the girls?"

He looked at her quizzically.

"Do they always get this way around you?"

When he failed to answer, she continued, "Do they always get really nervous and stand there sweating and blushing?"

Among those joining in the laughter were Susan and the others in the control booth, who now included members of Lady Gaga's troupe and also her vocal coach, a gray-haired, bespectacled man of sixty-six named Don Lawrence, who first heard her sing when she was thirteen, and whose clients have included Mick Jagger, Christina Aguilera, Whitney Houston, Bono, and Jon Bon Jovi.

Danny Bennett, who had been sitting near Don Lawrence, returned to the studio carrying a newspaper clipping from the Yonkers *Record*, dated August 26, 1951, bearing the headline GIRLS "GAGA" AS TONY CROONS A HIT. The article displayed a photograph of a youthful, dark-haired Tony Bennett in a tuxedo surrounded by four smiling young female fans; the caption explained that he had just serenaded them with one of his all-time hit tunes, "Because of You."

Lady Gaga began reading the article aloud, standing next to Bennett. "Girls 'gaga' as Tony croons a hit," she read, and moving closer to him she said, "See, I told you. You make women do that. Look what you did! . . . Oh, Tony, I would have been chasing you around. Oh, Tony, do you die when you read that?"

"Oh, you're right," Susan Bennett replied, her voice echoing through the speaker in the control room. "Gotta keep the girls off him."

"Keep Gaga off!" Lady Gaga corrected her, before turning to some-body on her staff and requesting a drink. A young man scurried into the studio carrying a glass of whiskey. Bennett watched as she took a sip. Then she announced, "Now that I've had a little bit to drink, I'm not so nervous." Again she turned to Bennett.

"Do women do that around you, too?" she persisted.

"What's that?" he asked.

"Do they just knock 'em back, just so they can be in your presence?" she asked. He grinned.

"Yes, they all do," she answered for him. "We're all very nervous around him." She took another swallow, holding the glass in one hand and the microphone in the other.

Dae's voice was heard over the speaker in the control room, asking, "All set?"—meaning, in effect, Shall we finally get to work?

"I'm all set," Lady Gaga said. Then she added, "Hey, Tony."

"Yes?"

"I missed you, baby."

Suddenly, the brassy up-tempo sound of the orchestra filled the studio, and immediately it was accompanied by the two singers' voices:

BENNETT: She gets too hungry for dinner at eight,
Loves the theatre but she never comes late.
GAGA: Eye-ha never bother with people I hay-yate.

They smoothly got through the song, taking a little more than two minutes, and after the conclusion Dae Bennett, in the control room, said, "OK, that sounds really good. We just need to do some inserts on the end, and we'll have everything."

"OK," Bennett said.

"Great," Gaga replied.

But then Bennett went on, "I think we should do it a couple more times, I really do, and get whatever's good there." He turned to Lady Gaga: "Is that all right with you?"

She agreed, saying, "We're having a good time."

She looked around at some of the guests standing in the hallway and the control room, and, seeing the dapper Leonard Riggio, and Joe Segreto in his seersucker suit, white shirt, blue-knit tie, and white shoes, she said to Bennett, "You know, all my friends—you have to meet them sometime, they're always in three-piece suits, with beautiful hats on. They like to go out and pretend like it's the fifties."

"Right," Bennett said. They agreed to do another take.

Gaga said, "I'm going to give it a little more character."

He started singing again, and when they finished she said, "It's like our third date now!"

Over the next half hour, they did six more takes, some with scatting, all of them acceptable to Bennett's sons, in the control room, but at the conclusion of each take neither Bennett nor Lady Gaga wanted the duet to end.

"Oh, fun!" she exclaimed, after yet another take. "We can do this all day?"

"Yes, I liked it," he said.

"Shall we do one more?" she asked.

"Whatever we want," he said. "We can do it till we're very happy with it."

"Oh, let's keep having fun. I'm having a good time."

"Good."

"Is your musical director happy?"

"So far," Dae Bennett replied over the speaker.

"Everybody's happy," Lady Gaga declared. "Happy faces!" she loudly announced, adding, "I've never done this without headphones. It's so liberating." She took another sip of whiskey.

For a different take, they decided to improvise some lyrics.

When Gaga burst out, "I like the Yankees," Bennett followed with "and Jeter's just fine."

Lady Gaga interrupted. "Maybe I should pick another Yankee. Posada's my favorite. But is he not playing anymore?"

Somebody shouted that he'd been benched.

"Makes me sad," Lady Gaga said, then improvised a new line: "I miss Posada!"

When they finally decided that there was a limit to their alacrity, and their duet was done for the day, they were called upon to do a short taped interview for the documentary film, which Danny was overseeing.

"Was it OK?" Lady Gaga asked Bennett, as they stepped off the platform.

"Aw, c'mon. It's the best thing that ever happened."

"I can't wait. I'm going to cry so hard when it comes out."

With Bennett and Lady Gaga sitting side by side in front of a camera, a staff member named Sylvia Weiner asked her to recount some of her feelings about working with Tony Bennett.

Lady Gaga replied that, when she knew she'd be recording a duet with him, first she decided she would have to change her wardrobe: "Well, I have to meet Mr. Bennett! What do I wear? Do I look classy? Do I look elegant? Do I look sexy? I don't know what he likes. So I tried a couple of different outfits on, and then I just ran out there, and"—turning toward him as she spoke—"I met your beautiful wife. It was wonderful."

"Well," Weiner went on, "tell us why 'Lady Is a Tramp' lent itself so well for your duet."

Lady Gaga thought for a moment, and then replied, "Well, 'cause I'm a tramp. And," she went on, gesturing at Bennett, "he knows it."

She laughed.

But he shook his head.

"I know that you're a lady," he said, emphatically. "Playing a tramp."

Credits

"Wartime Sunday," "The Kidnapping of Joe Bonanno," "Charlie Manson's Home on the Range," "A Matter of Fantasy," "Frank Sinatra Has a Cold," and "The Kingdoms, the Powers, and the Glories of the *New York Times*" were originally published in *Esquire*.

"On Writing 'Frank Sinatra Has a Cold'" was originally published as the Introduction to *The Best American Essays 1987*, ed. Gay Talese. (Boston: Ticknor and Fields, 1987).

"The Homeless Woman with Two Homes" was originally published in *New York Magazine* (October 30, 1989).

"Gino's Long Run," "Travels with a Diva," "Four Hundred Dresses," and "High Notes" were originally published in the *New Yorker*.

"The Kingdom and the Tower" was originally published in the *New York Observer* (July 2–9, 2007).

"I've Got the World on a String"
Written by Harold Arlen and Ted Koehler
Copyright ©1932 (Renewed) Ted Koehler Music Company and SA Music Company

A Note on the Author

Gay Talese is a journalist and international bestselling author whose works include *The Bridge*, *The Kingdom and the Power*, *Honor Thy Father*, *Thy Neighbor's Wife*, *Unto the Sons*, *A Writer's Life*, and in 2016, *The Voyeur's Motel*. He won the George Polk Award for career achievement in 2008. He lives in New York City with his wife Nan, the publisher of Nan A. Talese/Doubleday.

Lee Gutkind, founder and editor of *Creative Nonfiction* magazine, is Distinguished Writer in Residence in the Consortium for Science, Policy & Outcomes and Professor, School for the Future of Innovation in Society, Arizona State University.